NEW MERM

General editors:
William C. Carroll, Boston University
Brian Gibbons, University of Münster
Tiffany Stern, University of Oxford

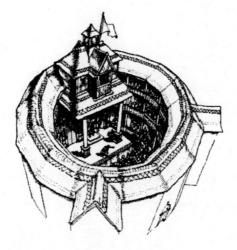

Reconstruction of an Elizabethan theatre
by C. Walter Hodges

NEW MERMAIDS

NEW MERMAIDS

CHRISTOPHER MARLOWE

TAMBURLAINE PARTS ONE AND TWO

edited by Anthony B. Dawson
Professor of English University of British Columbia

Bloomsbury Methuen Drama
An imprint of Bloomsbury Publishing Plc

BLOOMSBURY
LONDON · NEW DELHI · NEW YORK · SYDNEY

Bloomsbury Methuen Drama
An imprint of Bloomsbury Publishing Plc

Imprint previously known as Methuen Drama

50 Bedford Square	1385 Broadway
London	New York
WC1B 3DP	NY 10018
UK	USA

www.bloomsbury.com

**BLOOMSBURY, METHUEN DRAMA and the Diana logo are
trademarks of Bloomsbury Publishing Plc**

First New Mermaid Edition 1971
© Ernest Benn Limited 1971
Reprinted by Bloomsbury Methuen Drama 2012, 2013, 2014, 2015

© Bloomsbury Publishing PLC 1997

British Library Cataloguing-in-Publication Data
A catalogue record for this book is available from the British Library.

ISBN: PB: 978-0-7136-6814-8
ePDF: 978-1-4081-4445-9
ePUB: 978-1-4081-4446-6

Library of Congress Cataloging-in-Publication Data
A catalog record for this book is available from the Library of Congress.

Series: New Mermaids

Printed and bound in Great Britain

CONTENTS

ACKNOWLEDGEMENTS

IN PREPARING this edition I have incurred a number of debts. Previous editors have made the task considerably easier than it would otherwise have been, most especially Una Ellis-Fermor, J. S. Cunningham, Fredson Bowers and J. W. Harper. Al Braunmuller first suggested I undertake the project, and Brian Gibbons, the general editor of this series, has been unfailingly encouraging and exacting in his fulfilment of that role. I want also to express my gratitude to Anne Watts, of A & C Black, and to Louise McConnell, for their sharp-eyed help with the editing and for their patience with my many second thoughts. Paul Yachnin not only read several drafts of the Introduction and made, as he always does, dozens of helpful suggestions, but he also helped to locate some of the illustrations at the Folger Library. Joel Kaplan shared both his memories and his portfolio of photographs of the National Theatre production of *Tamburlaine* in 1976. T. R. Stockwell of the Shakespeare Institute kindly sent me a chapter of his thesis, containing details of the textual changes made for the 1992 RSC production. And a special expression of thanks to my graduate research assistant, Paul Collis, who spent long hours with me poring over the text, struggling with the minutiae of punctuation, reading the proofs aloud, and wrestling with the explanatory notes. Finally I want to remember my mother, Nancy Dawson, who died shortly before this edition appeared, but whose lifelong interest in the theatre inspired me years ago to follow the path I have chosen.

INTRODUCTION

THE AUTHOR

DESPITE much that is known about Christopher Marlowe, there hovers around his figure a tantalizing sense of mystery, an interpretive ambiguity that plays through both his life and his writing. In 1587, he burst on to the London theatre scene with the first 'blockbuster' hit of the whole period – *Tamburlaine*, a play whose popularity was matched only by the notoriety of its author. Performed by the Lord Admiral's Men, with the great Edward Alleyn in the title role, the play was what we now call Part One, since Part Two had not yet been written. Its author, the son of a Canterbury cobbler, was born in 1564, the same year as Shakespeare. He must have shown great promise in his studies since, despite his relatively humble background, he attended The King's School in Canterbury and then proceeded to Cambridge at the age of sixteen, receiving his BA in 1584, and his MA in 1587 (*Tamburlaine* was thus probably written while he was still a student). The university authorities were reluctant to award him his final degree, perhaps because of his prolonged absences from Cambridge during the previous three years. They had to be persuaded by a stiffly worded note from the Privy Council itself, specifying that Marlowe had been employed 'in matters touching the benefitt of his Countrie' and hence 'deserved to be rewarded for his faithfull dealinge'.[1] His 'good service' almost certainly involved spying or undercover work of some sort – it certainly was *not* play-writing. Six years later, on 30 May 1593, he was killed in suspicious circumstances by one Ingram Frizer, who claimed that he acted in self-defence after a quarrel arose about the paying of a bill for food and drink at the house of a gentlewoman of Deptford, Eleanor Bull. Of the four men present, including Marlowe, at least three had known connections with the Elizabethan espionage system; not surprisingly, a great deal of research has been devoted to establishing a political motive for Marlowe's murder – including the plausible suggestion that the Queen and her first minister were directly involved.[2] While proof remains elusive, there is little doubt that the official story is full of holes.

The uncertainty about his death is made all the more murky by the fact that Marlowe had a reputation as a notorious atheist

[1] See John Bakeless, *The Tragicall History of Christopher Marlowe* (Cambridge, Ma., 1942), I, p. 77, for a full text.

[2] David Riggs gathers extensive evidence for this conclusion in his splendid new biography, *The World of Christopher Marlowe* (London, 2004), pp. 328-37.

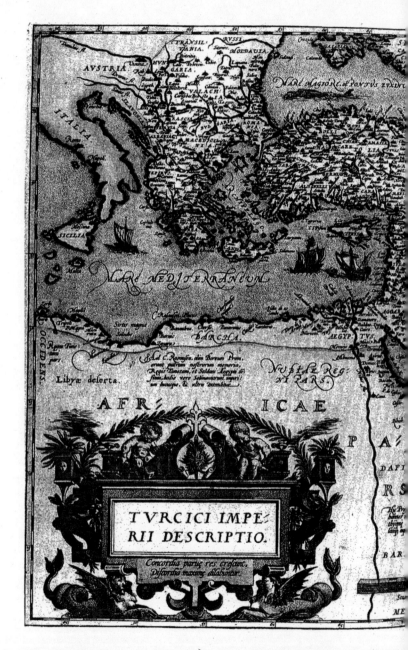

Map of Turkish Empire on which Tamburlaine's military campaigns can be traced

From Abraham Ortelius, *Theatrum Orbis Terrarum*, 1570 (by permission of the Folger Shakespeare Libary)

and free-thinker, a rebel against morals and religion, and was the subject of government investigation on that account. It is possible he used his unsavoury reputation as a kind of cover to gather information, although if this was the case it is likely that some government spies in the loosely structured, overlapping networks that made up the Elizabethan secret service, were unaware of it. Towards the end of his life, he seems to have been the victim of a smear campaign designed to discredit him and some of his associates (including, perhaps, Sir Walter Raleigh).[3] Just days before he was killed, a government agent named Richard Baines delivered a note to the Privy Council detailing Marlowe's 'damnable Judgement of Religion', e.g. that 'Moses was but a Jugler' and that the 'first beginning of Religoun was only to keep men in awe'. A few weeks earlier, Thomas Kyd, a former friend and fellow playwright, imprisoned and tortured as the suspected author of the 'Dutch Church libel' (an attack on foreigners that was signed 'Tamburlaine'), had informed against Marlowe, citing the latter as the owner of an incriminating 'atheistic' treatise (since shown to be harmless enough) found in Kyd's lodgings. Marlowe was detained, but he was not charged and remained free under supervision (even this has been cited as evidence for a plot against him since it allowed for the fateful meeting at Deptford a few weeks later). Shortly after Marlowe's death, Kyd, attempting to clear himself, wrote a pair of letters to the Lord Keeper attributing to his onetime fellow-lodger various outrageous and illegal opinions, including, for example, that the Apostle John was Christ's 'Alexis', i.e. his homosexual lover.[4] The letters probably reflect what Kyd had earlier told his interrogators. Just as Marlowe's undercover activities are impossible to reconstruct with complete confidence, so we will never know for certain what he really thought; the best evidence we have is the plays, which certainly do contain radical challenges to accepted views, but they are dramatic texts and tell us nothing definite.

Nevertheless, such uncertainty has not prevented scholars and critics from reading the plays as an expression of a single over-arching vision proceeding from a mind concerned with its own workings and aspirations. Over and over, *Tamburlaine* has been interpreted, in the words of one influential critic, as the product of the 'recklessly courageous' playwright whose act of play-making 'spurn[s] and subvert[s] his culture's metaphysical and

---

[3] See Charles Nicholl, *The Reckoning: The Murder of Christopher Marlowe* (London, 1992), for an historically detailed, but highly speculative account of Marlowe's life as a government agent.

[4] For the full texts of the Kyd and Baines documents, see Millar Maclure, ed., *Marlowe: The Critical Heritage 1588–1896* (London, 1979), pp. 32–8.

ethical certainties'.[5] In such a scenario, Marlowe himself becomes the ultimate Marlovian hero. To some extent, it must be admitted, Marlowe invites this response: he continually *dares* his audiences, challenging them to follow his speculative dramatic paths, creating aspiring, restless heroes who push beyond prescribed limits. We can imagine him on the afternoon of that first performance in 1587: only twenty-three but bold beyond his years, flushed with the excitement of secret government work and buoyed by artistic arrogance. He takes pleasure in provoking an audience both shocked and delighted by the challenges they could hardly help but feel. To begin to take the measure of Marlowe's effect on his contemporaries, we need imaginatively to resurrect the excitement at the brand-new Rose Theatre when Edward Alleyn began to speak the young writer's intoxicating words – much imitated and lampooned in the years to come but at that moment startlingly original, unlike anything that had been heard before.[6]

THE *TAMBURLAINE* PLAYS

Sights of Power

The first thing the audience heard was a prologue, spoken perhaps by Alleyn, though more likely by a less eminent member of the company. Like the rest of the play, the prologue is a kind of dare, and it offers a few clues about audience experience, which are corroborated to some degree by contemporary testimony:

> From jigging veins of rhyming mother wits
> And such conceits as clownage keeps in pay,
> We'll lead you to the stately tent of war,
> Where you shall hear the Scythian Tamburlaine
> Threat'ning the world with high astounding terms
> And scourging kingdoms with his conquering sword.
> View but his picture in this tragic glass,
> And then applaud his fortunes as you please.

This is clearly a challenge, almost a manifesto: away with the old, here comes the new (and considerably better). No more doggerel rhymes or clownage, but real poetry: 'high astounding terms' which the auditors will hear and respond to with necessary

---

[5] Stephen Greenblatt, *Renaissance Self-Fashioning* (Chicago, 1980), p. 220.

[6] There is no clear evidence that the earliest performances were at the Rose, but since Alleyn was performing there in the 1580s and since a few years later Henslowe's *Diary* indicates that both *Tamburlaine* plays were performed there, it is certainly not impossible.

present/past tense of prologues

awe. Notice the commanding tone and the nervous forward thrust of the future tense, different from the deference and the relaxed ease of the present tense typical of Shakespearean prologues (as, for example, in the Chorus speeches of *Henry V*). Where Shakespeare requests our attention, Marlowe simply declares: we *shall* hear and (it seems) be astounded. Marlowe's 'mighty line', in Ben Jonson's famous phrase, will take hold of us, exorcising all memory of the jigging veins of unskilled rhymers. But our experience will not be all aural. In fact, the sounds blend imperceptibly with the ravages of Tamburlaine's sword and the 'picture' that we are told to 'view'. The theatre is a mirror, a 'tragic glass', producing 'sights of power to grace my victory' (1, V, ii, 412), as Tamburlaine later puts it. He deploys these 'sights' to illustrate and confirm his power; he creates a design with the dead bodies of kings and potentates – the Turkish emperor in his cage, his hapless queen nearby, and the defeated king of Arabia; they are arranged on stage as signs of victory, marks of invincibility. Both Tamburlaine and Marlowe create visual emblems that lead to applause, even perhaps to wonder.

And so the prologue pushes us toward awe before we have even seen Tamburlaine, but then pulls back in a surprising but characteristic Marlovian move: 'And then applaud his fortunes as you please.' The last three words seem tossed off with casual aggressiveness; partly a concession to that original audience, they invite spectators to judge but then seem to disdain whatever judgement might be made. The final phrase also pushes us to reconsider the force of Tamburlaine's rhetoric as defined earlier in the prologue; it drives a wedge between the responses of his onstage and offstage audiences. Cosroe and Orcanes may be astounded, but will we also be? The curious falling away at the end of the prologue catches an ambivalent attitude that is recurrent not only in Marlowe's work generally but in his life as well. Consider his supposed portrait, which hangs in the dining hall of Corpus Christi, his Cambridge college. It carries the motto *Quod me nutrit me destruit* – that which sustains me also destroys me; his expression is assured, his doublet rich (for a scholarship boy it seems lavish), his stance confident. But the motto casts what we see into ironic perspective. It delivers a hint of the ambiguous mixture of commitment and betrayal that seems to have characterized his life as a spy as well as a poet, a suspected Catholic sympathizer as well as a government agent, an 'atheist' as well as a believer.[7] His plays, his portrait, his

[7] The portrait was only discovered in 1953 and may not even be Marlowe – another mark of uncertainty. See Nicholl, pp. 5–9.

biography, all challenge us to know, but keep hidden from us the means to do so; like Mephistophilis with Faustus, they tease us with uncertainty and then seem to scorn us for wanting to be certain.

Michael Goldman, in a perceptive essay, has drawn attention to the motif of *ravishment* in Marlowe – how his characters are ravished by a vision of bliss associated with a particular object, such as the crown in *Tamburlaine*, which is then discarded as mere trash, nothing but a stage prop, entirely external and hence worthless.[8] The same might be said for the audience's experience as Marlowe constructs it in both the prologue and the play as a whole. The picture created in and by the theatre induces wonder, but then that wonder is reduced or trivialized. We can make of it what we please. However, it is precisely in this arena that Marlowe's irony comes fully into play, not to disable wonder but to redirect it, to give it an intellectual edge. The combination of awe and disdain is at the core of the distinctively Marlovian form of theatrical wonder, and the effect is to place sceptical thought at the centre of the experience. Theatrical experience involves being ravished, but it also involves thinking about ravishment and even discarding it. T. S. Eliot used the phrase 'savage farce' to describe Marlowe's *Jew of Malta*; the inescapable doubleness in the term catches something of the ambivalence in the experience that I am describing.

Marlowe's audience was not immune to the poetics of ravishment. At the same time, there were those who reacted to the extravagant acting style of an Alleyn with disdain – suggesting a division among Elizabethan playgoers that reflects the text's ambivalence and in some ways parallels the controversies of modern critics. Joseph Hall, a satirist writing ten years after *Tamburlaine* was first produced, attacks the still popular play, but in doing so gives us a strong sense of its effect on its auditors: he imagines a high-pitched poet (a thinly disguised sketch of Marlowe), creating on

> his fainèd stage
> The stalking steps of his great personage,
> Graced with huf-cap termes and thundring threats
> That his poor hearers hayre quite upright sets.

If intellectuals like Hall scoffed, they may indeed have been reacting to an invitation built into the text; ordinary theatregoers were not so fastidious:

---

[8] 'Marlowe and the Histrionics of Ravishment', in Alvin Kernan, ed., *Two Renaissance Mythmakers* (Baltimore and London, 1977), pp. 22–40.

> There [i.e. on the stage] if he can with termes Italianate,
> Big-sounding sentences, and words of state,
> Faire patch me up his pure *Iambick* verse,
> He ravishes the gazing Scaffolders.[9]

Ravishing the scaffolders involves both wonder and magic. Magic, of course, is dependent on language; *words* have magical force (witness even in the popular imagination the force of a phrase like '*abracadabra*'), and are contained in secret books. This is the subject of Marlowe's most famous play, *Dr Faustus*, where the bliss and dross of magic are both foregrounded: 'Tis magic, magic, that hath ravished me' (I, i, 111), says Faustus at the outset, but the audience is then treated to an increasingly degraded display of magical tricks. Tamburlaine too is magical; he borrows omnipotence from the gods and displays his power in a series of shows designed to provoke wonder. Theatrical magic depends on both words and 'sights' of power; it starts, especially in the open Elizabethan theatre, with the actor and the person he plays. Thomas Nashe, in 1592, defending the theatre from some of its vociferous enemies, praises an actor for resurrecting the English hero, Lord Talbot, in Shakespeare's *1 Henry VI*:

> How would it have ioyed brave Talbot [asks Nashe] to thinke that after he had lyne two hundred yeares in his Tombe, he should triumphe againe on the Stage, and haue his bones newe embalmed with the teares of ten thousand spectators at least, (at seuerall times) who in the Tragedian that represents his person, imagine they behold him fresh bleeding.[10]

Although Nashe is probably referring here to Richard Burbage, the point he is making carries over to Burbage's great rival, Edward Alleyn, and indeed opens a window to an understanding of actorly representation on the Elizabethan stage generally. The passage conflates actor and historical character as the *source* of theatrical effect. It records a 'triumph' (a word suggestive of Tamburlaine) on the part of the actor as well as the character. 'Triumph' was in fact a technical term for a ceremonial funeral display, a rite that was as much secular as religious and that represented the power of the deceased in a grand theatrical show.[11] The action in the theatre thus becomes a 'triumph' in several senses: as a victory for both character and actor, and as

[9] Joseph Hall, from *Virgidemiarum* (I, iii), in Maclure, p. 41.

[10] Thomas Nashe, *Pierce Penilesse, His Supplication to the Divell* (1592). Ed. G. B. Harrison (London: Bodley Head, 1924), p. 87.

[11] See Michael Neill, ' "*Exeunt with a Dead March*": Funeral Pageantry on the Shakespearean Stage', in David Bergeron, ed., *Pageantry in the Shakespearean Theater* (Athens, Ga., 1985), p. 154.

a memorial for an historical hero. Nashe conflates the actor's power with that of the man he represents and locates the effect of the theatrical experience in the living body that revives the dead person.[12]

Much has been made about the differences between Alleyn and Burbage, the former usually depicted as old-fashioned and histrionic, the latter as 'modern' and psychological, commanding that inwardness that seems required by Shakespearean tragedy (Burbage was the first Hamlet, Othello, Macbeth). From a host of contemporary accounts it seems clear that Alleyn's style could be unabashedly sensational (Jonson called it 'scenicall strutting and furious vociferation' and Shakespeare satirized it in Ancient Pistol, the braggart soldier in 2 *Henry IV* and *Henry V*). But Thomas Heywood, writing in 1632, remembered Alleyn in different terms: he won

> The Attribute of peerelesse, being a man
> Whom we may ranke with (doing no one wrong)
> Proteus for shapes, and Roscius for a tongue,
> So could he speake, so vary ...[13]

By 1600 or so, Alleyn's style had no doubt become old-fashioned; we can catch a glimpse of it in the player-king in *Hamlet*, an affectionate tribute to such acting that counter-balances the satire in Pistol, and note the change in style indicated by Hamlet's advice to 'suit the action to the word, the word to the action ... [but] o'erstep not the modesty of nature' (III, ii, 17–19). But that such acting was undeniably effective is clear from the player-king's Hecuba speech, itself a close imitation of Marlowe's *Dido Queen of Carthage*. And judging from Heywood's testimony, it did not preclude an ability to change shapes at will, like Proteus, nor to speak subtly and eloquently, like Roscius, the greatest of Roman actors.

So the differences between Alleyn and Burbage may not have been so marked as has often been claimed. A change of style usually brings with it a noisy rejection of what came before, which obscures the many continuities. The key to imagining Alleyn's Tamburlaine is to recall not just the tendency to strut or to pour the soul into extravagant rhetoric; such moves Alleyn undoubtedly mastered. But, as Heywood reminds us, he was also a 'Proteus for shapes': he could 'vary' quickly and easily.

---

[12] I have developed an analysis of the 'person' of actor and character on the Elizabethan stage, and the participatory power generated by the actor's presence, in *The Culture of Playgoing in Shakespeare's England: A Collaborative Debate* (Cambridge, 2001), with Paul Yachnin, pp. 11–37, 101–7.

[13] For the Jonson and Heywood quotations, see Maclure, *op. cit.*, pp. 50 and 49.

shifts (?)

And there is the key – for without variation, furious vociferation would soon get wearisome. We may be apt to regard *Tamburlaine* as an unvarying series of high rhetorical speeches and linguistic conquests, but this is to miss the frequent shifts and changes of mood that a great actor needs to bring out on the stage. Tamburlaine can turn from unfeelingly ordering the slaughter of the Damascus virgins to a meditation on the beauty of Zenocrate and the failure of language to express it. He can condemn a man to death with a wrathful look (1, III, ii) or shift from despair over the death of Zenocrate to a disquisition on military fortification (2, II, iv).

His famous speech on beauty and poetry is a manifestation of a new susceptibility invading the armour of his heroic stature, and requires an answerable acting style, one capable of registering a slightly bewildered access to a hitherto unexamined inner life:

What is beauty saith my sufferings then?
If all the pens that ever poets held
Had fed the feeling of their masters' thoughts ...
If all the heavenly quintessence they still
From their immortal flowers of poesy,
Wherein as in a mirror we perceive
The highest reaches of a human wit,
If these had made one poem's period
And all combined in beauty's worthiness,
Yet should there hover in their restless heads
One thought, one grace, one wonder at the least,
Which into words no virtue can digest.   (1, V, ii, 97–110)

Although he has just declared that he would never 'change my martial observations ... for the love of Venus' (59–61), he is, like Othello, deeply tempted to do just that. Michael Goldman notes how the 'sense of the body resting in protective comfort ... of melting into repose ... is as important in Marlowe as the strenuous excitement of aspiration' (p. 36). Tamburlaine here reveals his susceptibility to such a sensual urge, the very feeling that he rejects so cruelly when it manifests itself in his slothful son in Part Two (evidence perhaps that in destroying his son he is lashing out against a part of himself). The power of beauty at least temporarily defeats his characteristic mastery of his world. And, at the same time, he registers the restless aspiration of poets to capture in words the fullness of their imaginings and recognizes that such an aspiration, like his own desire for conquest, can never be completely fulfilled.

Of course his meditation carries him through to a resolution *not* to 'harbour thoughts effeminate and faint', but even that is

couched in ambivalent terms and a tortured syntax that bespeaks
the almost unresolved conflict:

> But how unseemly is it for my sex . . .
> To harbour thoughts effeminate and faint!
> Save only that in beauty's just applause,
> With whose instinct the soul of man is touched –
> And every warrior that is rapt with love
> Of fame, of valour, and of victory,
> Must needs have beauty beat on his conceits –
> I thus conceiving and subduing both . . .   (1, V, ii, 111–20)

The syntax and even the semantics of the lines keep urging us
to take them in a different way, most powerfully at line 117 when
'rapt with love' seems to keep us in the tempting realm of Venus,
but then reveals itself in the next line to be referring to what
warriors are *supposed* to love – valour and victory, the world of
Mars. The struggle is revealed too in the fact that the long clause
beginning with 'Save' has no main verb. Tamburlaine, usually so
precisely articulate, is here disordered in his thinking and it takes
a special effort of his extraordinary will to 'subdue' what he has
conceived. It is the mark of the great man, as it is of the poet, to
conceive beauty, but the conquering hero must also subdue it.
Both actor and character must engage with beauty, with poetry,
with softness, and then thrust them firmly back into their proper
place so that he can declare at the end that 'virtue [in the sense
of personal and military power, what the Italians called *virtù*]
solely is the sum of glory'. Again, the intellectual current in the
wonder, the mixture of ravishment and disdain, calls for an alert,
subtle style of acting, and evokes a parallel response in the
audience.

Appraising the Hero

How, overall, are we to react to Tamburlaine? That is the most
vexed and most debated question about the play. Does Marlowe
temper our admiration with ironic displacements or is the whole
thing one mighty, nose-thumbing hurrah for a figure who challenges many of the pieties of Elizabethan orthodoxy? Most of
the original audience, if we are to trust the many contemporary
reports that Richard Levin has compiled, were delighted with
Tamburlaine, even if Joseph Hall or Marlowe's ambivalent friend,
Robert Greene, disapproved. Greene accused Marlowe of
'daring God out of heaven with that Atheist Tamburlan'[14] and
critics of our own time have been equally troubled. Uneasy about

---

[14] From Greene's *Perimedes the Blacksmith* (1588); see Maclure, p. 29.

Portrait of Tamburlaine, from Paulus Giovius, *Elogia Virorum Bellica Virtute Illustrium*, 1575 (by permission of the Folger Shakespeare Library)

identifying with the blasphemous Tamburlaine, such critics insist on ironic undercurrents in the play which they see as directives from Marlowe that we should curb our tendency towards admiration. Instead, we should regard Tamburlaine as an admonition, and his career as a moral exemplum illustrating the inevitable defeat of the aspiring mind, the implacability of death, or the self-destructiveness of the tyrant. Marlowe, in this view, was subtly showing his audience that neither Tamburlaine himself nor the theatrical excitement at his triumphs was to be trusted. Elements such as his cruelty to the virgins of Damascus, his callous treatment of Bajazeth, Zenocrate's sympathy for Bajazeth and Zabina and her pained uncertainty about Tamburlaine's likely triumph over her father, Tamburlaine's own hesitation between the pull of beauty and love that he associates with Zenocrate and the desire for power and triumph that characterizes him throughout – all these are adduced to show that even in the upward trajectory of Part One his aspirations are placed in a partially ironic context.

The pattern, so the argument goes, is even more evident in Part Two, where there is certainly some diminution of Tamburlaine's former invincibility, and some ironic distancing from him. Not only does he succumb to death, but we last see him with his hand stretched over a huge map that reminds him of the expanse of lands that yet remain unconquered. Earlier he executes his own son, Calyphas, with the equanimity of the perfect justicer; Calyphas of course is an effeminate weakling, no fit son for Tamburlaine. But we are not allowed to forget that he shares his father's flesh and even some of his yearning, as well as his mother's pity; beyond that he is given a sharp tongue and a sceptical wit that serve to counter his father's triumphs and undermine his brothers' aspirations. His sarcasm to his warlike brothers is characteristic:

> 'Twill please my mind as well to hear both you
> Have won a heap of honour in the field,
> And left your slender carcasses behind,
> As if I lay with you for company.   (2, IV, i, 36–9)

Also in Part Two there is the barbaric treatment of the Governor of Babylon and the drowning of its citizens, the comic-grotesque humiliation of the carthorse-kings, Almeda's betrayal of Tamburlaine (no servant would have dreamed of betraying him in Part One), and the bizarre incident of the burning of the Koran, which seems to bring about the divine retribution that leads to death (although here, as so often, the meaning of the sequence is left indefinite – wouldn't Renaissance Christian society approve the desecration of the Koran?). All these seem to qualify our admiration of the hero, to undermine it in ways that, for critics of this persuasion, point a moral. Tamburlaine may awe us by his aspiration and draw us to forbidden admiration, but like Milton's Satan he is hollow at the core and our very awe is a temptation that we must learn to resist.

This, it must be stressed, is a minority view and is likely to remain so. The plays evoke a response that seems incompatible with a simple moral lesson. More frequent has been the temptation to read *Tamburlaine*, and indeed all of Marlowe's plays, as a sign of the aspiring and subversive mind of their maker. Tamburlaine's challenge to orthodoxy parallels and dovetails with Marlowe's own. Some critics have delighted in the iconoclastic reach of both author and character, perhaps secretly linking their own more circumscribed aspirations with those of the ascendant shepherd-warrior. Tamburlaine's famous defiance of the fixed order of Elizabethan cultural orthodoxy sounds the oppositional note most brilliantly:

> Nature that framed us of four elements
> Warring within our breasts for regiment,
> Doth teach us all to have aspiring minds:
> Our souls, whose faculties can comprehend
> The wondrous architecture of the world
> And measure every wand'ring planet's course ...
> Wills us to wear ourselves and never rest
> Until we reach the ripest fruit of all,
> That perfect bliss and sole felicity,
> The sweet fruition of an earthly crown. (1, II, vii, 18–29)

The 'warring elements', 'aspiring minds', 'wand'ring planets', and 'restless spheres' evoke a world of constant conflict instead of the relative stasis favoured by Elizabethan cosmological and social theory. Tamburlaine justifies his usurpation of Cosroe's crown by the example of Jove, who 'thrust his doting father from his chair', and places his own 'thirst of reign' in the context of a universal struggle of contending desires. The last three lines tease the hearers with a promise of orthodox fulfilment but then with the insertion of 'earthly' instead of 'heavenly' turn that promise askew, asserting a set of values in direct conflict with ideological piety, though not with political practice. The speech thus underlines a contradiction in Elizabethan culture as a whole. Its effect on modern commentators has been equally contradictory, those of an iconoclastic bent reading it positively, the moralists seeing its descent into 'bathos' in the last line as a sign that Marlowe wants his audience not only to distance themselves from Tamburlaine's portrayal of his aspiring self but to condemn him for it.

Portrait of Bajazeth, from Paulus Giovius, *Elogia Virorum Bellica Virtute Illustrium*, 1575 (by permission of the Folger Shakespeare Library)

Other critics, more complexly, have seen in Tamburlaine a model of the 'Herculean hero', [15] a figure of amoral force inherited by Marlowe from classical sources. This model includes both aspiration and cruelty, godlike power and inhuman consistency of purpose; hence moralized critique misses the point. Cruelty is an essential part of what makes the hero great, and awe on the part of his audiences, both onstage and in the theatre, is entirely appropriate. This dialectical view seeks to get around the polarized terms in which the problem of response has frequently been posed: i.e., either Marlowe is being ironic or he is not; either Tamburlaine is a bloodthirsty tyrant or a marvellous, conquering hero, a kind of irresistible force whom we must admire, even if our moral sense recoils from some of his actions. But the idea of the hero as beyond criticism because of his Herculean status leaves out of consideration the sceptical component in Marlovian wonder. For one thing, Marlowe gets his effects, as J. R. Brown once remarked, from an intellectual concentration on widening perspectives available to the audience. [16] The invoking of the 'earthly crown' is one of those moments where the perspective temporarily widens. Marlowe's plays may not demand moral *judgement* but they do demand moral *inquiry*, as well as entranced seeing. This returns us to the kinds of theatrical effect I began by talking about – the mixture of wonder and critique that Marlowe's dramatic and rhetorical technique aims at. The effect is sceptical rather than moralistic.

Sequel and Sequence

That there is a pronounced difference between the two parts of what we now often think of as a single play is unarguable. Judging by the way Marlowe handled the historical material at his disposal, as well as by the prologue to Part Two, the original plan seems to have been to write just the one play. By the 1580s, when Marlowe was writing, there was already a substantial body of historical work adumbrating the story of the fourteenth-century Mongol conqueror, Timur Khan (1336–1405), whose career was the subject of a Latin treatise available in the library of Marlowe's Cambridge college. There were also two important English accounts: Thomas Fortescue's *The Forest, or Collections of Histories*, a translation of a Spanish work by Pedro Mexia, and George Whetstone's *The English Mirrour*, published in 1586. Part One of Marlowe's play covers the material contained in these sources, so that when he came to write Part Two he was

---

[15] See Eugene Waith, *The Herculean Hero* (London, 1962), pp. 62–87.
[16] 'Marlowe and the Actors', *TDR* 8.4 (Summer 1964), 170–71.

thrown back on other historical material (such as that behind
the sub-plot concerning the treachery of King Sigismund of
Hungary) and, more important, on his own invention. [17] This
suggests that Marlowe started out to write just the one play
but, gratified by his initial success, decided, in a manner not
unfamiliar to modern-day filmgoers, to write a sequel. This is
certainly what we are told in the prologue to Part Two:

> The general welcomes Tamburlaine received
> When he arrivèd last upon our stage,
> Hath made our poet pen his second part,
> Where death cuts off the progress of his pomp
> And murd'rous Fates throws all his triumphs down.

The question for criticism raised by this is whether the different
circumstances of their composition make the two plays irrevo-
cably separate, or whether they can be regarded as a single
work. One aspect of this much debated question can be quickly
dispatched: there is no necessary connection between Marlowe's
apparent change of plan and dramatic incoherence. It is perfectly
possible to make a sequel cohere with what one has already
written. But did Marlowe succeed in doing this? Did he even
want to? That is another question.

In itself, Part Two seems less unified than Part One. It has a
sub-plot (Sigismund's betrayal of Orcanes) and a multiplicity of
incidents (the Olympia–Theridamus intrigue, the scoffing of
Calyphas, the disquisition on military fortification) that con-
tribute little to either the triumphs of the hero or his being
thrown down by 'murd'rous Fates'. But Marlowe, like other
dramatists of his time, probably cared less about unity than
modern critics, until recently, have tended to do. It may, indeed,
have been enough that Part Two continues Tamburlaine's story,
once again making us gasp at his boldness and irreverence, and
complicates our amazement by emphasizing the scepticism that
plays less conspicuously through Part One. G. I. Duthie many
years ago sought to counter the view that the plays lacked unity
by showing how the two parts were each organized around a
central conflict that was only partially resolved: in Part One, the
focus is on Tamburlaine's ambivalent response to Beauty in the
person of Zenocrate, and in Part Two Death is the adversary
that both conquers and is conquered. Zenocrate is as crucial to
the design of Part Two as of Part One, since her death in the
second act is the initial crisis in the central conflict. Thus the

---

[17] One important way in which he put his invention to work was in the way he made
poetic and dramatic use of Ortelius's great atlas, *Theatrum Orbis Terrarum*, of 1570
(see pp. viii–ix). See E. Seaton, 'Marlowe's Map', *Essays and Studies* 10 (1924), 13–35.

two parts are united by analogy in that they share a pattern and each uses Zenocrate as a pivotal figure.[18]

From a post-modern perspective, such an argument may seem like special pleading, since the force of the argument depends on leaving a lot out. Nowadays, it no longer matters so much whether texts can be rescued from the threat of disunity; in some ways texts are thought *better* if they can be shown to be rifted or contradictory! Critics are as likely to look for gaps and breaks as for coherence. This may in some ways bring us closer to a critical component of Elizabethan aesthetic sensibilities. Like one of those early spectators, we are not likely to be bothered by, for example, the improbabilities of the Olympia–Theridamus episode; we may indeed see it as a sardonic representation of the differential power relations between men and women both in the rest of the play (especially in the Tamburlaine–Zenocrate relation) and in Elizabethan culture generally. Olympia, we remember, outwits her unwanted suitor, Tamburlaine's trusty, if a bit obtuse, lieutenant, by offering him an ointment to make him invulnerable and then agreeing to demonstrate its effectiveness by anointing herself and inviting him to stab her. Even though she has been pleading with him for two scenes to put her out of her misery, he fails to see the trick. This incident offers us a glimpse of a woman claiming a kind of control over her fate, despite the fact that she lives in a man's world epitomized in Tamburlaine. At the same time, such control cannot help but include her own self-victimization, indeed her death, at a man's willing/unwilling hands (we remember too that she seeks death because her husband has been killed by Tamburlaine's forces). The intrusion of this sequence into the play thus complicates the positive representation of Tamburlaine's triumph over Zenocrate, itself enabled by the latter's willing acceptance of her subjection and softened by Tamburlaine's almost overwhelming love for her. And the muted dismay that we sometimes see in Part One in conjunction with Zenocrate's acceptance of her situation (especially her pain at the slaughter in Damascus and her horror over the fate of 'the Turk and his great emperess' [V, ii, 257–309]), finds fuller textual expression in a completely different setting in Part Two. Although, then, they may be seen to work against the thrust of the play's apparent meaning, the Olympia scenes allow us to think of cultural realities (such as the complex exchanges involved in gender relations) that the rest of the play skims over.

One other feature of the Olympia–Theridamus episode may

[18] G. I. Duthie, 'The Dramatic Structure of Marlowe's *Tamburlaine*', *Essays and Studies* I, N.S., (1948), 101–26.

claim our attention – its cavalier disregard for the canons of believability. It is extraordinarily, even laughably, incredible. That even the dumbest of knights could be fooled by such a patent device strains our belief. But this may be seen as part of its disruptiveness. It is certainly true that instances of the impossible are frequent in Elizabethan drama, but Marlowe takes particular delight in them, and occasionally, as here, seems to use them as a challenge to his audience, especially when there is an element of blackly comic cruelty to be derived from them (as also with the poisoning of the nuns in *The Jew of Malta*). So Marlowe's sardonic brand of humour plays on the audience's expectations, unsettling and amusing at once. Such complicated amusement seems part of the effect especially of Part Two, where the text plays constantly with audience engagement.

The most famous instance of this is probably the scene of the burning of the Koran, which then leads directly into Tamburlaine's illness and death. A Christian audience would hardly expect the crucial turning point in Tamburlaine's tragic career to turn out to be the burning of a document that any orthodox Elizabethan would have regarded as heretical. Although it has been argued that Elizabethans would have regarded blasphemy of any sort, including the burning of another religion's sacred book, as grounds for retribution, the effect aimed at seems first to be surprise. Tamburlaine's rebuke is characteristically ambiguous:

> Now Mahomet, if thou have any power,
> Come down thyself and work a miracle,
> Thou art not worthy to be worshippèd
> That suffers flames of fire to burn the writ
> Wherein the sum of thy religion rests.
> Why send'st thou not a furious whirlwind down ...
> Or vengeance on the head of Tamburlaine?   (2, V, i, 185–93)

After this challenge, he instructs his followers to adore 'The God that sits in heaven, if any god,/For he is God alone, and none but he' (199–200). The phrase 'if any god' sounds an agnostic note – if any god exists? That may be how Robert Greene interpreted it and why he regarded 'Tamberlan' as an atheist. But at the same time the statement as a whole can be taken as a declaration of faith (there *is* a God in heaven and if you are going to adore 'any god' then it had better be him). If so, however, we have to wonder why a moment later the fatal distemper that will spell the end of Tamburlaine suddenly strikes. Is it this mysterious God who sits in heaven that initiates the distemper? Is it a revengeful Mahomet come down to work a miracle? We are never sure. Theatrically what is most striking is that Tamburlaine and his followers start a fire and throw the Turkish holy books into it; and this is followed immediately by the spectacle of the once invincible hero having to be helped off the stage, to the accompaniment of a vaunt that now, perhaps for the first time, seems unjustified: 'Sickness or death can never conquer me' (220).

We can feel in the seemingly successful revenge of Mohammed some of that delight in shocking that characterizes much of Marlowe, even sense the cool grin that must have accompanied some of the more outrageous statements attributed to him by government informers such as Richard Baines, who reported Marlowe's views 'that Christ was a bastard and his mother dishonest' or that 'all they that love not Tobacco and Boies were fooles'. [19] A less overt, but nevertheless real, challenge to the audience is issued by the very form of Part Two, which is more fluid and less tightly structured than its predecessor, episodic and level rather than coherent and incremental. The looseness of structure in the second play, along with its refusal to meet audience expectation and its ironic placing of Tamburlaine's power, challenges the coherence of the first play, suggesting perhaps an excess in the initial representation, something a bit too pat in the neat way that Part One is put together. So too the sights of power are re-configured, made harsher and less grandly rhetorical, so that the wonder associated with Tamburlaine's triumph in Part One itself comes into question. Part, that is, of the response to the second play is a sense of scepticism about the wonder one has experienced at the grandeur of the first. Just as Marlowe exploits the potential contradictions in Alleyn's acting style, ironizing as well as sustaining the vociferations of his leading player, so he here undermines the structure and genre of his own heroic drama by having it work against itself. All this adds up to a kind of creative disunity, a partially antagonistic relation between the two parts in which the relatively cohesive portrayal of Tamburlaine's rise in Part One is subjected to sceptical scrutiny by both the form of Part Two and its more interrogative content.

A strong dramatic marker of this interrogative element is the fact that audience expectation is consistently led astray. Thus the sub-plot casually displays the brutal irreligious politics of the Christian forces and their unscrupulous betrayal of the Moslems, and then over and over through the rest of the action the smooth predictability of Part One is cast aside in favour of an aesthetic of surprise and even disarray (examples include Almeda's betrayal of Tamburlaine, the failure of Tamburlaine's sons to

[19] Maclure, p. 37.

meet his expectations, the suddenness of Zenocrate's sickness and death, the Olympia incident, and Tamburlaine's retributive distemper). Although the prologue's prediction in Part Two that 'murd'rous Fates' will throw 'all his triumphs down' does in the end come true, even that is not entirely right, since the play ends with a 'triumph' in the sense of a ceremonial funeral procession which features the hearses of Zenocrate and Tamburlaine and the chariot drawn grotesquely by Orcanes and Jerusalem. This chariot, mounted now by Amyras, who inherits Tamburlaine's place behind the human cart-horses, is linked in the language to the chariot of Phaëton, the upstart son of Apollo who was unable to handle his unruly horses and ended by scorching earth and heaven as he himself was destroyed. The image catches something of the text's ambivalence toward Tamburlaine, but refers to his son, not him. Tamburlaine, instead, and again contrary to expectation, succeeds to some degree in 'triumphing' over death, paradoxically by accepting it.

There is a curiously Eucharistic note to Tamburlaine's final speeches to his sons, a sign of this paradoxical triumph. Amyras begins it, invoking the complex spiritual unity effected through the animating spirit of Tamburlaine's 'essence' incorporated in his sons' bodies ('subjects'), which are flesh of his flesh:

> Your soul gives essence to our wretched subjects,
> Whose matter is incorporate in your flesh.

Tamburlaine's response continues and broadens the motif:

> But sons, this subject, not of force enough
> To hold the fiery spirit it contains,
> Must part, imparting his impressions
> By equal portions into both your breasts;
> My flesh divided in your precious shapes
> Shall still retain my spirit, though I die,
> And live in all your seeds immortally.

(2, V, iii, 164–74)

The language here, especially the word-play on 'part', seems to invoke the idea of 'participation' and the theological debates throughout the sixteenth century surrounding the question of the 'real presence' of Christ in the Eucharist. Originating in Paul's description of the Lord's Supper as an act of 'participating' the body and blood of Christ (*1 Cor. 10*), the term 'participation' is central to various understandings of the meaning of Eucharistic representation, whether Catholic or Anglican, Lutheran or Reformed. Anglican apologist and theologian Richard Hooker reads the Eucharist as 'instrumentally a cause of that mystical participation'[20] which binds Christ to his people. As some critics and historians have argued, it is possible to see the secular theatre taking over certain ritual forms and practices and transmuting them into theatrical rather than religious events,[21] and I would suggest that this is what is happening here at the end of *Tamburlaine*, once again with a combination of corrosive irony and theatrical awe. Certainly the context for such resonances of the sacred is outrageous. The participatory power of Christ's body is being transferred (blasphemously) to Tamburlaine, whose flesh is 'divided' among his devotees and, retaining his essential 'spirit', will 'live in all your seeds immortally'. His spirit-and-flesh will invest them and their descendants with the possibility of immortal life. At the same time, by a peculiarly theatrical magic, the body of the actor, in the person of the character, participates in the process, imparting his flesh to the raucous spectators at the Rose in a temporary and secular re-enactment of Eucharistic communality. Like Burbage as Talbot, the actor bleeds for and before them, and thereby 'triumphs', producing wonder, even though it is a rifted and uneven wonder, shot through with scepticism and dismay.

Hence the ending of *Tamburlaine* never lets go of Marlowe's central vision of his hero, sustaining the awe he had promised from the outset and constantly re-casting it without purging it. The young dramatist is bold enough to link his hero with Christ as a figure in a re-enactment, a ritualized representation depending on the body of the actor but also tied directly to some of his culture's most reverberant images. He thus proclaims the power of the theatre to take over from the church the task of representation and at the same time checks that theatrical power by submitting it to a rigorous scrutiny, allowing Tamburlaine both to dazzle the spectators' imaginations and haunt their minds.

STAGE HISTORY

As I have already indicated, *Tamburlaine* was a major success on the London stages of the 1580s and '90s. I have speculated that its first performance in 1587 was at the newly built Rose Theatre, erected by entrepreneur Philip Henslowe, whose *Diary* is the best documentary source for our knowledge of the daily routines

---

[20] Richard Hooker, *Of the Laws of Ecclesiastical Polity*, ed. A. S. McGrade and Brian Vickers (London, 1975), p. 294. See also n. 11 above.

[21] See, for example, C.L. Barber, *Creating Elizabethan Tragedy: The Theater of Marlowe and Kyd* (Chicago, 1988), and Louis Montrose *The Purpose of Playing* (Chicago, 1996).

and repertory of the Elizabethan theatre.[22] Although the title page of the first edition (1590) declares only that the two 'Tragicall Discourses' had been 'sundrie times shewed upon Stages in the Citie of London', we learn from Henslowe that the Rose was the venue for frequent performances of the two parts of the play during the 1590s. Between August 1594 and November 1595, Part One was performed on its own eight times, and on seven other occasions was paired with Part Two, usually on successive days. With twenty-two performances in all, *Tamburlaine* was one of the most popular plays of those years, a fact that can be gauged not just from frequency of performance but from the gate receipts also recorded by Henslowe. (Marlowe's *Dr Faustus* was another of the five or six most lucrative plays of this specific period, along with a few other works that have long since disappeared.) Since Marlowe's relatively recent death, and the life that led up to it, were notorious, we can discern in the decision to bring *Tamburlaine* back to the public a shrewd move on the part of Henslowe and his actors to capitalize on the young author's notoriety. After 1595, *Tamburlaine* disappears from Henslowe's records, though allusions to it, usually satiric or parodic, keep cropping up in drama, ballads, epistles, prologues and the like throughout the period. It is probable that as long as Edward Alleyn remained on the boards (he went into retirement in 1597 for a few years, made a comeback in 1600, and retired permanently in 1605), the play would have been occasionally revived. Which bold actors essayed the part after Alleyn's withdrawal from acting is not clear, though there are allusions to performances during the reign of Charles I, including one in 1641, just before the closing of the theatres – in all likelihood the last before the twentieth century.[23]

We now know something about the Rose Theatre, since its archaeological remains were unearthed in 1989, during construction of an office building in south London. Its lineaments can be traced much more accurately than those of Shakespeare's more celebrated, but less substantial, Globe. Compared with other Elizabethan playhouses, the Rose was fairly small (like them it was essentially round, but its full diameter was only about 74 feet while that of the Globe was about 100 feet); still, it was capable of accommodating about 2,000 people, well-packed, before renovations were undertaken in 1592, and about 2,400 afterwards. Its stage too was small, compared to the known dimensions of the Fortune theatre which Henslowe built in 1600, for which a contract and building specifications have survived. Trapezoidal in shape, the stage was shallow (about 16 feet),

[22] R. A. Foakes and R. T. Rickert, eds., *Henslowe's Diary* (Cambridge, 1961).

[23] Bakeless, *The Tragicall History of Christopher Marlowe*, I, p. 203.

narrow at the front (24 feet 9 inches) and angling back to meet the 'tiring house' wall where it measured about 37 feet in width. There was a trap-door, probably used for the cremation of Olympia's husband and son (2, III, iv) and perhaps for the burning of the Koran (2, V, i); an upper playing area for the scaling of the walls of Babylon and the bizarre shooting of its Governor (2, V, i); and some kind of inner stage or discovery space to serve for locations such as Calyphas's tent (2, IV, i) and Zenocrate's bedchamber (2, II, iv, where the stage directions require an arras to be drawn open to begin the scene and closed at the end).[24] Since none of these additional playing areas is necessary for Part One, it is likely that Marlowe did not initially have a particular stage in mind and only made use of the facilities of the Rose when he was writing the second part. With a rapt audience crowded around the Rose's shallow stage, we can imagine the force of Marlowe's emblematic dramaturgy and understand the potentially electric effect of Tamburlaine's 'sights of power'. In a big scene, such as the banquet (1, IV, iv) with Bajazeth in his cage (a prop mentioned by Henslowe) and Tamburlaine resplendent in his 'cotte with coper lace' and 'breches of crymson vellvet' (also mentioned by Henslowe),[25] the busy stage, the parade of crowns, and the vaunting of the hero would no doubt have produced a stunning effect.

It was not until 1919 that a version of Marlowe's play was again acted, a much abridged, even truncated one, put together by Stephen Vincent Benet and Edgar Wooley at Yale University. Despite some high praise from student reviewer Thornton Wilder, this production was at best a mere shadow of the original. In 1951, the richly imaginative and trend-setting British director Tyrone Guthrie staged the play at the Old Vic, with Donald Wolfit in the title role. This was the first professional production since the mid-seventeenth century. Like all twentieth-century producers, Guthrie and Wolfit departed from their Renaissance counterparts by treating the two parts as a unit; they also cut the text considerably, reducing it to a single, manageable play. This involved eliminating the whole of the Sigismund and Olympia sub-plots in Part Two, the defeat and death of Arabia in Part One (mentioned but not shown), plus several minor characters and a whole range of long speeches. The idea was to make the text theatrically lean and fast-paced, and to pile up the atrocities (none of which was eliminated) so that Guthrie's vision of the play as a 'ritual dance' or 'savage Oratorio', an 'orgy of sadism

---

[24] The inner stage or 'study' may have been a free-standing structure put into place when called for, rather than a permanent feature of the playhouse.
[25] *Diary*, p. 319, pp. 321–2.

by the light of meteors', could be fully enacted.[26] The production was huge (over fifty actors), astounding, and horrifying. The emphasis was on blood-lust, with an element of wild gaiety also present, giving a verve and vibrancy to the continual killing that both shocked and exhilarated most of the critics. Guthrie used a thrust stage, with a small apron and upper level, and a single set representing a tented field. Bodies piled up on the apron in a procession of moving emblems, the visual effects adding continually to the sense of sadistic delight. The final victim, the Governor of Babylon, was hung in chains against the back wall while 'by some fiendish technical trick, his body appear[ed] to be riddled with arrows.'[27] Such extravagant zest led some critics to dismiss the play as worthless, while others commented on the relation between the play's horrors and the recent events in a Europe decimated by war and genocide. What seems clear is that Guthrie's one-sided vision of the play, while exciting and powerful, lacked subtlety and completely missed the intellectual, sceptical side of the play. In emphasizing lyrical cruelty, which then descended into madness in Part Two, Guthrie and Wolfit sought to establish a perspective on Tamburlaine's career, to explain his barbarity as a species of insanity. But this was to miss both the careful way in which Marlowe establishes multiple perspectives toward his hero even in Part One, and the irony by which Tamburlaine achieves a measure of triumph over death at the end of Part Two. And most of the critics emphasized the sheer theatricality, the 'mad dream cast among barbaric splendours and miseries' (in the words of *The Times*, 25 Sept.), rather than commenting on any putative ethical dimension. Nevertheless, this production, which was revived in 1956 for a brief North American season in Toronto and New York,[28] was crucial for the renewal of theatrical interest in *Tamburlaine*, and for initiating an intermittent series of productions in the years since. Of these, I will focus on the two most successful and far-reaching: Peter Hall and Albert Finney's brilliant production that opened the Olivier amphitheatre at the National Theatre in 1976, and Terry Hands and Antony Sher's return to savage spectacle at the Swan Theatre in Stratford-upon-Avon in 1992.

---

[26] Tyrone Guthrie, 'Introduction' to *Tamburlaine the Great* (an acting version prepared by Tyrone Guthrie and Donald Wolfit), pp. x–xi.

[27] *Daily Mail*, 25 Sept. 1951, quoted in George L. Geckle, *Tamburlaine and Edward II: Text and Performance* (London, 1988), p. 57.

[28] For the revival, Anthony Quayle replaced Wolfit in the title role. The production was well received in Toronto, but some New York critics, and more important, New York audiences, were in no mood to enjoy plays full of rhetorical and visual splendour but with little relation to American theatrical tradition or interest. The eight week run was cancelled after two weeks.

In the first of these, Peter Hall chose to approach the play from the point of view of its symmetrical design; he placed heavy emphasis, for example, on its recurrent focus on the number three – three colours for tents and battle regalia (white, red, black), three contributory kings, three sons, three physicians attending on both Zenocrate and Tamburlaine, etc. Such a stress on the emblematic and hieratic led to a more distanced but also subtler production than Guthrie's, one that, if it was neither so frightening nor so exhilarating as the Old Vic's, was more intellectually engaging as well as splendid and colourful (the costumes alone cost £27,000.[29]) Hence his approach, more intellectual than visceral, led to less sensational theatre than the earlier production, but caught more of Marlowe's subtlety and irony. Hall saw the text as 'an immorality play' (the phrase occurs in the programme and in several interviews with both Hall and Finney that were published around the time of the opening), with a morality play structure but without the corresponding message. Rather, the point is irreligious and brutal: 'human will alone is master of fortune and success' (programme), and the hieratic staging was designed to bring this idea across.

The battle scenes remained offstage, represented by a symbolic reddening of the lights and a percussive soundscape created by Harrison Birtwhistle. The action took place on a large round platform under a circular golden lighting grid, while at the 'back and sides, panels either reflected the current colour-scheme (white, red, or black) or slid back to reveal huge golden friezes of soldiers or horsemen'.[30] When required, these same panels provided walls to be scaled by attacking armies. There was as well a 'ceremoniously rising and descending trap' downstage (I. Wardle, *The Times*, 5 Oct. 1976), which served as a pit for some of the victims of Tamburlaine's power (such as Agydas or Olympia's husband and son) as well as for the burning of the Koran, and could be used with ironic force in moments such as the ascent of Zenocrate's deathbed in Part Two immediately after the descent of the dead Sigismund. Guthrie's sadistic emphasis on bodies was transformed by such stylized effects into a brilliant monumentality. Stage movement was formal and restrained. Only Tamburlaine moved freely. Bernard Levin complained that most of the characters stood in 'amphitheatrical semicircles and address[ed] the audience instead of each other', assuming 'the same hieratic pose' again and again (*Sunday Times*, 10 Oct. 1976). Another critic noted that when Tamburlaine

---

[29] Geckle, p. 69.

[30] J. S. Cunningham and Roger Warren, '*Tamburlaine the Great* Re-Discovered', *Shakespeare Survey* 31 (1978), 156. Further references in the text.

spoke, 'even the victims stop[ped] writhing' (John Elsom, *The Listener*, 14 Oct.). This is not to say that throats were not cut; they were, in 'full frontal slow motion' (Levin). There was an unmistakable element of barbarity, but this was balanced by the emphasis on ritual symmetry. Some critics, especially those whose interest in the play was literary as well as theatrical, found Hall's approach intensely engaging, mainly because it brought out subtleties that Guthrie's production could not deliver. For example, the strict symmetry of the scene when Tamburlaine confronts Bajazeth for the first time (1, III, iii, 60ff.) was strongly marked in the production, to the extent even of having Tamburlaine adjust the position of his throne slightly so as to match Bajazeth's exactly. The point was to suggest first how Tamburlaine, in this early phase of his career, is 'evolving his own style, assisted by the observant, half-parodic mimicry of imperial style' (Cunningham and Warren, 156–7), and also to underline Tamburlaine's confidence, his awareness that he is playing a game. Such self-awareness gives him an advantage since it allows him to mock Bajazeth's faith in ritual even as he imitates it. This fits neatly with the Marlovian pattern of reducing the value, through mockery, of the very thing to which one consciously devotes oneself – in this case imperial majesty. Finney's 'horribly appealing' Tamburlaine (Levin) thus combined humour and mischievousness in the development of his style, strutting provocatively, daring his audiences, both onstage and off, with his own self-delight. He encompassed, said Robert Cushman, 'the gamester in the part' (*Observer*, 10 Oct.), his whole performance marked by 'sheer high spirits and risky verve' (Cunningham and Warren, 157). Overall, then, within the stylized world of the production, the main character gained an element of fluency and flexibility that helped account for his extraordinary success.

The text that Hall used was relatively full. Unlike Guthrie he cut none of the subsidiary incidents, instead trimming lines where he could, with the result that about 1,000 lines were cut overall (out of a total of over 4,600). He also transposed a number of scenes, notably at the beginning of Part Two, which began with an aging but still impressive Tamburlaine instead of the Sigismund sub-plot, the first three scenes being played after I, iv–vi. Although Hall's text made for a long evening (over four and half hours including a half hour break between the two parts), it also provided a sense of the epic sweep of the whole chronicle, a feature missing from the much more severely cut versions of Guthrie or Benet-Wooley. The pace was quick despite the formality, so that the action 'develop[ed] with frenzied geometric progression' (Wardle). Robert Cushman was surprised and delighted at the pace of the early part of the play, how

Denis Quilley as Bajazeth, Barbara Jefford as Zabina, Albert Finney as Tamburlaine and Susan Fleetwood as Zenocrate in (Part One III.iii) the 1976 production at the Royal National Theatre (photo: Nobby Clark)

Tamburlaine threw off his cloak to reveal his bare legs and golden armour, won Zenocrate with an aria, sat himself in the midst of his spoils on an unfurled golden carpet, and reeled off another aria to win Theridamas, all before the end of the second scene. The impression of a slow pace that can sometimes arise from mere reading is shown to be misleading – things happen fast on Marlowe's stage, and this production enacted that speed without dropping the stylization.

The play does of course slow down a little as the relentless conquering in Part Two is interspersed with sub-plots and eddies of domestic turbulence. Tamburlaine's progress through these was marked by aging but not, as in Wolfit's characterization, a growing insanity. He retained to the end the restless aspiration that is the keynote, but as sickness struck he was forced to acknowledge his own mortality. This, according to Cunningham and Warren, made him much more than a Hitler-figure, giving him an ironic grandeur that caught the doubleness that Marlowe built into his portrayal. Perhaps the best sign of this ambiguity was the Koran-burning scene in Part Two, where ten large bundles were tossed into the flaming pit and Usumcasane looked on with 'grinning relish' like one of Hitler's book burners, while Tamburlaine stood above in his chariot, grimly challenging Mahomet to react. After a pause, Tamburlaine quietly concluded that 'Mahomet remains in hell', but then the chariot swung around and Tamburlaine's sudden distemper struck: 'the movement after challenging stillness raised the possibility of Mahomet's revenge, reinforced by the subsequent build-up of Callapine – only to shatter that possibility by Tamburlaine's triumphant routing of him' (Cunningham and Warren, 158).

The defeat of Callapine, the only battle that took place onstage, provided for John Elsom the 'one truly frightening moment' of the evening: the dying Tamburlaine 'hauled himself up for a last turn in his chariot, drawn by the kings of Trebizon and Soria, and charged Callapine and his army, scattering them before him'. So Tamburlaine, in his weakest state, shows his indomitable power just before succumbing to the one enemy he cannot defeat, his mortal nature showing finally that it is unequal to his aspirations. The production caught this irony not only in the inability of Tamburlaine's two remaining sons to match his power, but in the failed magnificence of his funeral triumph, as, draped across Zenocrate's coffin, he descended emblematically into the very pit that had been, ambiguously, the sign of both his victories and his atrocities (Cunningham and Warren, 158).

In the RSC production at the Swan Theatre in Stratford in 1992, Terry Hands and Antony Sher brought blood and ferocity back to *Tamburlaine*, topping the savagery of Guthrie's production in spectacular ways. The idea, in Hands's words, was to exhibit onstage 'the human animal with its teeth bared'. [31] During the rehearsal period, Hands showed tapes of African hunting dogs as a model for the behaviour of Tamburlaine and his crew, and a collage of photos in the programme highlighting images of human violence and atrocity is headed by a picture of the same snarling animal. Hands was clearly moving the play away from the hieratic ritual and symmetry of Peter Hall. The emphasis was on constant, restless movement, especially in Part One when the extraordinary athleticism of Sher as an actor was the pivot of the shifting spectacle. Bajazeth and his followers, wearing tusked helmets, entered on huge golden stilts – their greatness and the fragility and pretence of that greatness both registered by the stage image. They towered above Tamburlaine in the confrontation scene (III, iii), rushing about the open thrust stage as if to trample the shepherd underneath, but Tamburlaine, always too quick for them, leapt nimbly out of the way, seeming to stalk his enemies even as he escaped them. The stilts failed to give the Turks any advantage, but instead made 'them seem like evolutionary laggards, out-maneuvered by nippier opponents' (Paul Taylor, *Independent*, 3 Sept. 1992). To compare this restless, physically charged scene with the same one in Hall's production, with its ironic emphasis on status and its hieratic balance, is to go to the heart of the differences between the two versions. If Hall sought perspective and provoked thought as well as awe (perhaps responding to more of Marlowe than the RSC), Hands wanted to assault the audience. And it worked: sitting in the front row, within arm's length of the huge and precarious figures who kept dashing around the crowded stage, I felt myself in real physical danger.

In the ensuing onstage battle (kept offstage by Hall), Tamburlaine delivered the decisive blow to the mastodon-like Bajazeth by swinging down from the rafters like Tarzan and felling his foe with a kick. Bajazeth was later confined in a spherical iron cage, a kind of ribbed globe, the bottom half of which was used in Part Two for Tamburlaine's chariot. (The same shape also turned up in miniature in the orb that Callapine carried with him, a kind of ironic memento of his father who had brained himself against the bars in despair in the final scene of Part One.) Tamburlaine's triumph over the Turkish emperor was the motivation for one of the show's most dazzling effects: Sher shinnied up the rope dangling above the great round globe-like cage and then hung upside down, one hand and foot twisted

[31] From an interview with Terry Hands, conducted by Brian G. Myers, *Shakespeare Bulletin* (Spring 1993), 22.

into the rope, the other hand extended as he exulted over the fallen Bajazeth directly beneath; he then began to swing in flashing circles and slid slowly down, still headfirst, to the top of the cage. All the while, the sonorous verse of Tamburlaine's address to the stars that reigned at his nativity rang through the theatre: 'For I, the chiefest lamp of all the earth ... Will send up fire to your turning spheres / And cause the sun to borrow light of you' (IV, ii, 36ff.).

Earlier, Tamburlaine won over Theridamas with comparable dazzle: a sudden falling of a golden curtain, fashioned entirely of medallions netted together, provided a glittering backdrop for the vaulting Tamburlaine who leapt to his associates' bent knees and onto their shoulders, once again emphasizing the vertical axis of power. Like Finney, Sher delighted in his own charisma, but did so more overtly and emphatically, obviously enjoying the consternation of his adversaries, joking with his supporters like a feisty footballer, licking his lips in sensual anticipation whenever he approached Zenocrate in Part One, speaking her name in savoured syllables. But at the same time, he could manifest ambivalence, even disdain, for the kingly power that he sought, speaking 'Is it not passing brave to be a king' as a 'sardonic comment from a nomadic warrior' and mockingly crowning his own men. 'There is nothing much to being a king,' he implies, 'conquest is all that counts' (I. Wardle, *Independent on Sunday*, 6 Sept. 1992).

Like Guthrie's only more so, this production emphasized blood, turning the triumphing over the caged Bajazeth and Zabina into a sadistic orgy, with a huge bowl of blood at the centre into which bread was dipped before being eaten by the conquerors and forced on Bajazeth in a grotesque parody of communion. The same bloody bowl was used to redden clothing and bodies before the slaughter at Damascus, and the virgins there were sweet young girls ('uncomprehending angels strayed in from a school nativity play' [A. Barton, *TLS*, 11 Sept., 19]), whose cruel deaths made even the most loyal of Tamburlaine's followers vomit. Here the extremity became almost too much for even this deliberately stagy production to handle: it darkened the picture abruptly and totally, shifting what in the first few acts had seemed joyously amoral. Any subtlety in Marlowe's careful placement of episode and control of effect was sidelined, deliberately no doubt. Partly Sher's very brilliance as a showman told against subtlety, and the production went strongly for powerfully opposed images. Sher was weakest in the soft moments, such as the speech on beauty, but outstanding as a theatrician; he knew always that both Tamburlaine's power as a conqueror and his own as an actor were linked to spectacle and he took delight in

Antony Sher as blood-soaked Tamburlaine in the 1992 production by the Royal Shakespeare Company (photo: Ivan Kynel)

fashioning it according to his own fancies. Hence the shift to the spectacle of blood was not mainly a move to test our ambiguous responses to this sort of hero, as in Hall's more modulated version, but simply to turn our sympathies against this man of monstrous blood-lust while at the same time reminding us of the connection between our enjoyment of spectacle and our susceptibility to sheer power.

The text that Sher and Hands devised for this production points a further contrast with the Hall version. Like Guthrie in the early '50s, they cut the plays radically, reducing them to a conventional manageable length. All in all, they cut over 2,000 lines, almost 44% of the text.[32] Like Guthrie, they completely excised the Sigismund sub-plot, thus eliminating five complete scenes from Part Two. Although they retained part of the Olympia business, including the death of her husband and son, and the onset of Theridamas's violent love, they omitted both the previous scene in which she and her husband seek to defend their town against Tamburlaine's troops and, more regrettably, the bizarrely comic trick by which she outwits her overzealous suitor. Instead, Olympia simply leapt into the same burning cauldron that had consumed the bodies of her loved ones.

There was as well a good deal of clever, even judicious transposition of both lines and scenes; for example, I, iii in Part Two, which dramatizes Callapine's escape from Tamburlaine through the help of his jailer, Almeda, was placed after the scenes involving Tamburlaine and his family and supporters (I, iv–I, vi in the text), which, as in Hall's production, began the second part (as noted, Hands cut the first two scenes, while Hall transposed them to after the Tamburlaine sequence). This had an important effect because immediately before the interval the audience witnessed the bloody defeat of Turks and Egyptians and the triumphant crowning of Zenocrate, while upon their return to their seats they were given an entirely new perspective: Tamburlaine much older now, grizzled and slow, relaxing on a central couch surrounded by his grown children and thoughtful, sharply perceptive wife. The domestic scene begins with Zenocrate's searching question, 'Sweet Tamburlaine, when wilt thou leave these arms / And save thy sacred person free from scathe / And dangerous chances of the wrathful war?' (2, I, iv, 9–11). Although the lithe body and the aspiring mind were still very much in evidence,

---

[32] For this and other details of the cuts and transpositions made to the text, I am indebted to T. R. Stockwell, who kindly sent me the relevant sections of his Master's thesis on the Hands/Sher production, written for the Shakespeare Institute of the University of Birmingham.

we were reminded right away of the process that would lead eventually to his defeat, and given as well a perspective on it in Zenocrate's unheeded wishes and, tellingly, in Calyphas's sharp, defiant and even brave scepticism – he stood up to his father and refused to buy into the heroic myth. (Later, about to die for supposed cowardice, he never flinched as Tamburlaine garroted him.)

After the softness of Zenocrate's death, the slaughter became almost casual, and the cut text rushed both Tamburlaine and us to the inevitable conclusion. After the bitter dispatch of Calyphas and the enslavement of a brace or two of kings, the unceremonious dumping of the people of Babylon into the asphalt lake and the shooting of its Governor on high seemed almost routine. Here Hands came up with a brilliant stage image for the sheer waste of it all: he had the captive kings pull Tamburlaine's chariot by running on the spot to the accompaniment of wild chanting and drumming; there were 'still lands to be conquered' but as Tamburlaine's chariot 'pound[ed] without actually moving across the endless plains of Asia', it became apparent that such aspiration 'is ineluctably futile' (Barton).

This futility was the keynote of the final moments as well. After burning the Koran and challenging Mahomet, Tamburlaine was 'suddenly seized by a dire and pathetic lassitude' (M. Coveney, *Observer*, 6 Sept.), almost tipping into the fiery pit himself. This undid some of the glory and lyricism of the great speech from the previous scene in which Tamburlaine imagines his homecoming to 'Samarcanda streets', where he will rule in pomp 'Until my soul dissevered from this flesh / Shall mount the milk-white way and meet him [i.e. God] there' (IV, iii, 131–2). Sher delivered the speech lyrically until he got to the last four words, 'at which point his voice turn[ed] to thunder and he stab[bed] a challenging finger at the sky' (Wardle). But, as Tamburlaine's sudden weakness indicated, God ultimately won. And the point was reiterated at the end when the cuts and transpositions emphasized the pathetic unfulfillment of Tamburlaine's aspirations. Instead of ending, as the text does, with the quiet acceptance of inevitable death ('For Tamburlaine, the scourge of God, must die'), the performance provided a shortened version of Tamburlaine's handing over the reins to his son Amyras and then ended with his restless speech of aspiration, punctuated by the reiterated line, 'And shall I die and this unconquerèd?' Stumbling near the back of the stage, Tamburlaine had pulled around himself the huge black and gold curtain-map that had hung as a backdrop at the very beginning and reappeared strategically through the play, but as he spoke he seemed to forget the map, fixing his eyes on those vast spaces around him, seeing only those still unsubdued territories, the last echoing words repeated with a dying fall.

From Alleyn to Sher, it is spectacle, the exploitation of theatricality as a form of power, that has been the basis of *Tamburlaine* performance. But spectacle has been tempered by thought and variation. Productions have typically appealed to the same moral ambivalences that seem to have animated Marlowe when he wrote the plays. The young author already knew some of the less savoury aspects of Elizabethan power from the inside, but found himself at the same time fascinated by the deployment of spectacular images in both the theatre itself and the theatre of the world. In writing *Tamburlaine*, he appealed to the same ambiguous mix in his audience as he was conscious of in himself – that uncomfortable blend of moral revulsion, willing susceptibility to the power of spectacle, and greedy fascination with cruelty, on which the success of the play depends.

THE TEXT

The first edition of *Tamburlaine*, a black letter octavo containing both parts of the play (O1), was published in 1590. There are two extant copies, one in the Bodleian library, the other in the Huntington. Three more early editions followed, an octavo in 1593 (O2), another octavo in 1597 (O3), and a quarto (Q)[33] in 1605–6, the last being a two volume edition. O2 and O3 both derive (independently) from O1, while Q was based on O3. All the reprints correct some obvious errors in O1, but also introduce new errors of their own, while at the same time adding nothing substantially new. It is clear, then, that only O1 possesses independent authority and it, accordingly, must be the copy text.

O1 appears to be printed from a scribal or authorial manuscript, rather than from a theatrical one. Stage directions, even exit and entrance directions, are often omitted or left incomplete, scene breaks are omitted where they should appear or added where they should not (making for inconsistent principles of scene division), names of characters are inconsistently treated, and speech prefixes omitted; all of these are matters that would often be cleared up in order to prepare the script for performance, and would therefore be reflected in a playhouse manuscript.

---

[33] There has been some disagreement among scholars as to whether this edition is actually an octavo or a quarto; both its size and its signatures suggest the latter, but the way the paper was originally folded suggests an octavo (see Una Ellis-Fermor, ed., *Tamburlaine the Great* [London, 1930] p. 3 n. 6). I here follow J. S. Cunningham and others in designating it a quarto.

Hence editors have traditionally concluded that O1 does not have a theatrical provenance. At the same time, its relative clarity and freedom from error suggest a clean manuscript rather than authorial 'foul papers'; probably, then, it was printed from some sort of intermediate transcript made either by Marlowe or a scribe.

In the preface to the first edition, the printer, Richard Jones, declares that 'some fond and frivolous gestures' have deliberately been omitted from the printed text, despite (or perhaps because of) the fact that they were popular in the theatre. Exactly what was omitted, if anything, is not clear, nor is there any indication as to whether what has been left out was part of Marlowe's original script or something added extempore by actors. Jones's words suggest that what he had in front of him contained the offensive material which he then 'purposely' left out, but even this is uncertain since, as stated above, his manuscript was not a theatre-based one. Even as it stands, there is considerable variety of tone and texture in *Tamburlaine*, a fact that Elizabethan actors seem to have exploited, assuming that what Jones says about the theatre reflects actual practice. So, perhaps Jones was merely advertising his edition as something to appeal to the higher tastes of 'gentlemen readers and others that take pleasure in reading histories', thus distinguishing prospective buyers from those who found their pleasure in the raucous, considerably less rarefied atmosphere of the public theatre.

In this edition, the spelling and punctuation have been modernized, the most obvious misprints have been silently corrected, abbreviations expanded and speech prefixes regularized. Stage directions have occasionally been supplemented, proper names added, indications of 'asides' provided etc. All such changes appear in square brackets and are not therefore recorded in the notes.

The punctuation of O1, though at times it provides an indication of patterns of rhetorical phrasing appropriate to theatrical speech, is confusing to a modern reader and, indeed, it frequently fails to take the measure of Marlowe's complex syntax. It regularly introduces, for example, full stops into the middle of Marlowe's elaborate compound sentences, or breaks sentences up without adequate consideration of meaning, hence interfering with what T. S. Eliot long ago noted as one of Marlowe's most important verse accomplishments in *Tamburlaine* – the 'driving power' he achieved 'by reinforcing the sentence period against the line period'. In modernizing the punctuation, I have tried to make the meaning as clear as possible to the reader, while at the same time seeking to keep in mind the voice of the actor. Wherever possible, therefore, I have reduced the punctuation, keeping it light in order to facilitate the flow of the verse. Certainly the best way to grasp the text is to speak it aloud as one reads, using the punctuation as a guide to the voice which, ultimately, must make the meaning.

Where a reading of one of the later octavos or Q has been adopted, that fact has been indicated in the notes, but no attempt has been made to record all the substantive variants between O1 and the other early texts. Where I have adopted a reading suggested by previous editors, or introduced a new reading, the change is recorded in the notes (with the notation 'ed.'), but usually without indicating its history. In preparing the edition, I have incurred debts to many previous scholars, most especially J. W. Harper, who edited the earlier New Mermaid, Una Ellis-Fermor, whose 1930 edition has influenced all subsequent editions and whose annotations have frequently proved indispensable, and J. S. Cunningham, whose edition for the Revels series is the most thorough and far-reaching of modern texts.

FURTHER READING

Bakeless, John, *The Tragicall History of Christopher Marlowe*, Cambridge, Ma., 1942

Bartels, Emily C., *Spectacles of Strangeness: Imperialism, Alienation, and Marlowe*, Philadelphia, 1993

Brown, John Russell, 'Marlowe and the Actors', *Tulane Drama Review*, 8.4 (Summer 1964), 155–73

Burton, Jonathan, 'Anglo-Ottoman Relations and the Image of the Turk in *Tamburlaine*', *Journal of Medieval and Early Modern Studies*, Winter 2000, 30 (1) 125–56

Cartelli, Thomas, *Marlowe, Shakespeare and the Economy of Theatrical Experience*, Philadelphia, 1991

Ceresano, Susan P., '*Tamburlaine* and Edward Alleyn's Ring' *Shakespeare Survey* 1994 (47) 171–79

Cheney, Patrick, ed., *The Cambridge Companion to Christopher Marlowe*, Cambridge, 2004

Cunningham, J. S., ed., *Tamburlaine the Great*, Revels edition, Manchester, 1981

Deats, Sara M., and Logan, Robert A., eds, *Marlowe's Empery: Expanding his Critical Contexts*, Newark DE and London, 2002

Ellis-Fermor, Una, ed., *Tamburlaine the Great*, London, 1930

Friedenreich, K. et al, eds., '*A Poet and a filthie Play-maker': New Essays on Christopher Marlowe*, New York, 1988

Geckle, George L., *Tamburlaine and Edward II: Text and Performance*, London, 1988

Gillies, John, 'Marlowe, the Timur Myth, and the Motives of Geography' in John Gillies and Virginia Mason Vaughan, eds, *Playing the Globe: Genre and Geography in English Renaissance Drama* (Madison, NJ, 1998) 203–29

Goldman, Michael, 'Marlowe and the Histrionics of Ravishment', in Alvin Kernan, ed., *Two Renaissance Mythmakers*, Baltimore and London, 1977, pp. 22–40

Grantley, Darryll and Roberts, Peter, eds, *Christopher Marlowe and English Renaissance Culture*, Aldershot, England, 1996

Greenblatt, Stephen, *Renaissance Self-Fashioning*, Chicago, 1980

Kuriyama, Constance Brown, *Christopher Marlowe: A Renaissance Life* (Ithaca, NY, 2002)

Leggatt, Alexander, 'Killing the Hero: Tamburlaine and Falstaff' in Paul Budra and Betty Schellenberg, eds, *Part Two: Reflections on the Sequel* (Toronto, 1998) 53–67

Levin Richard, 'The Contemporary Perception of Marlowe's *Tamburlaine*', *Medieval and Renaissance Drama in English* 1 (1984), 51–70

Levin, Harry, *The Overreacher: A Study of Christopher Marlowe*, London, 1954

Maus, Katherine Eisaman, *Inwardness and Theater in the English Renaissance*, Chicago, 1995

Nicholl, Charles, *The Reckoning: The Murder of Christopher Marlowe*, London, 1992

Riggs, David, *The World of Christopher Marlowe*, London, 2004

Shepherd, Alan 'Endless Sacks: Soldiers' Desire in *Tamburlaine*' *Renaissance Quarterly*, Winter 1993 (46.4) 734–53

Taunton, Nina, 'Unlawful Presences: The Politics of Military Space and the Problem of Women in Tamburlaine' in Andrew Gordon and Bernhard Klein, eds, *Literature, Mapping, and the Politics of Space in Early Modern Britain* (Cambridge, 2001), 138-54

Thurn, David H., 'Sights of Power in *Tamburlaine*', *ELR* 19 (1989), 3–21

Vitkus, Daniel, *Turning Turk: English Theater and the Multicultural Mediterranean, 1570-1630*, New York, 2003

Waith, Eugene, *The Herculean Hero in Marlowe, Chapman, Shakespeare and Dryden*, London, 1962

Weil, Judith, *Christopher Marlowe: Merlin's Prophet*, Cambridge, 1977

White, Paul Whitfield, ed., *Marlowe, History, and Sexuality: New Critical Essays on Christopher Marlowe* (New York, NY, 1998)

Tamburlaine

the Great.

Who, from a Scythian Shepheard
by his rare and woonderfull Conquests
becamea most puissant and migh-
'tye Monarque.

And (for his tyranny, and terrour in
Warre) was tearmed,

The Scourge of God.

Deuided into two Tragicall Dij
courses, as they were sundrie times
shewed vpon Stages in the Citie
of London.

By the right honorable the Lord
Admyrall, his seruautes.

Now first, and newlie published.

LONDON.
Printed by Richard Ihones: at the signe
of the Rose and Crowne neere Hol-
borne Bridge. 1590.

[DRAMATIS PERSONAE

PROLOGUE
MYCETES, King of Persia
COSROE, his brother
CENEUS ⎫
ORTYGIUS ⎪   5
MEANDER ⎬ Persian lords
MENAPHON ⎪
THERIDAMAS ⎭
TAMBURLAINE, a Scythian shepherd
TECHELLES ⎫ his followers   10
USUMCASANE ⎭
AGYDAS ⎫ Median lords
MAGNETES ⎭
BAJAZETH, Emperor of the Turks
KING OF ARGIER ⎫   15
KING OF FEZ ⎬ tributary kings to Bajazeth
KING OF MOROCCO ⎭
ALCIDAMUS, King of Arabia
SOLDAN OF EGYPT
CAPOLIN, an Egyptian   20
GOVERNOR OF DAMASCUS
A SPY
MESSENGERS, including PHILEMUS
BASSOES, LORDS, CITIZENS, MOORS, SOLDIERS, and ATTENDANTS

ZENOCRATE, daughter of the Soldan of Egypt   25
ANIPPE, her maid
ZABINA, wife of Bajazeth
EBEA, her maid
VIRGINS OF DAMASCUS]

---

13 *Magnetes* The name appears nowhere in the text but has been adopted by editors
   from the speech prefix 'Mag.' in O1.
15 *Argier* Algeria
19 *Soldan* Sultan
24 *Bassoes* pashas

TO THE GENTLEMEN READERS: AND OTHERS
THAT TAKE PLEASURE IN READING HISTORIES

Gentlemen, and courteous readers whosoever: I have here published in print for your sakes, the two tragical discourses of the Scythian shepherd, Tamburlaine, that became so great a conqueror, and so mighty a monarch. My hope is that they will be now no less acceptable unto   5
you to read after your serious affairs and studies, than they have been (lately) delightful for many of you to see, when the same were showed in London upon stages. I have (purposely) omitted and left out some fond and frivolous gestures, digressing (and in my poor opinion) far unmeet   10
for the matter, which I thought, might seem more tedious unto the wise, than any way else to be regarded, though (haply) they have been of some vain conceited fondlings greatly gaped at, what times they were showed upon the stage in their graced deformities: nevertheless, now, to be   15
mixtured in print with such matter of worth, it would prove a great disgrace to so honourable and stately a history. Great folly were it in me to commend unto your wisdoms either the eloquence of the author that writ them, or the worthiness of the matter itself; I therefore leave unto your   20
learned censures, both the one and the other, and myself the poor printer of them unto your most courteous and favourable protection: which if you vouchsafe to accept, you shall evermore bind me to employ what travail and service I can, to the advancing and pleasuring of your   25
excellent degree.

Yours, most humble at commandment,
R. J., Printer

---

9 *fond* foolish
13 *fondlings* fools
21 *censures* judgements
28 *R.J.* Richard Jones, a printer and bookseller, for whom the two parts of *Tamburlaine* were entered in the Stationers' Register on 14 August 1590

5

THE PROLOGUE

From jigging veins of rhyming mother wits
And such conceits as clownage keeps in pay,
We'll lead you to the stately tent of war,
Where you shall hear the Scythian Tamburlaine
Threat'ning the world with high astounding terms   5
And scourging kingdoms with his conquering sword.
View but his picture in this tragic glass,
And then applaud his fortunes as you please.

1–3 These lines are Marlowe's challenge to the stage conventions of the time, proclaiming a new kind of verse, unrhymed and heroic, to replace the doggerel rhymes and jog-trot rhythms of the popular drama of the previous years. He rejects the whims and tricks ('conceits') of clowns and jesters, preferring a more elevated and 'stately' theme.

1 *mother wits* those who possess 'mother wit', i.e. native or natural wit (*O.E.D.*; here used contemptuously)

TAMBURLAINE THE GREAT

Act I, Scene i

[*Enter*] MYCETES, COSROE, MEANDER, THERIDAMAS,
ORTYGIUS, [MENAPHON], *with others*

MYCETES
Brother Cosroe, I find myself aggrieved
Yet insufficient to express the same,
For it requires a great and thund'ring speech.
Good brother, tell the cause unto my lords,
I know you have a better wit than I.   5

COSROE
Unhappy Persia, that in former age
Hast been the seat of mighty conquerors
That in their prowess and their policies
Have triumphed over Afric and the bounds
Of Europe, where the sun dares scarce appear   10
For freezing meteors and congealèd cold,
Now to be ruled and governed by a man
At whose birthday Cynthia with Saturn joined,
And Jove, the Sun, and Mercury denied
To shed their influence in his fickle brain!   15
Now Turks and Tartars shake their swords at thee,
Meaning to mangle all thy provinces.

MYCETES
Brother, I see your meaning well enough,
And through your planets I perceive you think
I am not wise enough to be a king.   20
But I refer me to my noblemen,
That know my wit and can be witnesses.
I might command you to be slain for this –
Meander, might I not?

MEANDER
Not for so small a fault, my sovereign lord.   25

MYCETES
I mean it not, but yet I know I might.

---

8 *policies* diplomacy
11 *meteors* any atmospheric phenomena
13–15 *At . . . brain* The unfavourable influence of Cynthia (the moon – a symbol of
   change and fickleness) and Saturn (stupidity) presided over Mycetes' birth,
   whereas Jove (Jupiter – magnanimity), Apollo (the sun – kingliness), and Mercury
   (wit) were absent.

9

Yet live, yea live, Mycetes wills it so.
Meander, thou my faithful counsellor,
Declare the cause of my conceivèd grief,
Which is, God knows, about that Tamburlaine　　　　30
That like a fox in midst of harvest time
Doth play upon my flocks of passengers,
And, as I hear, doth mean to pull my plumes.
Therefore 'tis good and meet for to be wise.

MEANDER
Oft have I heard your majesty complain　　　　35
Of Tamburlaine, that sturdy Scythian thief
That robs your merchants of Persepolis,
Treading by land unto the Western Isles,
And in your confines with his lawless train
Daily commits incivil outrages,　　　　40
Hoping (misled by dreaming prophecies)
To reign in Asia, and with barbarous arms
To make himself the monarch of the East.
But ere he march in Asia or display
His vagrant ensign in the Persian fields,　　　　45
Your grace hath taken order by Theridamas,
Charged with a thousand horse, to apprehend
And bring him captive to your highness' throne.

MYCETES
Full true thou speak'st, and like thyself, my lord,
Whom I may term a Damon for thy love.　　　　50
Therefore 'tis best, if so it like you all,
To send my thousand horse incontinent
To apprehend that paltry Scythian.
How like you this, my honourable lords?
Is it not a kingly resolution?　　　　55

COSROE
It cannot choose, because it comes from you.

---

32 *passengers* travellers, traders
36 *Scythian* Marlowe's atlas, Ortelius' *Theatrum Orbis Terrarum*, located Scythia on
　　the north shore of the Black Sea, west of Crimea, but the name was often used
　　to refer generally to a large area in central Asia. Marlowe seems to have used the
　　terms Scythian and Tartar interchangeably, the Scythians being a branch of the
　　Tartar race.
37 *Persepolis* the ancient capital of Persia, situated on the river Araxes
38 *the Western Isles* Britain
45 *vagrant ensign* nomadic banner
47 *Charged with* placed in command of
50 *Damon* Damon and Pythias provided the classic example of friendship.
52 *incontinent* immediately
56 *choose* be otherwise

MYCETES

    Then hear thy charge, valiant Theridamas,
    The chiefest captain of Mycetes' host,
    The hope of Persia, and the very legs
    Whereon our state doth lean, as on a staff   60
    That holds us up and foils our neighbour foes.
    Thou shalt be leader of this thousand horse,
    Whose foaming gall with rage and high disdain
    Have sworn the death of wicked Tamburlaine.
    Go frowning forth, but come thou smiling home,   65
    As did Sir Paris with the Grecian dame.
    Return with speed, time passeth swift away,
    Our life is frail and we may die today.

THERIDAMAS

    Before the moon renew her borrowed light,
    Doubt not, my lord and gracious sovereign,   70
    But Tamburlaine and that Tartarian rout
    Shall either perish by our warlike hands
    Or plead for mercy at your highness' feet.

MYCETES

    Go, stout Theridamas, thy words are swords,
    And with thy looks thou conquerest all thy foes.   75
    I long to see thee back return from thence
    That I may view these milk-white steeds of mine
    All loaden with the heads of killèd men,
    And from their knees, even to their hoofs below,
    Besmeared with blood; that makes a dainty show.   80

THERIDAMAS

    Then now, my lord, I humbly take my leave.   *Exit*

MYCETES

    Theridamas farewell ten thousand times.
    Ah Menaphon, why stay'st thou thus behind,
    When other men press forward for renown?
    Go Menaphon, go into Scythia   85
    And foot by foot follow Theridamas.

COSROE

    Nay, pray you let him stay, a greater task
    Fits Menaphon than warring with a thief:

66 *Grecian dame* Helen of Troy
74 *stout* powerful
87 *greater task* ed. (greater O1)

Create him prorex of Assyria
That he may win the Babylonians' hearts,   90
Which will revolt from Persian government
Unless they have a wiser king than you.

MYCETES

Unless they have a wiser king than you?
These are his words Meander, set them down.

COSROE

And add this to them, that all Asia   95
Lament to see the folly of their king.

MYCETES

Well here I swear by this my royal seat –

COSROE

[*Aside*] You may do well to kiss it then.

MYCETES

– Embossed with silk as best beseems my state,
To be revenged for these contemptuous words.   100
O where is duty and allegiance now?
Fled to the Caspian or the ocean main?
What, shall I call thee brother? No, a foe,
Monster of nature, shame unto thy stock
That dar'st presume thy sovereign for to mock.   105
Meander come, I am abused Meander.

Exit [MYCETES *with his train*]. COSROE *and*
MENAPHON *remain*

MENAPHON

How now, my lord, what, mated and amazed
To hear the king thus threaten like himself?

COSROE

Ah Menaphon, I pass not for his threats –
The plot is laid by Persian noblemen   110
And captains of the Median garrisons
To crown me emperor of Asia.
But this it is that doth excruciate
The very substance of my vexèd soul:
To see our neighbours that were wont to quake   115

---

89 *prorex* viceroy
   Assyria ed. (Africa O1), an emendation suggested by B. A. van Dam on the
   grounds that 'Africa' does not fit the context, and supported by Bowers and
   Cunningham in their editions
107 *mated* rendered helpless
109 *pass* care
111 *Median* from Media, the north-eastern part of the Persian empire, south of the
   Caspian Sea
113 *excruciate* torment

And tremble at the Persian monarch's name
Now sits and laughs our regiment to scorn;
And that which might resolve me into tears,
Men from the farthest equinoctial line
Have swarmed in troops into the Eastern India,   120
Lading their ships with gold and precious stones,
And made their spoils from all our provinces.

MENAPHON
This should entreat your highness to rejoice,
Since fortune gives you opportunity
To gain the title of a conqueror   125
By curing of this maimèd empery.
Afric and Europe bordering on your land
And continent to your dominions,
How easily may you with a mighty host
Pass into Graecia, as did Cyrus once,   130
And cause them to withdraw their forces home,
Lest you subdue the pride of Christendom.

COSROE
But Menaphon, what means this trumpet's sound?

MENAPHON
Behold, my lord, Ortygius and the rest,
Bringing the crown to make you emperor.   135

Enter ORTYGIUS *and* CENEUS *bearing a crown,*
with others

ORTYGIUS
Magnificent and mighty Prince Cosroe,
We in the name of other Persian states
And commons of this mighty monarchy,
Present thee with th'imperial diadem.

CENEUS
The warlike soldiers and the gentlemen   140
That heretofore have filled Persepolis

---

117 *sits and laughs* a common plural form in the play and in Elizabethan English
    generally
117 *regiment* rule, authority
118 *resolve* dissolve
126 *empery* empire
128 *continent to* touching, bordering upon
130 *Cyrus* the son of Cambises and founder of the Persian empire. He conquered
    the Greek settlements of Asia Minor ('Graecia').
132 *pride of Christendom* probably Byzantium (Constantinople)
135 s.d. CENEUS ed. (Conerus O1)
137 *states* noblemen
140 s.p. ed. (Conerus O1)

With Afric captains taken in the field,
Whose ransom made them march in coats of gold
With costly jewels hanging at their ears
And shining stones upon their lofty crests,   145
Now living idle in the wallèd towns,
Wanting both pay and martial discipline,
Begin in troops to threaten civil war
And openly exclaim against the king.
Therefore, to stay all sudden mutinies,   150
We will invest your highness emperor,
Whereat the soldiers will conceive more joy
Than did the Macedonians at the spoil
Of great Darius and his wealthy host.

COSROE
Well, since I see the state of Persia droop   155
And languish in my brother's government,
I willingly receive th'imperial crown
And vow to wear it for my country's good
In spite of them shall malice my estate.

ORTYGIUS
And in assurance of desired success,   160
We here do crown thee monarch of the East,
Emperor of Asia and of Persia,
Great lord of Media and Armenia,
Duke of Assyria and Albania,
Mesopotamia and of Parthia,   165
East India and the late-discovered isles,
Chief lord of all the wide vast Euxine Sea,
And of the ever-raging Caspian lake.
Long live Cosroe, mighty emperor!

COSROE
And Jove may never let me longer live   170
Than I may seek to gratify your love,
And cause the soldiers that thus honour me
To triumph over many provinces,
By whose desires of discipline in arms
I doubt not shortly but to reign sole king,   175
And with the army of Theridamas,

153–4 Alexander the Great defeated the Emperor Darius of Persia at the battle of
    Issus in 333 B.C.
159 *malice* show ill will to
164 *Assyria* ed. (Africa O1)
166 *late-discovered isles* perhaps the West Indies
167 *Euxine Sea* Black Sea
170 *Jove may never* may Jove never

Whither we presently will fly, my lords,
To rest secure against my brother's force.
ORTYGIUS
We knew, my lord, before we brought the crown,
Intending your investion so near   180
The residence of your despisèd brother,
The lords would not be too exasperate
To injure or suppress your worthy title.
Or, if they would, there are in readiness
Ten thousand horse to carry you from hence   185
In spite of all suspected enemies.
COSROE
I know it well, my lord, and thank you all.
ORTYGIUS
Sound up the trumpets then, God save the king!

                                          Exeunt

acknowledged symbolism

Act I, Scene ii

*daughter
of Sultan
of Egypt.*

[*Enter*] TAMBURLAINE *leading* ZENOCRATE, [*with*]
TECHELLES, USUMCASANE, [MAGNETES, AGYDAS *and*]
other Lords and Soldiers loaden with treasure

T's main followers

TAMBURLAINE
Come, lady, let not this appal your thoughts;
The jewels and the treasure we have ta'en
Shall be reserved, and you in better state
Than if you were arrived in Syria,
Even in the circle of your father's arms,   5
The mighty Soldan of Egyptia.
ZENOCRATE
Ah shepherd, pity my distressèd plight,
If, as thou seem'st, thou art so mean a man,
And seek not to enrich thy followers
By lawless rapine from a silly maid   10
Who, travelling with these Median lords
To Memphis from my uncle's country of Media,
Where all my youth I have been governèd,

177 *presently* immediately
180 *investion* investiture
182 *lords* ed. (Lord O1)
       exasperate exasperated
188 lineation ed.
  8 *mean* lowly (i.e. a shepherd)
 10 *silly* helpless

Have passed the army of the mighty Turk,
Bearing his privy signet and his hand   15
To safe conduct us thorough Africa.

MAGNETES

And since we have arrived in Scythia,
Besides rich presents from the puissant Cham,
We have his highness' letters to command
Aid and assistance if we stand in need.   20

TAMBURLAINE

But now you see these letters and commands
Are countermanded by a greater man,
And through my provinces you must expect
Letters of conduct from my mightiness
If you intend to keep your treasure safe.   25
But since I love to live at liberty,
As easily may you get the Soldan's crown
As any prizes out of my precinct,
For they are friends that help to wean my state
Till men and kingdoms help to strengthen it,   30
And must maintain my life exempt from servitude.
But tell me, madam, is your grace betrothed?

ZENOCRATE

I am, my lord, for so you do import.

TAMBURLAINE

I am a lord, for so my deeds shall prove,
And yet a shepherd by my parentage.   35
But, lady, this fair face and heavenly hue
Must grace his bed that conquers Asia
And means to be a terror to the world,
Measuring the limits of his empery
By east and west as Phoebus doth his course.   40
Lie here ye weeds that I disdain to wear!

[handwritten annotation: ^ garments (again, things i.e. clothes)]

15 *hand* signature (guaranteeing safe passage)
16 *thorough* 'Through' was often thus spelled and pronounced in Elizabethan verse
   when the metre demanded a disyllable. There are several examples in *Tamburlaine*.
18 *puissant* mighty
   Cham Tartar emperor
28 *precinct* province
29 *wean my state* nurture my power
33 *for . . . import* i.e. for you do appear to be a lord
40 *Phoebus* Apollo, the sun
41 *weeds* garments

[*He removes his shepherd's clothing to reveal his
armour beneath*]

This complete armour and this curtle-axe
Are adjuncts more beseeming Tamburlaine,
And, madam, whatsoever you esteem
Of this success and loss unvaluèd,   45
Both may invest you empress of the East.
And these that seem but silly country swains
May have the leading of so great an host
As with their weight shall make the mountains quake,
Even as when windy exhalations   50
Fighting for passage tilt within the earth.

TECHELLES

As princely lions when they rouse themselves,
Stretching their paws and threat'ning herds of beasts,
So in his armour looketh Tamburlaine.
Methinks I see kings kneeling at his feet   55
And he, with frowning brows and fiery looks,
Spurning their crowns from off their captive heads.

USUMCASANE

And making thee and me, Techelles, kings,
That even to death will follow Tamburlaine.

TAMBURLAINE

Nobly resolved, sweet friends and followers.   60
These lords perhaps do scorn our estimates
And think we prattle with distempered spirits.
But since they measure our deserts so mean,
That in conceit bear empires on our spears,
Affecting thoughts co-equal with the clouds,   65
They shall be kept our forcèd followers
Till with their eyes they view us emperors.

41 s.d. Such has been the practice of modern productions. The text itself does not
   preclude the possibility that after removing his shepherd's cloak Tamburlaine
   gestures to his men to bring him his armour, which he then dons with a theatrical
   flourish.
42 *curtle-axe* heavy slashing sword
45 *success* result
   loss unvaluèd the inestimable loss you have incurred
47 *these* Tamburlaine's followers
   silly . . . swains simple shepherds
51 *tilt* joust
63 *deserts* worth
64 *conceit* imagination
65 *Affecting* aspiring to
67 *they* O2–3, Q (thee O1)

ZENOCRATE
    The gods, defenders of the innocent,
    Will never prosper your intended drifts
    That thus oppress poor friendless passengers.   70
    Therefore at least admit us liberty,
    Even as thou hop'st to be eternizèd
    By living Asia's mighty emperor.

AGYDAS > Median lord
    I hope our lady's treasure and our own
    May serve for ransom to our liberties.   75
    Return our mules and empty camels back
    That we may travel into Syria
    Where her betrothèd lord Alcidamus
    Expects th'arrival of her highness' person.

MAGNETES
    And wheresoever we repose ourselves,   80
    We will report but well of Tamburlaine.

TAMBURLAINE
    Disdains Zenocrate to live with me?
    Or you, my lords, to be my followers?
    Think you I weigh this treasure more than you?
    Not all the gold in India's wealthy arms   85
    Shall buy the meanest soldier in my train.
    Zenocrate, lovelier than the love of Jove,
    Brighter than is the silver Rhodope,
    Fairer than whitest snow on Scythian hills,
    Thy person is more worth to Tamburlaine   90
    Than the possession of the Persian crown,
    Which gracious stars have promised at my birth.
    A hundred Tartars shall attend on thee
    Mounted on steeds swifter than Pegasus;
    Thy garments shall be made of Median silk,   95
    Enchased with precious jewels of mine own
    More rich and valurous than Zenocrate's;
    With milk-white harts upon an ivory sled
    Thou shalt be drawn amidst the frozen pools
    And scale the icy mountains' lofty tops,   100
    Which with thy beauty will be soon resolved;
    My martial prizes with five hundred men

69 *drifts* purposes
88 *Rhodope* a snow-capped mountain range in Thrace, famous for silver mines
94 *Pegasus* the mythical winged horse
96 *Enchased* adorned
97 *valurous* valuable
101 *resolved* melted

Won on the fifty-headed Volga's waves
Shall all we offer to Zenocrate,
And then myself to fair Zenocrate.   105
TECHELLES
What now? In love?
TAMBURLAINE
Techelles, women must be flatterèd,
But this is she with whom I am in love.

Enter a SOLDIER

SOLDIER
News, news!
TAMBURLAINE
How now, what's the matter?   110
SOLDIER
A thousand Persian horsemen are at hand,
Sent from the king to overcome us all.
TAMBURLAINE
How now, my lords of Egypt and Zenocrate?
Now must your jewels be restored again,
And I that triumphed so be overcome?   115
How say you, lordings, is not this your hope?
AGYDAS
We hope yourself will willingly restore them.
TAMBURLAINE
Such hope, such fortune, have the thousand horse.
Soft ye, my lords and sweet Zenocrate,
You must be forcèd from me ere you go.   120
A thousand horsemen! We five hundred foot!
An odds too great for us to stand against.
But are they rich? And is their armour good?
SOLDIER
Their plumèd helms are wrought with beaten gold,
Their swords enamelled, and about their necks   125
Hangs massy chains of gold down to the waist,
In every part exceeding brave and rich.
TAMBURLAINE
Then shall we fight courageously with them,
Or look you I should play the orator?
TECHELLES
No: cowards and faint-hearted runaways   130
Look for orations when the foe is near.
Our swords shall play the orators for us.

---

103 *fifty-headed ... waves* i.e. the numerous tributaries of the Volga river
127 *brave* splendid

USUMCASANE
    Come let us meet them at the mountain foot
    And with a sudden and an hot alarm
    Drive all their horses headlong down the hill.   135
TECHELLES
    Come let us march.
TAMBURLAINE
    Stay Techelles, ask a parley first.

                The Soldiers [*of* TAMBURLAINE] *enter*

    Open the mails, yet guard the treasure sure.
    Lay out our golden wedges to the view
    That their reflections may amaze the Persians,   140
    And look we friendly on them when they come.
    But if they offer word or violence
    We'll fight five hundred men-at-arms to one
    Before we part with our possession,
    And 'gainst the general we will lift our swords   145
    And either lanch his greedy thirsting throat
    Or take him prisoner, and his chains shall serve
    For manacles till he be ransomed home.
TECHELLES
    I hear them come, shall we encounter them?
TAMBURLAINE
    Keep all your standings and not stir a foot;   150
    Myself will bide the danger of the brunt.

                Enter THERIDAMAS *with others*

THERIDAMAS
    Where is this Scythian Tamburlaine?
TAMBURLAINE
    Whom seek'st thou Persian? I am Tamburlaine.
THERIDAMAS
    [*Aside*] Tamburlaine?
    A Scythian shepherd, so embellishèd   155
    With nature's pride and richest furniture?
    His looks do menace heaven and dare the gods,
    His fiery eyes are fixed upon the earth
    As if he now devised some stratagem,

138 *mails* packs, baggage
139 *wedges* ingots
146 *lanch* cut
151 *brunt* attack
154 lineation ed.
156 *furniture* equipment

Or meant to pierce Avernus' darksome vaults   160
And pull the triple-headed dog from hell.

TAMBURLAINE   *Co Infresting assoc's with T.*
[*To* TECHELLES] Noble and mild this Persian seems to
    be,
If outward habit judge the inward man.

TECHELLES
His deep affections make him passionate.

TAMBURLAINE
With what a majesty he rears his looks!   165
[*To* THERIDAMAS] In thee, thou valiant man of Persia,
I see the folly of thy emperor.
Art thou but captain of a thousand horse,
That by characters graven in thy brows
And by thy martial face and stout aspect,   170
Deservest to have the leading of an host?
Forsake thy king and do but join with me
And we will triumph over all the world.
I hold the Fates bound fast in iron chains
And with my hand turn Fortune's wheel about,   175
And sooner shall the sun fall from his sphere
Than Tamburlaine be slain or overcome.
Draw forth thy sword, thou mighty man-at-arms,
Intending but to raze my charmèd skin,
And Jove himself will stretch his hand from heaven   180
To ward the blow and shield me safe from harm.
See how he rains down heaps of gold in showers
As if he meant to give my soldiers pay,
And as a sure and grounded argument
That I shall be the monarch of the East,   185
He sends this Soldan's daughter rich and brave
To be my queen and portly emperess.
If thou wilt stay with me, renownèd man,
And lead thy thousand horse with my conduct,
Besides thy share of this Egyptian prize   190

160 *Avernus* a lake anciently regarded as the entrance to the underworld
161 *And* O1 catchword (To O1 text).
    triple-headed dog Cerberus, who guarded the entrance to the underworld
164 *affections* emotions
174 *Fates* the three goddesses, Clotho, Lachesis, and Atropos, who governed human
    destiny
176 According to Ptolemaic astronomy, the sun moved in an orbit around the earth.
179 *raze* graze
187 *portly* stately
    emperess original spelling here and elsewhere retained for the sake of the metre
189 *conduct* direction

Those thousand horse shall sweat with martial spoil
Of conquered kingdoms and of cities sacked.
Both we will walk upon the lofty cliffs,
And Christian merchants, that with Russian stems
Plow up huge furrows in the Caspian Sea,   195
Shall vail to us as lords of all the lake.
Both we will reign as consuls of the earth,
And mighty kings shall be our senators.
Jove sometime maskèd in a shepherd's weed,
And, by those steps that he hath scaled the heavens,   200
May we become immortal like the gods.
Join with me now in this my mean estate
(I call it mean, because being yet obscure
The nations far removed admire me not)
And when my name and honour shall be spread   205
As far as Boreas claps his brazen wings
Or fair Boötes sends his cheerful light,
Then shalt thou be competitor with me,
And sit with Tamburlaine in all his majesty.

THERIDAMAS
Not Hermes, prolocutor to the gods,   210
Could use persuasions more pathetical.

TAMBURLAINE
Nor are Apollo's oracles more true
Than thou shalt find my vaunts substantial.

TECHELLES
We are his friends, and if the Persian king
Should offer present dukedoms to our state,   215
We think it loss to make exchange for that
We are assured of by our friend's success.

USUMCASANE
And kingdoms at the least we all expect,
Besides the honour in assured conquests,

194 *merchants* merchant ships
    stems prows and hence, by synecdoche, ships
196 *vail* lower the topsail in homage
199 *maskèd ... weed* disguised himself as a shepherd
200 *that* by which
206–7 *As ... light* as far as Boreas (the north wind) blows or Boötes (a northern
    constellation) shines; i.e. the northern limit of the empire
208 *competitor* partner
210 *Hermes* the god of eloquence
    prolocutor spokesman
211 *pathetical* moving
213 *vaunts* boasts
215 *offer ... state* offer to make us dukes immediately

Where kings shall crouch unto our conquering swords   220
And hosts of soldiers stand amazed at us,
When with their fearful tongues they shall confess
These are the men that all the world admires.

THERIDAMAS
What strong enchantments 'tice my yielding soul?
Ah, these resolvèd noble Scythians!   225
But shall I prove a traitor to my king?

TAMBURLAINE
No, but the trusty friend of Tamburlaine.

THERIDAMAS
Won with thy words and conquered with thy looks,
I yield myself, my men and horse to thee
To be partaker of thy good or ill,   230
As long as life maintains Theridamas.

TAMBURLAINE
Theridamas my friend, take here my hand,
Which is as much as if I swore by heaven
And called the gods to witness of my vow –
Thus shall my heart be still combined with thine   235
Until our bodies turn to elements
And both our souls aspire celestial thrones.
Techelles and Casane, welcome him.

TECHELLES
Welcome, renownèd Persian, to us all.

USUMCASANE
Long may Theridamas remain with us.   240

TAMBURLAINE
These are my friends in whom I more rejoice
Than doth the King of Persia in his crown,
And by the love of Pylades and Orestes,
Whose statues we adore in Scythia,
Thyself and them shall never part from me   245
Before I crown you kings in Asia.
Make much of them, gentle Theridamas,
And they will never leave thee till the death.

THERIDAMAS
Nor thee nor them, thrice noble Tamburlaine,
Shall want my heart to be with gladness pierced   250

224 *tice* entice
225 *Ah* ed. (Are O1)
235 *still* forever
243 *Pylades and Orestes* Pylades was the faithful friend of Orestes, helping him in the
    murder of his mother and sharing his exile and suffering.
249–50 *Nor ... heart* Neither to thee nor to them ... shall my heart fail

To do you honour and security.
TAMBURLAINE
A thousand thanks, worthy Theridamas.
And now, fair madam, and my noble lords,
If you will willingly remain with me,
You shall have honours as your merits be,   255
Or else you shall be forced with slavery.
AGYDAS
We yield unto thee, happy Tamburlaine.
TAMBURLAINE
For you then, madam, I am out of doubt.
ZENOCRATE
I must be pleased perforce, wretched Zenocrate!

                                        Exeunt

                              Persian lords

Act II, Scene i

[*Enter*] COSROE, MENAPHON, ORTYGIUS, CENEUS,
                with other Soldiers

COSROE
Thus far are we towards Theridamas
And valiant Tamburlaine, the man of fame,
The man that in the forehead of his fortune
Bears figures of renown and miracle.
But tell me that hast seen him, Menaphon,   5
What stature wields he, and what personage?
MENAPHON
Of stature tall and straightly fashionèd,
Like his desire, lift upwards and divine;
So large of limbs, his joints so strongly knit,
Such breadth of shoulders as might mainly bear   10
Old Atlas' burden; 'twixt his manly pitch,
A pearl more worth than all the world is placed,
Wherein by curious sovereignty of art
Are fixed his piercing instruments of sight,
Whose fiery circles bear encompassèd   15

251 *security* protection
  3–4 An allusion to the supposed Muslim belief that Allah wrote every man's fate
     in signs upon his forehead.
  8 *lift* lifted
  10 *mainly* entirely
  11 *Atlas' burden* Atlas the Titan bore the heavens upon his shoulders.
     pitch shoulders
  12 *pearl* i.e. his head

A heaven of heavenly bodies in their spheres
That guides his steps and actions to the throne
Where honour sits invested royally;
Pale of complexion, wrought in him with passion,
Thirsting with sovereignty, with love of arms,   20
His lofty brows in folds do figure death,
And in their smoothness, amity and life;
About them hangs a knot of amber hair,
Wrapped in curls as fierce Achilles' was,
On which the breath of heaven delights to play,   25
Making it dance with wanton majesty;
His arms and fingers long and sinewy,
Betokening valour and excess of strength –
In every part proportioned like the man
Should make the world subdued to Tamburlaine.   30

COSROE
Well hast thou portrayed in thy terms of life
The face and personage of a wondrous man.
Nature doth strive with Fortune and his stars
To make him famous in accomplished worth,
And well his merits show him to be made   35
His fortune's master and the king of men
That could persuade at such a sudden pinch,
With reasons of his valour and his life,
A thousand sworn and overmatching foes.
Then, when our powers in points of swords are joined   40
And closed in compass of the killing bullet,
Though strait the passage and the port be made
That leads to palace of my brother's life,
Proud is his fortune if we pierce it not.
And when the princely Persian diadem   45
Shall overweigh his weary witless head

15–17 *Whose ... throne* The glowing spheres of his eyes contain a constellation of
    stars and planets favourable to his gaining the throne.
21 *in folds* when furrowed
24 *Achilles* the greatest Greek warrior in the Trojan war
26 *wanton* unrestrained
27 *sinewy* ed. (snowy O1)
29–30 *In ... Tamburlaine* Each separate part of him is perfectly proportioned, as he
    himself is, to subdue the world.
31 *terms of life* vivid terms
37 *pinch* critical situation
41 *compass* range
42 *port* entrance
42–4 Cosroe compares his brother's body to a besieged town, his heart, the seat of
    his life, to the palace.

And fall like mellowed fruit, with shakes of death,
In fair Persia noble Tamburlaine
Shall be my regent and remain as king.

ORTYGIUS

In happy hour we have set the crown   50
Upon your kingly head, that seeks our honour
In joining with the man ordained by heaven
To further every action to the best.

CENEUS

He that with shepherds and a little spoil
Durst in disdain of wrong and tyranny   55
Defend his freedom 'gainst a monarchy,
What will he do supported by a king,
Leading a troop of gentlemen and lords,
And stuffed with treasure for his highest thoughts?

COSROE

And such shall wait on worthy Tamburlaine.   60
Our army will be forty thousand strong
When Tamburlaine and brave Theridamas
Have met us by the river Araris,
And all conjoined to meet the witless king
That now is marching near to Parthia,   65
And with unwilling soldiers faintly armed,
To seek revenge on me and Tamburlaine –
To whom, sweet Menaphon, direct me straight.

MENAPHON

I will my lord.   *Exeunt*

Act II, Scene ii

[*Enter*] MYCETES, MEANDER, *with other Lords
and Soldiers*

MYCETES

Come, my Meander, let us to this gear.
I tell you true my heart is swoll'n with wrath
On this same thievish villain Tamburlaine,
And of that false Cosroe, my traitorous brother.
Would it not grieve a king to be so abused,   5

55 *Durst* dared
63 *river Araris* probably the Araxes, which flows into the Caspian Sea
65 *Parthia* a kingdom south-east of the Caspian
1 *gear* business
3–4 *On, of* here used interchangeably to mean 'because of'
5 *abused* deceived

And have a thousand horsemen ta'en away?
And, which is worst, to have his diadem
Sought for by such scald knaves as love him not?
I think it would. Well then, by heavens I swear,
Aurora shall not peep out of her doors,　　　　　　　10
But I will have Cosroe by the head
And kill proud Tamburlaine with point of sword.
Tell you the rest, Meander, I have said.

MEANDER
Then having passed Armenian deserts now,
And pitched our tents under the Georgian hills,　　　15
Whose tops are covered with Tartarian thieves
That lie in ambush, waiting for a prey,
What should we do but bid them battle straight
And rid the world of those detested troops,
Lest if we let them linger here a while　　　　　　　20
They gather strength by power of fresh supplies?
This country swarms with vile outrageous men
That live by rapine and by lawless spoil,
Fit soldiers for the wicked Tamburlaine,
And he that could with gifts and promises　　　　　25
Inveigle him that led a thousand horse
And make him false his faith unto his king,
Will quickly win such as are like himself.
Therefore cheer up your minds, prepare to fight.
He that can take or slaughter Tamburlaine　　　　　30
Shall rule the province of Albania.
Who brings that traitor's head Theridamas
Shall have a government in Media,
Beside the spoil of him and all his train.
But if Cosroe (as our spials say,　　　　　　　　　35
And as we know) remains with Tamburlaine,
His highness' pleasure is that he should live
And be reclaimed with princely lenity.

[*Enter a* SPY]

SPY
An hundred horsemen of my company

8 *scald* scurvy, low
10 *Aurora* goddess of the dawn
15 *pitched* O2–3, Q (pitch O1)
18 *straight* immediately
27 *false* betray
31 *Albania* in Ortelius' atlas, the district lying along the west coast of the Caspian
35 *spials* spies

Scouting abroad upon these champion plains   40
Have viewed the army of the Scythians,
Which make reports it far exceeds the king's.

MEANDER

Suppose they be in number infinite,
Yet being void of martial discipline,
All running headlong after greedy spoils   45
And more regarding gain than victory,
Like to the cruel brothers of the earth
Sprung of the teeth of dragons venomous,
Their careless swords shall lanch their fellows' throats
And make us triumph in their overthrow.   50

MYCETES

Was there such brethren, sweet Meander, say,
That sprung of teeth of dragons venomous?

MEANDER

So poets say, my lord.

MYCETES

And 'tis a pretty toy to be a poet.
Well, well, Meander thou art deeply read   55
And, having thee, I have a jewel sure.
Go on, my lord, and give your charge I say,
Thy wit will make us conquerors today.

MEANDER

Then noble soldiers, to entrap these thieves
That live confounded in disordered troops,   60
If wealth or riches may prevail with them
We have our camels laden all with gold,
Which you that be but common soldiers
Shall fling in every corner of the field,
And while the base-born Tartars take it up,   65
You, fighting more for honour than for gold,
Shall massacre those greedy-minded slaves;
And when their scattered army is subdued
And you march on their slaughtered carcasses,
Share equally the gold that bought their lives   70
And live like gentlemen in Persia.
Strike up the drum and march courageously,
Fortune herself doth sit upon our crests.

MYCETES

He tells you true, my masters, so he does.

---

40 *champion plains* stretches of level grassland
47–8 Cadmus sowed the earth with dragons' teeth from which sprang armed men
     who began to fight one another.
54 *toy* trifling pastime

Drums, why sound ye not when Meander speaks?   75

Exeunt

Act II, Scene iii

[*Enter*] COSROE, TAMBURLAINE, THERIDAMAS,
TECHELLES, USUMCASANE, ORTYGIUS, *with others*

COSROE
   Now, worthy Tamburlaine, have I reposed
   In thy approvèd fortunes all my hope –
   What think'st thou, man, shall come of our attempts?
   For even as from assurèd oracle,
   I take thy doom for satisfaction.   5
TAMBURLAINE
   And so mistake you not a whit, my lord,
   For fates and oracles of heaven have sworn
   To royalize the deeds of Tamburlaine
   And make them blest that share in his attempts.
   And doubt you not but, if you favour me   10
   And let my fortunes and my valour sway
   To some direction in your martial deeds,
   The world will strive with hosts of men-at-arms
   To swarm unto the ensign I support.
   The host of Xerxes, which by fame is said   15
   To drink the mighty Parthian Araris,
   Was but a handful to that we will have.
   Our quivering lances shaking in the air
   And bullets like Jove's dreadful thunderbolts,
   Enrolled in flames and fiery smouldering mists,   20
   Shall threat the gods more than Cyclopian wars;
   And with our sun-bright armour as we march

1 *reposed* placed
2 *approvèd* successfully tried
5 *doom* judgement, opinion
  satisfaction certainty
7 *of* ed. (O1 omits)
8 *royalize* celebrate, make famous
11–12 *sway . . . in* have some authority over
15–16 The vast army assembled by Xerxes for the invasion of Greece was said to
  have drunk rivers dry.
19 *bullets* projectiles
20 *Enrolled* enfolded
21 *Cyclopian wars* Marlowe apparently identifies the Cyclopes with the Titans who
  warred against Jove.

We'll chase the stars from heaven and dim their eyes
That stand and muse at our admirèd arms.

THERIDAMAS
You see, my lord, what working words he hath,   25
But when you see his actions top his speech,
Your speech will stay or so extol his worth
As I shall be commended and excused
For turning my poor charge to his direction.
And these his two renownèd friends, my lord,   30
Would make one thrust and strive to be retained
In such a great degree of amity.

TECHELLES
With duty and with amity we yield
Our utmost service to the fair Cosroe.

COSROE
Which I esteem as portion of my crown.   35
Usumcasane and Techelles both,
When she that rules in Rhamnis' golden gates
And makes a passage for all prosperous arms
Shall make me solely emperor of Asia,
Then shall your meeds and valours be advanced   40
To rooms of honour and nobility.

TAMBURLAINE
Then haste, Cosroe, to be king alone,
That I with these my friends and all my men
May triumph in our long-expected fate.
The king your brother is now hard at hand: 45
Meet with the fool, and rid your royal shoulders
Of such a burden as outweighs the sands
And all the craggy rocks of Caspea.

[Enter a MESSENGER]

MESSENGER
My lord, we have discovered the enemy
Ready to charge you with a mighty army.   50

COSROE
Come, Tamburlaine, now whet thy wingèd sword
And lift thy lofty arm into the clouds

---

25 *working* effective, moving
26 *top* ed. (stop O1) exceed
27 *Your . . . stay* you will be at a loss for words
33 *and* Q (O1 omits)
37 *Rhamnis' golden gates* the temple of Nemesis (Vengeance) at Rhamnus in Attica
40 *meeds* merits
41 *rooms* places
48 *Caspea* the Caspian Sea

That it may reach the king of Persia's crown
And set it safe on my victorious head.

TAMBURLAINE

See where it is, the keenest curtle-axe   55
That e'er made passage thorough Persian arms.
These are the wings shall make it fly as swift
As doth the lightning or the breath of heaven,
And kill as sure as it swiftly flies.

COSROE

Thy words assure me of kind success.   60
Go, valiant soldier, go before and charge
The fainting army of that foolish king.

TAMBURLAINE

Usumcasane and Techelles come,
We are enough to scare the enemy,
And more than needs to make an emperor.   [*Exeunt*]   65

Act II, Scene iv

how does the obj. work on stage?

To the battle, and MYCETES *comes out alone with
his crown in his hand, offering to hide it*

MYCETES

Accursed be he that first invented war!
They knew not, ah, they knew not, simple men,
How those were hit by pelting cannon shot
Stand staggering like a quivering aspen leaf
Fearing the force of Boreas' boisterous blasts.   5
In what a lamentable case were I
If nature had not given me wisdom's lore?
For kings are clouts that every man shoots at,
Our crown the pin that thousands seek to cleave.
Therefore in policy I think it good   10
To hide it close, a goodly stratagem,
And far from any man that is a fool.
So shall I not be known, or if I be,
They cannot take away my crown from me.

60 *kind* favourable
  Scene iv ed. (O1 omits)
  II, iv, s.d. *offering* endeavouring
 3 *those were* those who were
 5 *Boreas* the north wind
 8 *clouts* The clout is the central mark of the target in archery.
 9 *pin* nail holding the clout in place
11 *close* secretly

Here will I hide it in this simple hole.   15

Enter TAMBURLAINE

TAMBURLAINE
What, fearful coward, straggling from the camp
When kings themselves are present in the field?
MYCETES
Thou liest.
TAMBURLAINE
Base villain, dar'st thou give the lie?
MYCETES
Away, I am the king! Go, touch me not!   20
Thou break'st the law of arms unless thou kneel
And cry me 'Mercy, noble king!'
TAMBURLAINE
Are you the witty king of Persia?
MYCETES
Ay, marry, am I; have you any suit to me?
TAMBURLAINE
I would entreat you to speak but three wise words.   25
MYCETES
So I can when I see my time.
TAMBURLAINE
Is this your crown?
MYCETES
Ay, didst thou ever see a fairer?
TAMBURLAINE
You will not sell it, will ye?
MYCETES
Such another word, and I will have thee executed.   30
Come give it me.
TAMBURLAINE
No, I took it prisoner.
MYCETES
You lie, I gave it you.
TAMBURLAINE
Then 'tis mine.
MYCETES
No, I mean, I let you keep it.   35
TAMBURLAINE
Well, I mean you shall have it again.
Here, take it for a while, I lend it thee
Till I may see thee hemmed with armèd men:

19 *give the lie* accuse a person of lying
23 *witty* wise

Then shalt thou see me pull it from thy head.
Thou art no match for mighty Tamburlaine.   [*Exit*]   40

MYCETES
O gods, is this Tamburlaine the thief?
I marvel much he stole it not away.
           Sound trumpets to the battle, and he runs in

Act II, Scene v

[*Enter*] COSROE, TAMBURLAINE, THERIDAMAS,
MENAPHON, MEANDER, ORTYGIUS, TECHELLES,
USUMCASANE, *with others*

TAMBURLAINE
Hold thee, Cosroe, wear two imperial crowns.
Think thee invested now as royally,
Even by the mighty hand of Tamburlaine,
And if as many kings as could encompass thee
With greatest pomp had crowned thee emperor.   5

COSROE
So do I, thrice renownèd man-at-arms,
And none shall keep the crown but Tamburlaine:
Thee do I make my regent of Persia
And general lieutenant of my armies.
Meander, you that were our brother's guide   10
And chiefest counsellor in all his acts,
Since he is yielded to the stroke of war,
On your submission we with thanks excuse
And give you equal place in our affairs.

MEANDER
Most happy emperor, in humblest terms   15
I vow my service to your majesty
With utmost virtue of my faith and duty.

COSROE
Thanks, good Meander. Then Cosroe reign
And govern Persia in her former pomp.
Now send embassage to thy neighbour kings   20
And let them know the Persian king is changed
From one that knew not what a king should do
To one that can command what 'longs thereto.
And now we will to fair Persepolis

Scene v ed. (O1 omits)
17 *virtue* commitment
23 *'longs* belongs

With twenty thousand expert soldiers. 25
The lords and captains of my brother's camp
With little slaughter take Meander's course
And gladly yield them to my gracious rule.
Ortygius and Menaphon, my trusty friends,
Now will I gratify your former good 30
And grace your calling with a greater sway.

ORTYGIUS
And as we ever aimed at your behoof
And sought your state all honour it deserved,
So will we with our powers and our lives
Endeavour to preserve and prosper it. 35

COSROE
I will not thank thee, sweet Ortygius –
Better replies shall prove my purposes.
And now, Lord Tamburlaine, my brother's camp
I leave to thee and to Theridamas
To follow me to fair Persepolis. 40
Then will we march to all those Indian mines
My witless brother to the Christians lost
And ransom them with fame and usury.
And till thou overtake me, Tamburlaine,
Staying to order all the scattered troops, 45
Farewell lord regent and his happy friends –
I long to sit upon my brother's throne.

MENAPHON
Your majesty shall shortly have your wish
And ride in triumph through Persepolis.

     Exeunt [all except] TAMBURLAINE, TECHELLES,
       THERIDAMAS, [*and*] USUMCASANE

TAMBURLAINE
And ride in triumph through Persepolis? 50
Is it not brave to be a king, Techelles?
Usumcasane and Theridamas,
Is it not passing brave to be a king

27 *course* example
30 *gratify ... good* repay your service
31 *grace ... sway* give you a more authoritative position
32 *aimed* O3, Q (and O1)
 behoof profit
33 *sought your state* sought for your position
37 *Better replies* i.e. actions
38 *camp* troops
43 *with ... usury* to our glory and advantage
51 *brave* wonderful
53 *passing* exceedingly

*link to ceremon- /
memorialising*

And ride in triumph through Persepolis?
TECHELLES
O, my lord, 'tis sweet and full of pomp.   55
USUMCASANE
To be a king is half to be a god.
THERIDAMAS
A god is not so glorious as a king.
I think the pleasure they enjoy in heaven
Cannot compare with kingly joys in earth.
To wear a crown enchased with pearl and gold,   60
Whose virtues carry with it life and death,
To ask and have, command and be obeyed,
When looks breed love, with looks to gain the prize –
Such power attractive shines in princes' eyes.
TAMBURLAINE
Why, say, Theridamas, wilt thou be a king?   65
THERIDAMAS
Nay, though I praise it, I can live without it.
TAMBURLAINE
What says my other friends, will you be kings?
TECHELLES
Ay, if I could, with all my heart my lord.
TAMBURLAINE
Why that's well said, Techelles, so would I,
And so would you, my masters, would you not?   70
USUMCASANE
What then, my lord?
TAMBURLAINE
Why then, Casane, shall we wish for ought
The world affords in greatest novelty
And rest attemptless, faint and destitute?
Methinks we should not. I am strongly moved   75
That if I should desire the Persian crown
I could attain it with a wondrous ease,
And would not all our soldiers soon consent
If we should aim at such a dignity?
THERIDAMAS
I know they would, with our persuasions.   80
TAMBURLAINE
Why then, Theridamas, I'll first assay
To get the Persian kingdom to myself,

61 *virtues* powers
73 *in ... novelty* no matter how new and rare
75 *moved* inwardly convinced
81 *assay* attempt

Then thou for Parthia, they for Scythia and Media.
And if I prosper, all shall be as sure
As if the Turk, the Pope, Afric and Greece   85
Came creeping to us with their crowns apace.

TECHELLES
Then shall we send to this triumphing king
And bid him battle for his novel crown?

USUMCASANE
Nay quickly then, before his room be hot.

TAMBURLAINE
'Twill prove a pretty jest, in faith, my friends.   90

THERIDAMAS
A jest to charge on twenty thousand men?
I judge the purchase more important far.

TAMBURLAINE
Judge by thyself, Theridamas, not me,
For presently Techelles here shall haste
And bid him battle ere he pass too far   95
And lose more labour than the gain will quite.
Then shalt thou see the Scythian Tamburlaine
Make but a jest to win the Persian crown.
Techelles, take a thousand horse with thee
And bid him turn his back to war with us   100
That only made him king to make us sport.
We will not steal upon him cowardly,
But give him warning and more warriors.
Haste thee, Techelles, we will follow thee.
What saith Theridamas?

THERIDAMAS
                    Go on, for me.   [*Exeunt*] 105

Act II, Scene vi

[*Enter*] COSROE, MEANDER, ORTYGIUS, MENAPHON,
with other Soldiers

COSROE
What means this devilish shepherd to aspire

---

86 *apace* immediately
88 *novel* newly gained
89 *before . . . hot* before he is well established in his new position
92 *purchase* undertaking
94 *presently* immediately
96 *than . . . quite* than the benefit of defeating Cosroe would requite
105 *for me* as far as I am concerned

With such a giantly presumption
To cast up hills against the face of heaven
And dare the force of angry Jupiter?
But as he thrust them underneath the hills   5
And pressed out fire from their burning jaws,
So will I send this monstrous slave to hell
Where flames shall ever feed upon his soul.

MEANDER
Some powers divine, or else infernal, mixed
Their angry seeds at his conception: 10
For he was never sprung of human race
Since with the spirit of his fearful pride
He dares so doubtlessly resolve of rule
And by profession be ambitious.

ORTYGIUS
What god or fiend or spirit of the earth,   15
Or monster turned into a manly shape,
Or of what mould or mettle he be made,
What star or state soever govern him,
Let us put on our meet encountering minds
And, in detesting such a devilish thief,   20
In love of honour and defence of right
Be armed against the hate of such a foe,
Whether from earth or hell or heaven he grow.

COSROE
Nobly resolved, my good Ortygius.
And since we all have sucked one wholesome air   25
And with the same proportion of elements
Resolve, I hope we are resembled
Vowing our loves to equal death and life.
Let's cheer our soldiers to encounter him,
That grievous image of ingratitude,   30
That fiery thirster after sovereignty,
And burn him in the fury of that flame
That none can quench but blood and empery.
Resolve, my lords and loving soldiers, now

3 *cast ... heaven* i.e. as did the Titans who warred against Jupiter
5 *them* i.e. the Titans. Recalling Enceladus' imprisonment beneath Mount Aetna,
  Marlowe imagines all the defeated Titans as imprisoned under mountains.
13 *doubtlessly* without hesitation
   resolve of determine to
14 *by profession* openly
19 *Let ... minds* let us put ourselves in a proper frame of mind to meet the challenge
26–7 *And ... Resolve* and will decompose into the same elements
27 *resembled* alike in
34 *Resolve* Be resolute

To save your king and country from decay.   35
Then strike up drum, and all the stars that make
The loathsome circle of my dated life
Direct my weapon to his barbarous heart,
That thus opposeth him against the gods
And scorns the powers that govern Persia.   [*Exeunt*]   40

Act II, Scene vii

Enter to the battle, and after the battle enter COSROE
wounded, THERIDAMAS, TAMBURLAINE, TECHELLES,
USUMCASANE, *with others*

COSROE
Barbarous and bloody Tamburlaine,
Thus to deprive me of my crown and life!
Treacherous and false Theridamas,
Even at the morning of my happy state,
Scarce being seated in my royal throne,   5
To work my downfall and untimely end!
An uncouth pain torments my grievèd soul
And death arrests the organ of my voice,
Who, entering at the breach thy sword hath made,
Sacks every vein and artier of my heart.   10
Bloody and insatiate Tamburlaine!
TAMBURLAINE
The thirst of reign and sweetness of a crown,
That caused the eldest son of heavenly Ops
To thrust his doting father from his chair
And place himself in the empyreal heaven,   15
Moved me to manage arms against thy state.
What better precedent than mighty Jove?
Nature that framed us of four elements

37 *dated* limited, transitory
    II, vii, s.d. The stage direction here suggests that the battle begins onstage, moves
    offstage, and culminates in the re-entry of the wounded Cosroe and Tamburlaine
    victorious. In O1 there is no new scene here, nor any indication that Cosroe and
    his followers leave the stage at the end of II, vi, prior to the onset of the battle.
 7 *uncouth* strange, novel
10 *artier* artery
13 *eldest . . . Ops* Jupiter, the yougest (not the eldest) son of Saturn and Ops
15 *empyreal heaven* empyrean, i.e. the outermost sphere of the universe, with a
    sardonic pun on 'imperial'
18 *four elements* i.e. the earth, water, air, and fire of ancient physiology

Warring within our breasts for regiment,
Doth teach us all to have aspiring minds: 20
Our souls, whose faculties can comprehend
The wondrous architecture of the world
And measure every wand'ring planet's course,
Still climbing after knowledge infinite
And always moving as the restless spheres,   25
Wills us to wear ourselves and never rest
Until we reach the ripest fruit of all,
That perfect bliss and sole felicity,
The sweet fruition of an earthly crown.

THERIDAMAS
And that made me to join with Tamburlaine,   30
For he is gross and like the massy earth
That moves not upwards nor by princely deeds
Doth mean to soar above the highest sort.

TECHELLES
And that made us, the friends of Tamburlaine,
To lift our swords against the Persian king.   35

USUMCASANE
For as when Jove did thrust old Saturn down,
Neptune and Dis gained each of them a crown,
So do we hope to reign in Asia,
If Tamburlaine be placed in Persia.

COSROE
The strangest men that ever nature made!   40
I know not how to take their tyrannies.
My bloodless body waxeth chill and cold
And with my blood my life slides through my wound.
My soul begins to take her flight to hell
And summons all my senses to depart.   45
The heat and moisture, which did feed each other
For want of nourishment to feed them both
Is dry and cold, and now doth ghastly death

19 *regiment* rule
25 *restless spheres* the eternally revolving hollow globes that were believed to carry
   the planets and the stars around the earth. See Introduction, p. xx.
31–3 *For ... sort* anyone who does not aspire to soar upwards is gross and earth-
   bound
37 Neptune, the god of the sea, and Dis, the god of the underworld, were the
   brothers of Jove (i.e., Jupiter).
46–8 *The heat ... cold* 'Blood, the element which combines the properties of moisture and heat, being removed, the balance of the "temperament" or constitution
   is destroyed and only the properties of cold and dryness, those of the melancholy
   humour in the constitution of man, and of the earth in the material universe,
   remain' (Ellis-Fermor).

With greedy talents gripe my bleeding heart
And like a harpy tires on my life.   50
Theridamas and Tamburlaine, I die,
And fearful vengeance light upon you both.

[*Dies.* TAMBURLAINE] *takes the crown and puts it on*

TAMBURLAINE
Not all the curses which the Furies breathe
Shall make me leave so rich a prize as this.
Theridamas, Techelles, and the rest,   55
Who think you now is king of Persia?
ALL
Tamburlaine! Tamburlaine!
TAMBURLAINE
Though Mars himself, the angry god of arms,
And all the earthly potentates conspire
To dispossess me of this diadem,   60
Yet will I wear it in despite of them
As great commander of this eastern world,
If you but say that Tamburlaine shall reign.
ALL
Long live Tamburlaine and reign in Asia!
TAMBURLAINE
So now it is more surer on my head   65
Than if the gods had held a parliament
And all pronounced me king of Persia.   [*Exeunt*]

g Emperor of the Turks.

Act III, Scene i

[*Enter*] BAJAZETH, *the* KINGS OF FEZ, MOROCCO *and*
ARGIER, [BASSOES], *with others, in great pomp*

BAJAZETH
Great kings of Barbary and my portly bassoes,
We hear the Tartars and the eastern thieves
Under the conduct of one Tamburlaine
Presume a bickering with your emperor,
And thinks to rouse us from our dreadful siege   5

49 *talents* talons
50 *harpy* O2 (Harpyr O1), monstrous bird of prey with a woman's face
   tires tears flesh in feeding (a term from falconry)
53 *Furies* the avenging deities of classical mythology
59 *potentates* monarchs
 1 *Barbary* the north coast of Africa
   bassoes pashas

Of the famous Grecian Constantinople.
You know our army is invincible:
As many circumcisèd Turks we have
And warlike bands of Christians renied
As hath the ocean or the Terrene sea   10
Small drops of water when the moon begins
To join in one her semi-circled horns.
Yet would we not be braved with foreign power,
Nor raise our siege before the Grecians yield
Or breathless lie before the city walls.   15

KING OF FEZ

Renownèd emperor and mighty general,
What if you sent the bassoes of your guard
To charge him to remain in Asia,
Or else to threaten death and deadly arms
As from the mouth of mighty Bajazeth?   20

BAJAZETH

Hie thee, my basso, fast to Persia,
Tell him thy lord the Turkish emperor,
Dread lord of Afric, Europe and Asia,
Great king and conqueror of Graecia,
The ocean, Terrene, and the coal-black sea,   25
The high and highest monarch of the world,
Wills and commands (for say not I entreat)
Not once to set his foot in Africa,
Or spread his colours in Graecia,
Lest he incur the fury of my wrath.   30
Tell him I am content to take a truce
Because I hear he bears a valiant mind.
But if presuming on his silly power
He be so mad to manage arms with me,
Then stay thou with him, say I bid thee so,   35
And if before the sun have measured heaven
With triple circuit thou regreet us not,
We mean to take his morning's next arise
For messenger he will not be reclaimed,
And mean to fetch thee in despite of him.   40

  9 *renied* apostate
10 *Terrene sea* the Mediterranean
11–12 *moon . . . horns* i.e. when the moon is full and the tides are high
13 *braved with* harassed by
33 *silly* weak, unskilled
38 *his* the sun's
39 *For . . . reclaimed* as a sign that Tamburlaine will not relent

BASSO
> Most great and puissant monarch of the earth,
> Your basso will accomplish your behest
> And show your pleasure to the Persian
> As fits the legate of the stately Turk.

KING OF ARGIER
> They say he is the king of Persia,   45
> But if he dare attempt to stir your siege
> 'Twere requisite he should be ten times more,
> For all flesh quakes at your magnificence.

BAJAZETH
> True, Argier, and tremble at my looks.

KING OF MOROCCO
> The spring is hindered by your smothering host,   50
> For neither rain can fall upon the earth
> Nor sun reflex his virtuous beams thereon,
> The ground is mantled with such multitudes.

BAJAZETH
> All this is true as holy Mahomet,
> And all the trees are blasted with our breaths.   55

KING OF FEZ
> What thinks your greatness best to be achieved
> In pursuit of the city's overthrow?

BAJAZETH
> I will the captive pioners of Argier
> Cut off the water that by leaden pipes
> Runs to the city from the mountain Carnon;   60
> Two thousand horse shall forage up and down
> That no relief or succour come by land;
> And all the sea my galleys countermand.
> Then shall our footmen lie within the trench,
> And with their cannons mouthed like Orcus' gulf   65
> Batter the walls, and we will enter in:
> And thus the Grecians shall be conquerèd.   [*Exeunt*]

Act III, Scene ii

[*Enter*] AGYDAS, ZENOCRATE, ANIPPE, *with others*

[AGYDAS]
> Madam Zenocrate, may I presume

41 *puissant* mighty
52 *reflex* cast
58 *pioners* advance guard of trench-diggers
63 *countermand* control
65 *Orcus' gulf* hell. Orcus was one of several names for Hades.

To know the cause of these unquiet fits
That work such trouble to your wonted rest?
'Tis more than pity such a heavenly face
Should by heart's sorrow wax so wan and pale,   5
When your offensive rape by Tamburlaine,
Which of your whole displeasures should be most,
Hath seemed to be digested long ago.

ZENOCRATE
Although it be digested long ago,
As his exceeding favours have deserved,   10
And might content the Queen of Heaven as well
As it hath changed my first conceived disdain,
Yet, since, a farther passion feeds my thoughts
With ceaseless and disconsolate conceits,
Which dyes my looks so lifeless as they are,   15
And might, if my extremes had full events,
Make me the ghastly counterfeit of death.

AGYDAS
Eternal heaven sooner be dissolved,
And all that pierceth Phoebe's silver eye,
Before such hap fall to Zenocrate.   20

ZENOCRATE
Ah, life and soul, still hover in his breast,
And leave my body senseless as the earth,
Or else unite you to his life and soul,
That I may live and die with Tamburlaine.

       Enter [behind], TAMBURLAINE *with* TECHELLES
               and others

AGYDAS
With Tamburlaine? Ah, fair Zenocrate,   25
Let not a man so vile and barbarous,
That holds you from your father in despite
And keeps you from the honours of a queen,
Being supposed his worthless concubine,
Be honoured with your love but for necessity.   30
So now the mighty Soldan hears of you,
Your highness needs not doubt but in short time

  6 *rape* seizure
11 *Queen of Heaven* Juno
14 *conceits* fancies
16 *extremes* violent passions
    events expression in action
17 *counterfeit* likeness
19 *all ... eye* all that the moon beholds
31 *So* Provided that

He will with Tamburlaine's destruction
Redeem you from this deadly servitude.

ZENOCRATE
Leave to wound me with these words,   35
And speak of Tamburlaine as he deserves.
The entertainment we have had of him
Is far from villainy or servitude,
And might in noble minds be counted princely.

AGYDAS
How can you fancy one that looks so fierce,   40
Only disposed to martial stratagems?
Who when he shall embrace you in his arms
Will tell how many thousand men he slew,
And when you look for amorous discourse
Will rattle forth his facts of war and blood,   45
Too harsh a subject for your dainty ears.

ZENOCRATE
As looks the sun through Nilus' flowing stream,
Or when the morning holds him in her arms,
So looks my lordly love, fair Tamburlaine;
His talk much sweeter than the Muses' song   50
They sung for honour 'gainst Pierides,
Or when Minerva did with Neptune strive,
And higher would I rear my estimate
Than Juno, sister to the highest god,
If I were matched with mighty Tamburlaine.   55

AGYDAS
Yet be not so inconstant in your love,
But let the young Arabian live in hope
After your rescue to enjoy his choice.
You see though first the King of Persia,
Being a shepherd, seemed to love you much,   60
Now in his majesty he leaves those looks,
Those words of favour and those comfortings,
And gives no more than common courtesies.

ZENOCRATE
Thence rise the tears that so distain my cheeks,

35 *Leave* Cease

37 *entertainment* treatment

40 *fancy* love

50–1 The nine daughters of King Pierus were defeated by the Muses in a singing
contest and transformed into birds.

52 Minerva (Athene, goddess of wisdom) and Neptune (Poseidon, god of the sea)
strove for control of Athens.

Fearing his love through my unworthiness.   65

TAMBURLAINE goes to her, and takes her away lovingly
by the hand, looking wrathfully on AGYDAS,
and says nothing.

[*Exeunt all except* AGYDAS]

AGYDAS
Betrayed by fortune and suspicious love,
Threatened with frowning wrath and jealousy,
Surprised with fear of hideous revenge,
I stand aghast; but most astonièd
To see his choler shut in secret thoughts   70
And wrapped in silence of his angry soul.
Upon his brows was portrayed ugly death,
And in his eyes the fury of his heart,
That shine as comets, menacing revenge,
And casts a pale complexion on his cheeks.   75
As when the seaman sees the Hyades
Gather an army of Cimmerian clouds
(Auster and Aquilon with wingèd steeds
All sweating tilt about the watery heavens
With shivering spears enforcing thunderclaps,   80
And from their shields strike flames of lightning),
All fearful folds his sails and sounds the main,
Lifting his prayers to the heavens for aid
Against the terror of the winds and waves:
So fares Agydas for the late-felt frowns   85
That sent a tempest to my daunted thoughts,
And makes my soul divine her overthrow.

65 *Fearing his love* fearing to lose his love
69 *astonièd* astonished
74 *comets* signs of disaster
76 *Hyades* a constellation of seven stars which were supposed to bring rain if they
rose at the same time as the sun
77 *Cimmerian* dark. The Cimmerii were said to live in perpetual darkness.
78 *Auster and Aquilon* the south and north winds
79 *tilt* fight
82 *sounds the main* measures the depth of the waves
87 *divine* foretell

Enter TECHELLES *with a naked dagger* [*and* USUMCASANE]

TECHELLES

See you, Agydas, how the king salutes you.
He bids you prophesy what it imports.

AGYDAS

I prophesied before and now I prove   90
The killing frowns of jealousy and love.
He needed not with words confirm my fear,
For words are vain where working tools present
The naked action of my threatened end.
It says, Agydas, thou shalt surely die,   95
And of extremities elect the least.
More honour and less pain it may procure
To die by this resolvèd hand of thine
Than stay the torments he and heaven have sworn.
Then haste, Agydas, and prevent the plagues   100
Which thy prolongèd fates may draw on thee;
Go wander free from fear of tyrant's rage,
Removèd from the torments and the hell
Wherewith he may excruciate thy soul.
And let Agydas by Agydas die,   ` 105
And with this stab slumber eternally.

                              [*Stabs himself*]

TECHELLES

Usumcasane, see how right the man
Hath hit the meaning of my lord the king.

USUMCASANE

Faith, and Techelles, it was manly done,
And since he was so wise and honourable,   110
Let us afford him now the bearing hence
And crave his triple-worthy burial.

TECHELLES

Agreed Casane, we will honour him.

                      [*Exeunt, bearing out the body*]

---

89 *imports.* O3, Q (imports. *Exit* O1–2)
89ff. The precise stage movement is uncertain here. Perhaps Techelles enters alone
    at 1. 87, menaces Agydas and exits two lines later (as O1 seems to indicate). But
    O1 has no stage direction indicating re-entry at l. 106. It seems simpler to imagine
    both of Tamburlaine's men entering at l. 87 and threatening Agydas, who might
    even take the proffered dagger. Techelles and Usumcasane then step back to
    observe Agydas's soliloquy and suicide and come forward at 1. 106 to comment
    and bear away the body.
90 *prove* find by experience
99 *stay* await

Act III, Scene iii

[*Enter*] TAMBURLAINE, TECHELLES, USUMCASANE,
THERIDAMAS, BASSO, ZENOCRATE, *with others*

TAMBURLAINE
  Basso, by this thy lord and master knows
  I mean to meet him in Bithynia.
  See how he comes! Tush, Turks are full of brags
  And menace more than they can well perform.
  He meet me in the field and fetch thee hence!   5
  Alas, poor Turk, his fortune is too weak
  T'encounter with the strength of Tamburlaine.
  View well my camp, and speak indifferently,
  Do not my captains and my soldiers look
  As if they meant to conquer Africa?   10
BASSO
  Your men are valiant but their number few,
  And cannot terrify his mighty host.
  My lord, the great commander of the world,
  Besides fifteen contributory kings
  Hath now in arms ten thousand janissaries   15
  Mounted on lusty Mauritanian steeds
  Brought to the war by men of Tripoli,
  Two hundred thousand footmen that have served
  In two set battles fought in Graecia,
  And for the expedition of this war,   20
  If he think good, can from his garrisons
  Withdraw as many more to follow him.
TECHELLES
  The more he brings, the greater is the spoil,
  For when they perish by our warlike hands
  We mean to seat our footmen on their steeds   25
  And rifle all those stately janissars.
TAMBURLAINE
  But will those kings accompany your lord?
BASSO
  Such as his highness please, but some must stay

---

2 *Bithynia* a district in Asia Minor south of the Black Sea
3 *See . . . comes* i.e. Bajazeth has not yet arrived
8 *indifferently* without prejudice
15 *janissaries* Turkish soldiers
16 *Mauritanian steeds* Mauritania in north-west Africa on the Barbary coast was
   famous for its horses.
26 *rifle* pillage

To rule the provinces he late subdued.

TAMBURLAINE

[*To his men*] Then fight courageously, their crowns are
    yours.   30
This hand shall set them on your conquering heads
That made me emperor of Asia.

USUMCASANE

Let him bring millions infinite of men,
Unpeopling western Africa and Greece,
Yet we assure us of the victory.   35

THERIDAMAS

Even he, that in a trice vanquished two kings
More mighty than the Turkish emperor,
Shall rouse him out of Europe and pursue
His scattered army till they yield or die.

TAMBURLAINE

Well said, Theridamas, speak in that mood,   40
For 'will' and 'shall' best fitteth Tamburlaine,
Whose smiling stars gives him assurèd hope
Of martial triumph, ere he meet his foes.
I, that am termed the scourge and wrath of God,
The only fear and terror of the world,   45
Will first subdue the Turk, and then enlarge
Those Christian captives which you keep as slaves,
Burdening their bodies with your heavy chains
And feeding them with thin and slender fare
That naked row about the Terrene sea,   50
And, when they chance to breathe and rest a space,
Are punished with bastones so grievously
That they lie panting on the galley's side
And strive for life at every stroke they give.
These are the cruel pirates of Argier,   55
That damnèd train, the scum of Africa,
Inhabited with straggling runagates,
That make quick havoc of the Christian blood.
But, as I live, that town shall curse the time
That Tamburlaine set foot in Africa.   60

29 *late* lately
38 *rouse* cause to rise from cover
46 *enlarge* set free
52 *bastones* cudgels
56 *train* troop
57 *runagates* apostates, deserters

Enter BAJAZETH *with his Bassoes and contributory* KINGS
[OF FEZ, MOROCCO, *and* ARGIER, ZABINA *and* EBEA]

BAJAZETH
    Bassoes and janissaries of my guard,
    Attend upon the person of your lord,
    The greatest potentate of Africa.
TAMBURLAINE
    Techelles and the rest, prepare your swords,
    I mean t'encounter with that Bajazeth.   65
BAJAZETH
    Kings of Fez, Morocco and Argier,
    He calls me Bajazeth, whom you call lord!
    Note the presumption of this Scythian slave!
    I tell thee, villain, those that lead my horse
    Have to their names titles of dignity,   70
    And dar'st thou bluntly call me Bajazeth?
TAMBURLAINE
    And know thou, Turk, that those which lead my horse
    Shall lead thee captive thorough Africa.
    And dar'st thou bluntly call me Tamburlaine?
BAJAZETH
    By Mahomet my kinsman's sepulchre   75
    And by the holy Alcoran, I swear
    He shall be made a chaste and lustless eunuch,
    And in my sarell tend my concubines,
    And all his captains that thus stoutly stand
    Shall draw the chariot of my emperess,   80
    Whom I have brought to see their overthrow.
TAMBURLAINE
    By this my sword that conquered Persia,
    Thy fall shall make me famous through the world.
    I will not tell thee how I'll handle thee,
    But every common soldier of my camp   85
    Shall smile to see thy miserable state.
KING OF FEZ
    What means the mighty Turkish emperor
    To talk with one so base as Tamburlaine?
KING OF MOROCCO
    Ye Moors and valiant men of Barbary,
    How can ye suffer these indignities?   90

70 *to* in addition to
76 *Alcoran* Koran
78 *sarell* seraglio, harem

KING OF ARGIER
　Leave words and let them feel your lances' points,
　Which glided through the bowels of the Greeks.
BAJAZETH
　Well said, my stout contributory kings,
　Your threefold army and my hugy host
　Shall swallow up these base-born Persians.　　　　　95
TECHELLES
　Puissant, renowned and mighty Tamburlaine,
　Why stay we thus prolonging all their lives?
THERIDAMAS
　I long to see those crowns won by our swords
　That we may reign as kings of Africa.
USUMCASANE
　What coward would not fight for such a prize?　　　100
TAMBURLAINE
　Fight all courageously and be you kings.
　I speak it, and my words are oracles.
BAJAZETH
　Zabina, mother of three braver boys
　Than Hercules, that in his infancy
　Did pash the jaws of serpents venomous,　　　　　105
　Whose hands are made to grip a warlike lance,
　Their shoulders broad for complete armour fit,
　Their limbs more large and of a bigger size
　Than all the brats ysprung from Typhon's loins,
　Who, when they come unto their father's age,　　　110
　Will batter turrets with their manly fists,
　Sit here upon this royal chair of state,
　And on thy head wear my imperial crown
　Until I bring this sturdy Tamburlaine
　And all his captains bound in captive chains.　　　115
ZABINA
　Such good success happen to Bajazeth.
TAMBURLAINE
　Zenocrate, the loveliest maid alive,
　Fairer than rocks of pearl and precious stone,
　The only paragon of Tamburlaine,
　Whose eyes are brighter than the lamps of heaven　120

　94 *hugy* huge
105 *pash* smash, crush
109 *ysprung* sprung
　　Typhon's Typhon was a hundred-headed giant, the father of various monsters,
　　including Hydra (see 140 below).
119 *paragon* match, consort

And speech more pleasant than sweet harmony,
That with thy looks canst clear the darkened sky
And calm the rage of thund'ring Jupiter,
Sit down by her, adornèd with my crown
As if thou wert the empress of the world.   125
Stir not, Zenocrate, until thou see
Me march victoriously with all my men,
Triumphing over him and these his kings
Which I will bring as vassals to thy feet.
Till then take thou my crown, vaunt of my worth,   130
And manage words with her as we will arms.

ZENOCRATE
And may my love, the King of Persia,
Return with victory and free from wound.

BAJAZETH
Now shalt thou feel the force of Turkish arms,
Which lately made all Europe quake for fear.   135
I have of Turks, Arabians, Moors and Jews
Enough to cover all Bithynia.
Let thousands die, their slaughtered carcasses
Shall serve for walls and bulwarks to the rest;
And as the heads of Hydra, so my power,   140
Subdued, shall stand as mighty as before:
If they should yield their necks unto the sword,
Thy soldiers' arms could not endure to strike
So many blows as I have heads for thee.
Thou knowest not, foolish-hardy Tamburlaine,   145
What 'tis to meet me in the open field,
That leave no ground for thee to march upon.

TAMBURLAINE
Our conquering swords shall marshal us the way
We use to march upon the slaughtered foe,
Trampling their bowels with our horses' hoofs –   150
Brave horses, bred on the white Tartarian hills.
My camp is like to Julius Caesar's host
That never fought but had the victory,
Nor in Pharsalia was there such hot war
As these my followers willingly would have.   155

---

130 *vaunt of* extol
131 *manage . . . arms* fight her with words as we shall fight with weapons
139 *bulwarks* ramparts, defences
140 *Hydra* a many-headed monster, whose heads grew back as quickly as they were
    cut off
148 *marshal* point out, lead
154 *Pharsalia* Julius Caesar defeated Pompey in 48 B.C. at the battle of Pharsalus.

Legions of spirits fleeting in the air
Direct our bullets and our weapons' points,
And make your strokes to wound the senseless air;
And when she sees our bloody colours spread,
Then Victory begins to take her flight,   160
Resting herself upon my milk-white tent.
But come, my lords, to weapons let us fall.
The field is ours, the Turk, his wife and all.

Exit, with his followers

BAJAZETH
Come, kings and bassoes, let us glut our swords
That thirst to drink the feeble Persians' blood.   165

Exit, with his followers

ZABINA
Base concubine, must thou be placed by me
That am the empress of the mighty Turk?

ZENOCRATE
Disdainful Turkess and unreverend boss,
Call'st thou me concubine that am betrothed
Unto the great and mighty Tamburlaine?   170

ZABINA
To Tamburlaine the great Tartarian thief?

ZENOCRATE
Thou wilt repent these lavish words of thine
When thy great basso-master and thyself
Must plead for mercy at his kingly feet
And sue to me to be your advocates.   175

ZABINA
And sue to thee? I tell thee, shameless girl,
Thou shalt be laundress to my waiting-maid.
How lik'st thou her, Ebea, will she serve?

EBEA
Madam, she thinks perhaps she is too fine,
But I shall turn her into other weeds,   180
And make her dainty fingers fall to work.

ZENOCRATE
Hear'st thou, Anippe, how thy drudge doth talk,
And how my slave, her mistress, menaceth?
Both for their sauciness shall be employed
To dress the common soldiers' meat and drink,   185
For we will scorn they should come near ourselves.

158 *your ... air* ed. (our ... lure O1)
168 *boss* fat woman
180 *weeds* clothing

ANIPPE
    Yet sometimes let your highness send for them
    To do the work my chambermaid disdains.
               They sound [to] the battle within, and stay

ZENOCRATE
    Ye gods and powers that govern Persia
    And made my lordly love her worthy king,   190
    Now strengthen him against the Turkish Bajazeth,
    And let his foes like flocks of fearful roes
    Pursued by hunters fly his angry looks,
    That I may see him issue conqueror.

ZABINA
    Now Mahomet, solicit God himself   195
    And make him rain down murdering shot from heaven
    To dash the Scythians' brains, and strike them dead
    That dare to manage arms with him
    That offered jewels to thy sacred shrine
    When first he warred against the Christians.   200
            [Trumpets sound] to the battle again

ZENOCRATE
    By this the Turks lie weltering in their blood
    And Tamburlaine is lord of Africa.

ZABINA
    Thou art deceived, I heard the trumpets sound
    As when my emperor overthrew the Greeks
    And led them captive into Africa.   205
    Straight will I use thee as thy pride deserves;
    Prepare thyself to live and die my slave.

ZENOCRATE
    If Mahomet should come from heaven and swear
    My royal lord is slain or conquerèd,
    Yet should he not persuade me otherwise   210
    But that he lives and will be conqueror.

      BAJAZETH *flies [across the stage] and* [TAMBURLAINE]
    pursues him [off]. The battle [is] short, and they [re-]enter.
             BAJAZETH *is overcome*

TAMBURLAINE
    Now, king of bassoes, who is conqueror?
BAJAZETH
    Thou, by the fortune of this damnèd foil.

188 s.d. Trumpets announce the battle and then cease.
192 *roes* small deer
213 *foil* ed. (soile O1) defeat

TAMBURLAINE
Where are your stout contributory kings?

Enter TECHELLES, THERIDAMAS, USUMCASANE

TECHELLES
We have their crowns, their bodies strew the field.   215
TAMBURLAINE
Each man a crown? Why kingly fought i'faith.
Deliver them into my treasury.
ZENOCRATE
Now let me offer to my gracious lord
His royal crown again, so highly won.
TAMBURLAINE
Nay, take the Turkish crown from her, Zenocrate,   220
And crown me emperor of Africa.
ZABINA
No Tamburlaine, though now thou gat the best,
Thou shalt not yet be lord of Africa.
THERIDAMAS
Give her the crown, Turkess, you were best.
He takes it from her and gives it [*to*] ZENOCRATE
ZABINA
Injurious villains, thieves, runagates,   225
How dare you thus abuse my majesty?
THERIDAMAS
Here madam, you are empress, she is none.
TAMBURLAINE
Not now, Theridamas, her time is past:
The pillars that have bolstered up those terms
Are fallen in clusters at my conquering feet.   230
ZABINA
Though he be prisoner, he may be ransomed.
TAMBURLAINE
Not all the world shall ransom Bajazeth.
BAJAZETH
Ah, fair Zabina, we have lost the field,
And never had the Turkish emperor
So great a foil by any foreign foe.   235
Now will the Christian miscreants be glad,
Ringing with joy their superstitious bells
And making bonfires for my overthrow.
But ere I die those foul idolators

222 *gat the best* got the upper hand
225 *runagates* vagabonds
229 *terms* statuary busts set on pillars

Shall make me bonfires with their filthy bones,   240
For though the glory of this day be lost,
Afric and Greece have garrisons enough
To make me sovereign of the earth again.

TAMBURLAINE
Those wallèd garrisons will I subdue
And write myself great lord of Africa.   245
So from the East unto the furthest West
Shall Tamburlaine extend his puissant arm.
The galleys and those pilling brigandines
That yearly sail to the Venetian gulf
And hover in the straits for Christians' wrack,   250
Shall lie at anchor in the Isle Asant
Until the Persian fleet and men-of-war,
Sailing along the oriental sea,
Have fetched about the Indian continent
Even from Persepolis to Mexico,   255
And thence unto the Straits of Jubalter,
Where they shall meet and join their force in one,
Keeping in awe the Bay of Portingale
And all the ocean by the British shore.
And by this means I'll win the world at last.   260

BAJAZETH
Yet set a ransom on me Tamburlaine.

TAMBURLAINE
What, think'st thou Tamburlaine esteems thy gold?
I'll make the kings of India ere I die
Offer their mines to sue for peace to me,
And dig for treasure to appease my wrath.   265
Come bind them both and one lead in the Turk.
The Turkess let my love's maid lead away.
                                              They bind them

BAJAZETH
Ah villains, dare ye touch my sacred arms?
O Mahomet, O sleepy Mahomet!

ZABINA
O cursèd Mahomet that mak'st us thus   270
The slaves to Scythians rude and barbarous!

247 *puissant* powerful
248 *pilling brigandines* pillaging pirate ships
250 *wrack* destruction
251 *Isle Asant* Zante, off the west coast of Greece
252–59 Tamburlaine imagines his fleet circumnavigating the globe, going east across
    the Indian Ocean ('oriental sea') and the Pacific to Mexico and thence to
    Gibraltar ('Jubaltar') and the Bay of Biscay ('Portingale').

TAMBURLAINE
 Come bring them in, and for this happy conquest
 Triumph, and solemnize a martial feast.   *Exeunt*

Act IV, Scene i

[*Enter*] SOLDAN OF EGYPT, *with three or four Lords,*
CAPOLIN, [MESSENGER]

SOLDAN
 Awake, ye men of Memphis, hear the clang
 Of Scythian trumpets! Hear the basilisks
 That, roaring, shake Damascus' turrets down!
 The rogue of Volga holds Zenocrate,
 The Soldan's daughter, for his concubine,   5
 And with a troop of thieves and vagabonds
 Hath spread his colours to our high disgrace
 While you faint-hearted base Egyptians
 Lie slumb'ring on the flowery banks of Nile,
 As crocodiles that unaffrighted rest   10
 While thund'ring cannons rattle on their skins.
[MESSENGER]
 Nay, mighty Soldan, did your greatness see
 The frowning looks of fiery Tamburlaine,
 That with his terror and imperious eyes
 Commands the hearts of his associates,   15
 It might amaze your royal majesty.
SOLDAN
 Villain, I tell thee, were that Tamburlaine
 As monstrous as Gorgon, prince of hell,
 The Soldan would not start a foot from him.
 But speak, what power hath he?
MESSENGER   Mighty lord,   20
 Three hundred thousand men in armour clad,
 Upon their prancing steeds, disdainfully
 With wanton paces trampling on the ground;
 Five hundred thousand footmen threat'ning shot,
 Shaking their swords, their spears and iron bills,   25
 Environing their standard round, that stood
 As bristle-pointed as a thorny wood;

 2 *basilisks* large cannons
18 *Gorgon* Demogorgon, a devil
23 *wanton* insolent in triumph, merciless
25 *bills* long-handled axes, halberds

Their warlike engines and munition
Exceed the forces of their martial men.

SOLDAN
Nay, could their numbers countervail the stars,   30
Or ever-drizzling drops of April showers,
Or withered leaves that autumn shaketh down,
Yet would the Soldan by his conquering power
So scatter and consume them in his rage,
That not a man should live to rue their fall.   35

CAPOLIN
So might your highness, had you time to sort
Your fighting men and raise your royal host.
But Tamburlaine by expedition
Advantage takes of your unreadiness.

SOLDAN
Let him take all th'advantages he can;   40
Were all the world conspired to fight for him,
Nay, were he devil, as he is no man,
Yet in revenge of fair Zenocrate,
Whom he detaineth in despite of us,
This arm should send him down to Erebus   45
To shroud his shame in darkness of the night.

MESSENGER
Pleaseth your mightiness to understand,
His resolution far exceedeth all:
The first day when he pitcheth down his tents,
White is their hue, and on his silver crest   50
A snowy feather spangled white he bears,
To signify the mildness of his mind
That satiate with spoil refuseth blood;
But when Aurora mounts the second time,
As red as scarlet is his furniture –   55
Then must his kindled wrath be quenched with blood,
Not sparing any that can manage arms;
But if these threats move not submission,
Black are his colours, black pavilion,
His spear, his shield, his horse, his armour, plumes,   60
And jetty feathers menace death and hell;

Symbolism of tent colours? (handwritten marginal note)

---

28 *engines* instruments of assault
30 *countervail* equal in number
38 *expedition* speed
45 *Erebus* the son of Chaos and the brother of Night, whose name came to signify
   the dark region beneath the earth
54 *Aurora* goddess of the dawn
55 *furniture* military equipment

Without respect of sex, degree or age,
He razeth all his foes with fire and sword.

SOLDAN

Merciless villain, peasant ignorant
Of lawful arms or martial discipline:
Pillage and murder are his usual trades.   65
The slave usurps the glorious name of war.
See, Capolin, the fair Arabian king
That hath been disappointed by this slave
Of my fair daughter and his princely love,   70
May have fresh warning to go to war with us,
And be revenged for her disparagement.   [*Exeunt*]

Act IV, Scene ii

> [*Enter*] TAMBURLAINE [*all in white*], TECHELLES,
> THERIDAMAS, USUMCASANE, ZENOCRATE, ANIPPE,
> *two Moors drawing* BAJAZETH *in his cage,*
> *and his wife* [ZABINA] *following him*

TAMBURLAINE

Bring out my footstool.
                    They take [BAJAZETH] *out of the cage*

BAJAZETH

Ye holy priests of heavenly Mahomet,
That, sacrificing, slice and cut your flesh,
Staining his altars with your purple blood,
Make heaven to frown and every fixèd star   5
To suck up poison from the moorish fens,
And pour it in this glorious tyrant's throat!

TAMBURLAINE

The chiefest god, first mover of that sphere
Enchased with thousands ever-shining lamps,
Will sooner burn the glorious frame of heaven   10
Than it should so conspire my overthrow.
But, villain, thou that wishest this to me,
Fall prostrate on the low disdainful earth
And be the footstool of great Tamburlaine,
That I may rise into my royal throne.   15

---

7 *glorious* boastful
8–9 Tamburlaine invokes the Aristotelian conception of God as the 'prime mover',
  who initiates the movement of the outermost sphere whose motion causes that
  of the other heavenly spheres.

BAJAZETH

    First shalt thou rip my bowels with thy sword
    And sacrifice my heart to death and hell,
    Before I yield to such a slavery.

TAMBURLAINE

    Base villain, vassal, slave to Tamburlaine,
    Unworthy to embrace or touch the ground   20
    That bears the honour of my royal weight,
    Stoop, villain, stoop! Stoop, for so he bids
    That may command thee piecemeal to be torn,
    Or scattered like the lofty cedar trees
    Struck with the voice of thund'ring Jupiter.   25

BAJAZETH

    Then as I look down to the damnèd fiends,
    Fiends, look on me, and thou, dread god of hell,
    With ebon sceptre strike this hateful earth
    And make it swallow both of us at once!

                 [TAMBURLAINE] *gets up upon him to his chair*

TAMBURLAINE

    Now clear the triple region of the air,   30
    And let the majesty of heaven behold
    Their scourge and terror tread on emperors.
    Smile, stars that reigned at my nativity
    And dim the brightness of their neighbour lamps,
    Disdain to borrow light of Cynthia,   35
    For I, the chiefest lamp of all the earth,
    First rising in the east with mild aspect,
    But fixèd now in the meridian line,
    Will send up fire to your turning spheres
    And cause the sun to borrow light of you.   40
    My sword struck fire from his coat of steel,
    Even in Bithynia, when I took this Turk,
    As when a fiery exhalation,
    Wrapped in the bowels of a freezing cloud,
    Fighting for passage, makes the welkin crack,   45
    And casts a flash of lightning to the earth.

28 *ebon* black
30 An allusion to the contemporary belief that the air, between the earth and the
    sphere of fire, was divided into three 'regions' according to distance from the
    earth and temperature.
35 *Cynthia* the moon
38 *the meridian line* an imaginary arc through the sky, running from north to south
    directly above the observer's head so that the sun passed through it at noon
43 *exhalation* a vapour drawn from the earth's atmosphere
45 *makes* ed. (make O1)
    welkin sky

But ere I march to wealthy Persia,
Or leave Damascus and the Egyptian fields,
As was the fame of Clymen's brain-sick son
That almost brent the axle-tree of heaven,   50
So shall our swords, our lances and our shot
Fill all the air with fiery meteors.
Then, when the sky shall wax as red as blood,
It shall be said I made it red myself,
To make me think of naught but blood and war.   55

ZABINA
Unworthy king, that by thy cruelty
Unlawfully usurp'st the Persian seat,
Dar'st thou that never saw an emperor
Before thou met my husband in the field,
Being thy captive, thus abuse his state,   60
Keeping his kingly body in a cage,
That roofs of gold and sun-bright palaces
Should have prepared to entertain his grace,
And treading him beneath thy loathsome feet,
Whose feet the kings of Africa have kissed?   65

TECHELLES
You must devise some torment worse, my lord,
To make these captives rein their lavish tongues.

TAMBURLAINE
Zenocrate, look better to your slave.

ZENOCRATE
She is my handmaid's slave, and she shall look
That these abuses flow not from her tongue.   70
Chide her Anippe.

ANIPPE
Let these be warnings for you then, my slave,
How you abuse the person of the king,
Or else I swear to have you whipped stark naked.

BAJAZETH
Great Tamburlaine, great in my overthrow,   75
Ambitious pride shall make thee fall as low
For treading on the back of Bajazeth,

---

49 *Clymen's* O2 (Clymenes; Clymeus O1)
  Phaëton, son of Clymen and the sun god Apollo, met disaster when he tried to
  drive his father's horses across the sky.
50 *brent* burnt
  axle-tree of heaven the axis of the universe on which all of the heavenly spheres
  were believed to turn
60 *state* high rank
67 *lavish* free-speaking

That should be horsèd on four mighty kings.

TAMBURLAINE
Thy names and titles and thy dignities
Are fled from Bajazeth, and remain with me,   80
That will maintain it against a world of kings.
Put him in again.

                    [*They put* BAJAZETH *into the cage*]

BAJAZETH
Is this a place for mighty Bajazeth?
Confusion light on him that helps thee thus.

TAMBURLAINE
There, whiles he lives, shall Bajazeth be kept   85
And where I go be thus in triumph drawn,
And thou his wife shall feed him with the scraps
My servitors shall bring thee from my board.
For he that gives him other food than this
Shall sit by him and starve to death himself.   90
This is my mind, and I will have it so.
Not all the kings and emperors of the earth,
If they would lay their crowns before my feet,
Shall ransom him or take him from his cage.
The ages that shall talk of Tamburlaine,   95
Even from this day to Plato's wondrous year,
Shall talk how I have handled Bajazeth.
These Moors that drew him from Bithynia
To fair Damascus, where we now remain,
Shall lead him with us wheresoe'er we go.   100
Techelles, and my loving followers,
Now may we see Damascus' lofty towers,
Like to the shadows of Pyramides
That with their beauties graced the Memphian fields.
The golden statue of their feathered bird   105
That spreads her wings upon the city walls
Shall not defend it from our battering shot.
The townsmen mask in silk and cloth of gold,
And every house is as a treasury –
The men, the treasure, and the town is ours.   110

84 *helps* treats
96 *Plato's wondrous year* In *Timaeus* (39 D) Plato writes of the future year when all
      of the planets will have returned to their original positions.
102–4 Tamburlaine compares the towers of Damascus to the Egyptian ('Memphian')
      pyramids.
105 *statue* O3, Q (stature O1)
      bird the ibis, a bird sacred to the Egyptians
108 *mask* dress

THERIDAMAS
Your tents of white now pitched before the gates
And gentle flags of amity displayed,
I doubt not but the governor will yield,
Offering Damascus to your majesty.
TAMBURLAINE
So shall he have his life, and all the rest.   115
But if he stay until the bloody flag
Be once advanced on my vermilion tent,
He dies, and those that kept us out so long.
And when they see me march in black array,
With mournful streamers hanging down their heads,   120
Were in that city all the world contained,
Not one should 'scape, but perish by our swords.
ZENOCRATE
Yet would you have some pity for my sake,
Because it is my country's and my father's.
TAMBURLAINE
Not for the world, Zenocrate, if I have sworn.   125
Come, bring in the Turk.   *Exeunt*

Act IV, Scene iii

[*Enter*] SOLDAN, [KING OF] ARABIA, CAPOLIN, *with streaming colours; and Soldiers*

SOLDAN
Methinks we march as Meleager did,
Environèd with brave Argolian knights,
To chase the savage Calydonian boar,
Or Cephalus with lusty Theban youths
Against the wolf that angry Themis sent   5
To waste and spoil the sweet Aonian fields.
A monster of five hundred thousand heads,
Compact of rapine, piracy and spoil,

120 *streamers* long and narrow pointed flags, pennons
   IV, iii, s.d. 1 *streaming* O3, Q (steaming O1)
   1–3 Meleager was a warrior who, along with other Greek ('Argolian') knights,
     hunted a wild boar sent by Artemis. Although he killed the boar, the incident led
     to his own death. See Ovid, *Metamorphoses* viii, 270ff.
   3 *Calydonian* O2 (Caldonian O1)
   4 *Cephalus* a hunter who destroyed a wild beast that was ravaging the Theban
     territories. See Ovid, *Metamorphoses* vii, 759ff.
   5 *Themis* a Greek deity, the symbol of order and justice
   6 *Aonian* Theban

The scum of men, the hate and scourge of God,
Raves in Egyptia and annoyeth us.   10
My lord, it is the bloody Tamburlaine,
A sturdy felon and a base-bred thief
By murder raisèd to the Persian crown,
That dares control us in our territories.
To tame the pride of this presumptuous beast,   15
Join your Arabians with the Soldan's power;
Let us unite our royal bands in one
And hasten to remove Damascus' siege.
It is a blemish to the majesty
And high estate of mighty emperors   20
That such a base usurping vagabond
Should brave a king or wear a princely crown.

KING OF ARABIA
Renownèd Soldan, have ye lately heard
The overthrow of mighty Bajazeth
About the confines of Bithynia?   25
The slavery wherewith he persecutes
The noble Turk and his great emperess?

SOLDAN
I have, and sorrow for his bad success.
But, noble lord of great Arabia,
Be so persuaded that the Soldan is   30
No more dismayed with tidings of his fall,
Than in the haven when the pilot stands
And views a stranger's ship rent in the winds
And shiverèd against a craggy rock.
Yet in compassion of his wretched state,   35
A sacred vow to heaven and him I make,
Confirming it with Ibis' holy name,
That Tamburlaine shall rue the day, the hour,
Wherein he wrought such ignominious wrong
Unto the hallowed person of a prince,   40
Or kept the fair Zenocrate so long,
As concubine, I fear, to feed his lust.

KING OF ARABIA
Let grief and fury hasten on revenge.
Let Tamburlaine for his offences feel
Such plagues as heaven and we can pour on him.   45
I long to break my spear upon his crest

---

25 *confines* borders
28 *bad success* ill fortune
37 *Ibis* See note to IV, ii, 105 above.

And prove the weight of his victorious arm;
For fame I fear hath been too prodigal
In sounding through the world his partial praise.

SOLDAN
Capolin, hast thou surveyed our powers?   50

CAPOLIN
Great emperors of Egypt and Arabia,
The number of your hosts united is
A hundred and fifty thousand horse,
Two hundred thousand foot, brave men-at-arms,
Courageous and full of hardiness,   55
As frolic as the hunters in the chase
Of savage beasts amid the desert woods.

KING OF ARABIA
My mind presageth fortunate success,
And, Tamburlaine, my spirit doth foresee
The utter ruin of thy men and thee.   60

SOLDAN
Then rear your standards, let your sounding drums
Direct our soldiers to Damascus' walls.
Now, Tamburlaine, the mighty Soldan comes
And leads with him the great Arabian king
To dim thy baseness and obscurity,   65
Famous for nothing but for theft and spoil,
To raze and scatter thy inglorious crew
Of Scythians and slavish Persians.   *Exeunt*

Act IV, Scene iv

The banquet, and to it cometh TAMBURLAINE *all in scarlet,*
[ZENOCRATE], THERIDAMAS, TECHELLES, USUMCASANE,
the Turk [BAJAZETH *in his cage,* ZABINA], *with others*

TAMBURLAINE
Now hang our bloody colours by Damascus,
Reflexing hues of blood upon their heads
While they walk quivering on their city walls,
Half dead for fear before they feel my wrath.
Then let us freely banquet and carouse   5
Full bowls of wine unto the god of war,

47 *prove* test
49 *partial* biased
56 *frolic* merry
65 *thy baseness and obscurity* i.e. Tamburlaine's low birth
 2 *Reflexing* casting

That means to fill your helmets full of gold
And make Damascus' spoils as rich to you
As was to Jason Colchos' golden fleece.
And now, Bajazeth, hast thou any stomach?   10

BAJAZETH
Ay, such a stomach, cruel Tamburlaine, as I could willingly feed upon thy blood-raw heart.

TAMBURLAINE
Nay, thine own is easier to come by, pluck out that and
'twill serve thee and thy wife. Well Zenocrate, Techelles,
and the rest, fall to your victuals.   15

BAJAZETH
Fall to, and never may your meat digest!
Ye Furies that can mask invisible,
Dive to the bottom of Avernus' pool
And in your hands bring hellish poison up
And squeeze it in the cup of Tamburlaine!   20
Or, wingèd snakes of Lerna, cast your stings
And leave your venoms in this tyrant's dish!

ZABINA
And may this banquet prove as ominous
As Progne's to th'adulterous Thracian king
That fed upon the substance of his child.   25

ZENOCRATE
My lord, how can you suffer these
Outrageous curses by these slaves of yours?

TAMBURLAINE
To let them see, divine Zenocrate,
I glory in the curses of my foes,
Having the power from the empyreal heaven   30
To turn them all upon their proper heads.

TECHELLES
I pray you give them leave, madam, this speech is a
goodly refreshing to them.

---

9 *Jason* a Greek hero who led his Argonauts to Colchis in quest of the golden fleece
10–11 *stomach* (1) hunger, (2) anger
15 *victuals* food
18 *Avernus' pool* See note to I, ii, 160 above.
21 *Lerna* a region near Argos where Hercules killed the Hydra
24–5 After Tereus, King of Thrace, had raped his sister-in-law Philomela, his wife
    Progne revenged herself by tricking him into eating the body of Itys, their son.
    See *Metamorphoses* vi, 433ff.
26–7 lineation ed.
30 *empyreal heaven* See note to II, vii, 15 above.
31 *proper* own

THERIDAMAS
>But if his highness would let them be fed, it would do
>them more good.   35

TAMBURLAINE
>Sirrah, why fall you not to? Are you so daintily brought
>up, you cannot eat your own flesh?

BAJAZETH
>First legions of devils shall tear thee in pieces.

USUMCASANE
>Villain, knowest thou to whom thou speakest?

TAMBURLAINE
>O let him alone. Here, eat sir, take it from my sword's   40
>point, or I'll thrust it to thy heart.
>   [BAJAZETH] *takes it and stamps upon it*

THERIDAMAS
>He stamps it under his feet, my lord.

TAMBURLAINE
>Take it up, villain, and eat it, or I will make thee slice
>the brawns of thy arms into carbonadoes and eat them.

USUMCASANE
>Nay, 'twere better he killed his wife, and then she shall   45
>be sure not to be starved, and he be provided for a
>month's victual beforehand.

TAMBURLAINE
>Here is my dagger, dispatch her while she is fat, for if
>she live but a while longer, she will fall into a con-
>sumption with fretting, and then she will not be worth   50
>the eating.

THERIDAMAS
>Dost thou think that Mahomet will suffer this?

TECHELLES
>'Tis like he will, when he cannot let it.

TAMBURLAINE
>Go to, fall to your meat. What, not a bit? Belike he hath
>not been watered today, give him some drink.   55

They give him water to drink, and he flings it on the ground

>Fast and welcome, sir, while hunger make you eat. How
>now, Zenocrate, doth not the Turk and his wife make a
>goodly show at a banquet?

44 *brawns* muscles
   carbonadoes thin strips of meat
52 *suffer* allow
53 *let* prevent
56 *while* until

ZENOCRATE
Yes, my lord.

THERIDAMAS
Methinks 'tis a great deal better than a consort of music.   60

TAMBURLAINE
Yet music would do well to cheer up Zenocrate. Pray
thee tell, why art thou so sad? If thou wilt have a song,
the Turk shall strain his voice. But why is it?

ZENOCRATE
My lord, to see my father's town besieged,
The country wasted where myself was born,   65
How can it but affect my very soul?
If any love remain in you, my lord,
Or if my love unto your majesty
May merit favour at your highness' hands,
Then raise your siege from fair Damascus' walls,   70
And with my father take a friendly truce.

TAMBURLAINE
Zenocrate, were Egypt Jove's own land,
Yet would I with my sword make Jove to stoop.
I will confute those blind geographers
That make a triple region in the world,   75
Excluding regions which I mean to trace,
And with this pen reduce them to a map,
Calling the provinces, cities and towns
After my name and thine, Zenocrate.
Here at Damascus will I make the point   80
That shall begin the perpendicular –
And wouldst thou have me buy thy father's love
With such a loss? Tell me Zenocrate.

60 *consort of music* company of musicians
63 *strain his voice* i.e. sing
75 *triple region* Asia, Africa, and Europe
77 *this pen* i.e. his sword
80–81 Although Ellis-Fermor suggests that 'perpendicular' here should be read as
    meridian, the more likely explanation is provided by D. K. Anderson, who argues
    that Marlowe is referring to the archaic 'T-in-O' maps of the medieval known
    world, which featured a 'T' circumscribed by an 'O'. The upper half of the
    circle, above the cross-bar, is the east, representing Asia, the lower left quadrant
    represents Europe (north and west) and the lower right quadrant Africa (south
    and west), with the lines of the 'T' standing for bodies of water. Tamburlaine
    imagines such maps being re-drawn to place Damascus, rather than the traditional
    Jerusalem, at the 'point' where vertical and horizontal lines meet, i.e. the spiritual
    centre of the world. See *N & Q* N.S. 21.8 (1974), 284–6.

ZENOCRATE
> Honour still wait on happy Tamburlaine:
> Yet give me leave to plead for him, my lord.   85

TAMBURLAINE
> Content thyself, his person shall be safe,
> And all the friends of fair Zenocrate,
> If with their lives they will be pleased to yield,
> Or may be forced to make me emperor –
> For Egypt and Arabia must be mine.   90
> [*To* BAJAZETH] Feed, you slave, thou may'st think thyself
> happy to be fed from my trencher.

BAJAZETH
> My empty stomach, full of idle heat,
> Draws bloody humours from my feeble parts,
> Preserving life by hasting cruel death.   95
> My veins are pale, my sinews hard and dry,
> My joints benumbed – unless I eat, I die.

ZABINA
> Eat, Bajazeth. Let us live in spite of them, looking some
> happy power will pity and enlarge us.

TAMBURLAINE
> Here, Turk, wilt thou have a clean trencher?   100

BAJAZETH
> Ay, tyrant, and more meat.

TAMBURLAINE
> Soft, sir, you must be dieted, too much eating will make
> you surfeit.

THERIDAMAS
> So it would, my lord, 'specially having so small a walk,
> and so little exercise.   105

Enter a second course of crowns

TAMBURLAINE
> Theridamas, Techelles, and Casane, here are the cates
> you desire to finger, are they not?

---

84 *still* forever
92 *trencher* wooden platter
93–7 Bajazeth's hunger draws blood, one of the four chief fluids of the body ('humours'), into his stomach, and away from his limbs and sinews, thus drying and weakening them. Hence his body, in working to preserve life, works against itself to hasten his death.
99 *looking . . . us* hoping that some favourable power will pity and free us
105 s.d. At this point, kingly crowns and perhaps also delicacies in the shape of crowns are brought in.
106 *cates* delicacies

THERIDAMAS
  Ay, my lord, but none save kings must feed with these.
TECHELLES
  'Tis enough for us to see them, and for Tamburlaine
  only to enjoy them.   110
TAMBURLAINE
  Well, here is now to the Soldan of Egypt, the King of
  Arabia, and the Governor of Damascus. Now take these
  three crowns, and pledge me, my contributory kings. I
  crown you here, Theridamas, King of Argier; Techelles,
  King of Fez; and Usumcasane, King of Morocco. How   115
  say you to this, Turk? These are not your contributory
  kings.
BAJAZETH
  Nor shall they long be thine, I warrant them.
TAMBURLAINE
  Kings of Argier, Morocco, and of Fez,
  You that have marched with happy Tamburlaine   120
  As far as from the frozen place of heaven
  Unto the watery morning's ruddy bower,
  And thence by land unto the torrid zone,
  Deserve these titles I endow you with
  By valour and by magnanimity.   125
  Your births shall be no blemish to your fame,
  For virtue is the fount whence honour springs,
  And they are worthy she investeth kings.
THERIDAMAS
  And since your highness hath so well vouchsafed,
  If we deserve them not with higher meeds   130
  Than erst our states and actions have retained,
  Take them away again and make us slaves.
TAMBURLAINE
  Well said, Theridamas. When holy fates
  Shall 'stablish me in strong Egyptia,
  We mean to travel to th'antarctic pole,   135
  Conquering the people underneath our feet,
  And be renowned as never emperors were.

122 *bower* O3, Q (hour O1)
125 *valour* ed. (value O1)
126 *births* humble origins
127 *virtue* power and ability
129 *vouchsafed* granted (the crowns)
130 *meeds* merits
131 *erst* formerly
    retained warranted
136 *underneath our feet* i.e. who live in the southern hemisphere

Zenocrate, I will not crown thee yet,
Until with greater honours I be graced.   [*Exeunt*]

Act V, Scene i

[*Enter*] *the* GOVERNOR OF DAMASCUS, *with three or four*
Citizens, and four VIRGINS *with branches of laurel*
in their hands

GOVERNOR
Still doth this man or rather god of war
Batter our walls and beat our turrets down,
And to resist with longer stubbornness
Or hope of rescue from the Soldan's power,
Were but to bring our wilful overthrow   5
And make us desperate of our threatened lives.
We see his tents have now been alterèd
With terrors to the last and cruellest hue.
His coal-black colours everywhere advanced
Threaten our city with a general spoil,   10
And if we should with common rites of arms
Offer our safeties to his clemency,
I fear the custom proper to his sword,
Which he observes as parcel of his fame
Intending so to terrify the world,   15
By any innovation or remorse
Will never be dispensed with till our deaths.
Therefore for these our harmless virgins' sakes,
Whose honours and whose lives rely on him,
Let us have hope that their unspotted prayers,   20
Their blubbered cheeks and hearty humble moans,
Will melt his fury into some remorse,
And use us like a loving conqueror.
FIRST VIRGIN
If humble suits or imprecations –
Uttered with tears of wretchedness and blood   25
Shed from the heads and hearts of all our sex,

13 *proper ... sword* which is a part of his code of war
14 *parcel* an essential part
16 *innovation* change of mind
   remorse pity
21 *blubbered* tear-stained
   hearty heart-felt
24 *imprecations* prayers

Some made your wives, and some your children –
Might have entreated your obdurate breasts
To entertain some care of our securities
Whiles only danger beat upon our walls,   30
These more than dangerous warrants of our death
Had never been erected as they be,
Nor you depend on such weak helps as we.

GOVERNOR
Well, lovely virgins, think our country's care,
Our love of honour, loath to be enthralled   35
To foreign powers and rough imperious yokes,
Would not with too much cowardice or fear
Before all hope of rescue were denied
Submit yourselves and us to servitude.
Therefore in that your safeties and our own,   40
Your honours, liberties and lives were weighed
In equal care and balance with our own,
Endure as we the malice of our stars,
The wrath of Tamburlaine and power of wars,
Or be the means the overweighing heavens   45
Have kept to qualify these hot extremes,
And bring us pardon in your cheerful looks.

SECOND VIRGIN
Then here before the majesty of heaven
And holy patrons of Egyptia,
With knees and hearts submissive we entreat   50
Grace to our words and pity to our looks,
That this device may prove propitious,
And through the eyes and ears of Tamburlaine
Convey events of mercy to his heart,
Grant that these signs of victory we yield   55
May bind the temples of his conquering head
To hide the folded furrows of his brows
And shadow his displeasèd countenance
With happy looks of ruth and lenity.
Leave us, my lord and loving countrymen,   60
What simple virgins may persuade, we will.

GOVERNOR
Farewell, sweet virgins, on whose safe return

27 *made* being
31 *warrants* signs (i.e. Tamburlaine's black colours)
45 *overweighing* overruling
54 *events* results
59 *ruth* pity
      lenity mercy

Depends our city, liberty, and lives.

Exeunt [all except the VIRGINS]

Act V, Scene ii

[*Enter*] TAMBURLAINE, TECHELLES, THERIDAMAS,
USUMCASANE, *with others:* TAMBURLAINE *all in black,
and very melancholy*

TAMBURLAINE

What, are the turtles frayed out of their nests?
Alas poor fools, must you be first shall feel
The sworn destruction of Damascus?
They know my custom. Could they not as well
Have sent ye out when first my milk-white flags   5
Through which sweet mercy threw her gentle beams,
Reflexing them on your disdainful eyes,
As now, when fury and incensèd hate
Flings slaughtering terror from my coal-black tents
And tells for truth submissions comes too late?   10

FIRST VIRGIN

Most happy king and emperor of the earth,
Image of honour and nobility
For whom the powers divine have made the world,
And on whose throne the holy Graces sit,
In whose sweet person is comprised the sum   15
Of nature's skill and heavenly majesty,
Pity our plights! O pity poor Damascus!
Pity old age, within whose silver hairs
Honour and reverence evermore have reigned.
Pity the marriage bed, where many a lord   20
In prime and glory of his loving joy
Embraceth now with tears of ruth and blood
The jealous body of his fearful wife,
Whose cheeks and hearts, so punished with conceit
To think thy puissant never-stayèd arm   25

V, ii Though this is not strictly a new scene, most editors retain O1's scene division
    here.
1 *turtles frayed* turtle-doves frightened
2 *fools* helpless ones
7 *Reflexing* reflecting
10 *submissions* the act of yielding
14 *Graces* three daughters of Jupiter, bestowers of beauty and charm
23 *jealous* apprehensive
24 *punished with conceit* tormented by the thought

Will part their bodies and prevent their souls
From heavens of comfort yet their age might bear,
Now wax all pale and withered to the death;
As well for grief our ruthless governor
Have thus refused the mercy of thy hand,   30
Whose sceptre angels kiss and Furies dread,
As for their liberties, their loves or lives.
O then for these and such as we ourselves,
For us, for infants, and for all our bloods
That never nourished thought against thy rule,   35
Pity, O pity, sacred emperor,
The prostrate service of this wretched town –
And take in sign thereof this gilded wreath,
Whereto each man of rule hath given his hand
And wished as worthy subjects happy means   40
To be investers of thy royal brows,
Even with the true Egyptian diadem.

TAMBURLAINE
Virgins, in vain ye labour to prevent
That which mine honour swears shall be performed.
Behold my sword, what see you at the point?   45

[FIRST] VIRGIN
Nothing but fear and fatal steel, my lord.

TAMBURLAINE
Your fearful minds are thick and misty then,
For there sits Death, there sits imperious Death,
Keeping his circuit by the slicing edge.
But I am pleased you shall not see him there.   50
He now is seated on my horsemen's spears,
And on their points his fleshless body feeds.
Techelles, straight go charge a few of them
To charge these dames, and show my servant Death
Sitting in scarlet on their armèd spears.   55

[VIRGINS]
O pity us!

26–7 *prevent . . . From* deprive . . . of
29–32 *As well . . . lives* i.e. the people of Damascus are as pained by their Governor's
refusal as they are by their personal losses.
34 *bloods* i.e. spirits
40 *happy means* fortunate opportunity
41–2 i.e. to crown Tamburlaine
49 *circuit* Death is likened to a judge whose circuit, or journey in a particular district
to hold court sessions, is equal to the distance reached by Tamburlaine's sword.
52 *fleshless body* the medieval image of Death as a skeleton
55 *scarlet* (1) judge's robe, (2) blood

TAMBURLAINE
        Away with them I say and show them Death.
                    [TECHELLES *and others*] *take them away*
        I will not spare these proud Egyptians
        Nor change my martial observations
        For all the wealth of Gihon's golden waves,   60
        Or for the love of Venus, would she leave
        The angry god of arms and lie with me.
        They have refused the offer of their lives
        And know my customs are as peremptory
        As wrathful planets, death, or destiny.   65

                    Enter TECHELLES

        What, have your horsemen shown the virgins Death?
TECHELLES
        They have, my lord, and on Damascus' walls
        Have hoisted up their slaughtered carcasses.
TAMBURLAINE
        A sight as baneful to their souls I think
        As are Thessalian drugs or mithridate.   70
        But go, my lords, put the rest to the sword.
                    Exeunt [*all except* TAMBURLAINE]
        Ah fair Zenocrate, divine Zenocrate,
        Fair is too foul an epithet for thee,
        That in thy passion for thy country's love
        And fear to see thy kingly father's harm   75
        With hair dishevelled wip'st thy watery cheeks;
        And like to Flora in her morning's pride,
        Shaking her silver tresses in the air,
        Rain'st on the earth resolvèd pearl in showers
        And sprinklest sapphires on thy shining face,   80
        Where Beauty, mother to the Muses, sits
        And comments volumes with her ivory pen,

---

59 *observations* customary practices
60 *Gihon* the second river of Eden (*Genesis* 2:13)
62 *god of arms* Mars, the lover of Venus
64 *peremptory* absolute
69 *baneful* deadly
70 *Thessalian* Thessaly was traditionally regarded as the land of witchcraft and strange drugs.
    mithridate Here, apparently, poison. But generally mithridate was regarded as an antidote to poison.
77ff. The looseness of the syntax here may indicate Tamburlaine's uncharacteristically rapt and uncertain state.
77 *Flora* the Roman goddess of springtime and flowers
79 *resolvèd pearl* i.e. tears

Taking instructions from thy flowing eyes –
Eyes when that Ebena steps to heaven
In silence of thy solemn evening's walk,   85
Making the mantle of the richest night,
The moon, the planets, and the meteors, light.
There angels in their crystal armours fight
A doubtful battle with my tempted thoughts
For Egypt's freedom and the Soldan's life,   90
His life that so consumes Zenocrate,
Whose sorrows lay more siege unto my soul
Than all my army to Damascus' walls;
And neither Persians' sovereign nor the Turk
Troubled my senses with conceit of foil   95
So much by much as doth Zenocrate.
What is beauty saith my sufferings then?
If all the pens that ever poets held
Had fed the feeling of their masters' thoughts,
And every sweetness that inspired their hearts,   100
Their minds, and muses on admirèd themes,
If all the heavenly quintessence they still
From their immortal flowers of poesy,
Wherein as in a mirror we perceive
The highest reaches of a human wit,   105
If these had made one poem's period
And all combined in beauty's worthiness,
Yet should there hover in their restless heads
One thought, one grace, one wonder at the least,
Which into words no virtue can digest.   110
But how unseemly is it for my sex,
My discipline of arms and chivalry,
My nature and the terror of my name,
To harbour thoughts effeminate and faint!
Save only that in beauty's just applause,   115
With whose instinct the soul of man is touched –
And every warrior that is rapt with love

---

84 *Ebena* No such deity is known. The sense here is Zenocrate's eyes at night light
     up the various heavenly bodies.
91 *consumes* wastes with anxiety
95 *conceit of foil* the thought of defeat
101 *muses* meditations
102 *quintessence* most essential part
     still distil
105 *wit* imagination
106–7 *made ... worthiness* been combined to form a single poem in beauty's praise
110 *Which ... digest* which no power can express in words
114 *faint* weak

Of fame, of valour, and of victory,
Must needs have beauty beat on his conceits –
I thus conceiving and subduing both 120
That which hath stooped the topmost of the gods,
Even from the fiery-spangled veil of heaven,
To feel the lovely warmth of shepherds' flames
And march in cottages of strewèd weeds,
Shall give the world to note, for all my birth, 125
That virtue solely is the sum of glory
And fashions men with true nobility.
Who's within there?
           Enter two or three [ATTENDANTS]
Hath Bajazeth been fed today?
ATTENDANT
Ay, my lord. 130
TAMBURLAINE
Bring him forth, and let us know if the town be ran-
sacked.
                         [*Exeunt* ATTENDANTS]

Enter TECHELLES, THERIDAMAS, USUMCASANE, *and others*

TECHELLES
The town is ours, my lord, and fresh supply
Of conquest and of spoil is offered us.
TAMBURLAINE
That's well, Techelles. What's the news? 135

115–27 A notoriously difficult passage, coming just at a crucial point in Tamburlaine's
development as a character. He suggests (somewhat paradoxically) that, though
it may be 'unseemly' (l. 111) for great warriors like himself to be affected by love,
it is also inevitable, since the soul of man is properly stirred by the prompting
('instinct') of beauty (ll. 115–16). The long concessive clause beginning at l. 115
('Save' = except) is incomplete, leading to a break at l. 120; at that point,
Tamburlaine turns to his own power over the incursions of beauty: he is able
both to conceive of it in his soul *and* subdue it (l. 120). He thereby outdoes even
the highest ('topmost') of the gods, who have typically 'stooped' to the power of
Beauty by coming down to earth disguised as shepherds and the like, and hence
shown themselves unable to master temptation. Thus Tamburlaine is able to
show the world that, despite his low birth (l. 125), his 'virtue' (i.e. his power and
self-command as a warrior) is the noblest attribute of men. See Introduction,
pp. xvi–xvii.
119 *beat on his conceits* impinge on his thoughts
121 *stooped the topmost* ed. (stopt the tempest O1). An emendation suggested by G.
I. Duthie.
122 *fiery-spangled veil* stars
124 *cottages of strewèd weeds* simple dwellings with rushes strewn on the floor
126 *sum* the highest attainable point
130 s.p. ed. (An. O1)

TECHELLES
    The Soldan and the Arabian king together
    March on us with such eager violence
    As if there were no way but one with us.
TAMBURLAINE
    No more there is not, I warrant thee, Techelles.

    They bring in [BAJAZETH,] *the Turk* [*in his cage,*
    followed by ZABINA]

THERIDAMAS
    We know the victory is ours, my lord,   140
    But let us save the reverend Soldan's life
    For fair Zenocrate that so laments his state.
TAMBURLAINE
    That will we chiefly see unto, Theridamas,
    For sweet Zenocrate, whose worthiness
    Deserves a conquest over every heart.   145
    And now, my footstool, if I lose the field,
    You hope of liberty and restitution.
    Here let him stay, my masters, from the tents,
    Till we have made us ready for the field.
    Pray for us, Bajazeth, we are going.   150
                Exeunt [*all except* BAJAZETH *and* ZABINA]
BAJAZETH
    Go, never to return with victory!
    Millions of men encompass thee about
    And gore thy body with as many wounds!
    Sharp forkèd arrows light upon thy horse!
    Furies from the black Cocytus lake   155
    Break up the earth and with their firebrands
    Enforce thee run upon the baneful pikes!
    Volleys of shot pierce through thy charmèd skin
    And every bullet dipped in poisoned drugs,
    Or roaring cannons sever all thy joints,   160
    Making thee mount as high as eagles soar!
ZABINA
    Let all the swords and lances in the field
    Stick in his breast, as in their proper rooms!
    At every pore let blood come dropping forth,
    That ling'ring pains may massacre his heart   165
    And madness send his damnèd soul to hell!

155 *Cocytus* a river in the underworld, though here Marlowe refers to it as a lake
157 *Enforce thee* force thee to
163 *as in ... rooms* as if that were their proper home

BAJAZETH

Ah fair Zabina, we may curse his power,
The heavens may frown, the earth for anger quake,
But such a star hath influence in his sword
As rules the skies and countermands the gods   170
More than Cimmerian Styx or destiny.
And then shall we in this detested guise,
With shame, with hunger, and with horror aye
Griping our bowels with retorquèd thoughts,
And have no hope to end our ecstasies.   175

ZABINA

Then is there left no Mahomet, no God,
No fiend, no fortune, nor no hope of end
To our infamous monstrous slaveries?
Gape earth, and let the fiends infernal view
A hell as hopeless and as full of fear   180
As are the blasted banks of Erebus,
Where shaking ghosts with ever-howling groans
Hover about the ugly ferryman
To get a passage to Elysium.
Why should we live O wretches, beggars, slaves,   185
Why live we, Bajazeth, and build up nests
So high within the region of the air
By living long in this oppression,
That all the world will see and laugh to scorn
The former triumphs of our mightiness   190
In this obscure infernal servitude?

BAJAZETH

O life more loathsome to my vexèd thoughts
Than noisome parbreak of the Stygian snakes,
Which fills the nooks of hell with standing air,

171 *Styx* the chief river of Hades, here described as black (Cimmerian)
172 *we in* 'Live' or 'continue' is understood after 'we' – its omission may be a sign of Bajazeth's anguish.
173 *aye* forever
174 *retorquèd* twisted back upon themselves
175 *ecstasies* frenzies
181 *Erebus* hell. See note to IV, i. 45 above.
183–4 lineation ed.
183 *ferryman* Charon, who conveyed the souls of the dead across the river Styx to the underworld ('Elysium').
185 The 'O' in mid-line is probably a cry, not an apostrophe.
186–7 *build ... air* subsist on false hopes. Cf. the expression 'to build castles in the air'.
193 *parbreak* vomit
194 *standing* stagnant

Infecting all the ghosts with cureless griefs!   195
O dreary engines of my loathèd sight
That sees my crown, my honour and my name
Thrust under yoke and thraldom of a thief,
Why feed ye still on day's accursèd beams
And sink not quite into my tortured soul?   200
You see my wife, my queen and emperess,
Brought up and proppèd by the hand of fame,
Queen of fifteen contributory queens,
Now thrown to rooms of black abjection,
Smearèd with blots of basest drudgery,   205
And villainess to shame, disdain and misery.
Accursèd Bajazeth, whose words of ruth
That would with pity cheer Zabina's heart
And make our souls resolve in ceaseless tears,
Sharp hunger bites upon and gripes the root   210
From whence the issues of my thoughts do break.
O poor Zabina, O my queen, my queen,
Fetch me some water for my burning breast
To cool and comfort me with longer date,
That in the shortened sequel of my life   215
I may pour forth my soul into thine arms
With words of love, whose moaning intercourse
Hath hitherto been stayed with wrath and hate
Of our expressless banned inflictions.

ZABINA
Sweet Bajazeth, I will prolong thy life   220
As long as any blood or spark of breath
Can quench or cool the torments of my grief.
                                        She goes out

BAJAZETH
Now Bajazeth, abridge thy baneful days
And beat thy brains out of thy conquered head,
Since other means are all forbidden me   225
That may be ministers of my decay.
O highest lamp of ever-living Jove,
Accursèd day infected with my griefs,

196 *engines* instruments (i.e. his eyes)
204 *abjection* degradation
206 *villainess* servant
209 *resolve* dissolve
214 *date* term of life
219 *expressless* inexpressible
    banned cursed
226 *ministers ... decay* instruments of death

Can this be linked to suicide of Agydas?

Hide now thy stainèd face in endless night
And shut the windows of the lightsome heavens.   230
Let ugly Darkness with her rusty coach
Engirt with tempests wrapped in pitchy clouds
Smother the earth with never-fading mists,
And let her horses from their nostrils breathe
Rebellious winds and dreadful thunderclaps,   235
That in this terror Tamburlaine may live,
And my pined soul, resolved in liquid air,
May still excruciate his tormented thoughts.
Then let the stony dart of senseless cold
Pierce through the centre of my withered heart   240
And make a passage for my loathèd life.

He brains himself against the cage

Enter ZABINA

ZABINA
What do mine eyes behold, my husband dead?
His skull all riven in twain, his brains dashed out?
The brains of Bajazeth, my lord and sovereign!
O Bajazeth, my husband and my lord,   245
O Bajazeth, O Turk, O emperor, give him his liquor?
Not I. Bring milk and fire, and my blood I bring him
again, tear me in pieces, give me the sword with a ball
of wildfire upon it! Down with him, down with him! Go
to, my child, away, away, away! Ah, save that infant, save   250
him, save him! I, even I, speak to her – the sun was
down. Streamers white, red, black, here, here, here!
Fling the meat in his face! Tamburlaine, Tamburlaine,
let the soldiers be buried. Hell, death, Tamburlaine, hell,
make ready my coach, my chair, my jewels, I come, I   255
come, I come!

She runs against the cage and brains herself

[*Enter*] ZENOCRATE *and* ANIPPE

ZENOCRATE
Wretched Zenocrate, that livest to see
Damascus' walls dyed with Egyptian blood,
Thy father's subjects and thy countrymen,
The streets strowed with dissevered joints of men,   260
And wounded bodies gasping yet for life.

'brains' no verb

237 *pined* tormented
   resolved dissolved
   air O3, Q (ay O1)
238 *excruciate* torment

But most accursed, to see the sun-bright troop
Of heavenly virgins and unspotted maids,
Whose looks might make the angry god of arms
To break his sword and mildly treat of love,   265
On horsemen's lances to be hoisted up
And guiltlessly endure a cruel death;
For every fell and stout Tartarian steed
That stamped on others with their thund'ring hooves,
When all their riders charged their quivering spears   270
Began to check the ground and rein themselves,
Gazing upon the beauty of their looks.
Ah Tamburlaine, wert thou the cause of this,
That term'st Zenocrate thy dearest love,
Whose lives were dearer to Zenocrate   275
Than her own life or aught save thine own love?
But see another bloody spectacle!
Ah wretched eyes, the enemies of my heart,
How are ye glutted with these grievous objects
And tell my soul more tales of bleeding ruth!   280
See, see, Anippe if they breathe or no.

ANIPPE
No breath nor sense nor motion in them both.
Ah madam, this their slavery hath enforced,   *? apostropha (?.)*
And ruthless cruelty of Tamburlaine.

ZENOCRATE
Earth, cast up fountains from thy entrails,   285
And wet thy cheeks for their untimely deaths:
Shake with their weight in sign of fear and grief.
Blush, heaven, that gave them honour at their birth
And let them die a death so barbarous.
Those that are proud of fickle empery   290
And place their chiefest good in earthly pomp,
Behold the Turk and his great emperess!
Ah Tamburlaine, my love, sweet Tamburlaine,
That fights for sceptres and for slippery crowns,
Behold the Turk and his great emperess!   295
Thou, that in conduct of thy happy stars
Sleep'st every night with conquest on thy brows

268 *fell and stout* fierce and proud
270 *charged* levelled for the charge
271 *check the ground* paw the ground, hesitate
276 *aught* anything
280 *bleeding ruth* pitiable suffering
290 *empery* imperial rule
296 *in conduct* under the guidance

And yet wouldst shun the wavering turns of war,
In fear and feeling of the like distress
Behold the Turk and his great emperess!   300
Ah mighty Jove and holy Mahomet,
Pardon my love! O pardon his contempt
Of earthly fortune and respect of pity,
And let not conquest ruthlessly pursued
Be equally against his life incensed,   305
In this great Turk and hapless emperess.
And pardon me that was not moved with ruth
To see them live so long in misery.
Ah what may chance to thee, Zenocrate?

ANIPPE
Madam, content yourself and be resolved,   310
Your love hath Fortune so at his command
That she shall stay and turn her wheel no more
As long as life maintains his mighty arm
That fights for honour to adorn your head.

Enter [PHILEMUS,] *a Messenger*

ZENOCRATE
What other heavy news now brings Philemus?   315
PHILEMUS
Madam, your father and th'Arabian king,
The first affecter of your excellence,
Comes now as Turnus 'gainst Aeneas did,
Armèd with lance into th'Egyptian fields,
Ready for battle 'gainst my lord the king.   320
ZENOCRATE
Now shame and duty, love and fear, presents
A thousand sorrows to my martyred soul.
Whom should I wish the fatal victory
When my poor pleasures are divided thus,
And racked by duty from my cursèd heart?   325
My father and my first-betrothèd love
Must fight against my life and present love,
Wherein the change I use condemns my faith
And makes my deeds infamous through the world.

---

303 *respect of* regard for. Zenocrate prays that Tamburlaine's 'contempt' for sym-
    pathetic feeling may be pardoned.
306 *In* as in
317 *affecter* lover
318 *Turnus* leader of the Italian forces against the encroaching Trojans, and rival of
    Aeneas for Lavinia's hand, defeated by Aeneas at the end of the *Aeneid*
328 *change I use* shift of allegiance I have made

But as the gods to end the Trojans' toil   330
Prevented Turnus of Lavinia
And fatally enriched Aeneas' love,
So for a final issue to my griefs,
To pacify my country and my love,
Must Tamburlaine by their resistless powers,   335
With virtue of a gentle victory,
Conclude a league of honour to my hope;
Then as the powers divine have preordained,
With happy safety of my father's life
Send like defence of fair Arabia.   340

They sound to the battle. And TAMBURLAINE *enjoys the*
victory, after [which the KING OF] ARABIA *enters wounded*

KING OF ARABIA
What cursèd power guides the murdering hands
Of this infamous tyrant's soldiers
That no escape may save their enemies,
Nor fortune keep themselves from victory?
Lie down, Arabia, wounded to the death,   345
And let Zenocrate's fair eyes behold
That as for her thou bear'st these wretched arms
Even so for her thou diest in these arms,
Leaving thy blood for witness of thy love.

ZENOCRATE
Too dear a witness for such love, my lord.   350
Behold Zenocrate, the cursed object
Whose fortunes never masterèd her griefs –
Behold her wounded in conceit for thee
As much as thy fair body is for me.

KING OF ARABIA
Then shall I die with full contented heart   355
Having beheld divine Zenocrate
Whose sight with joy would take away my life,
As now it bringeth sweetness to my wound,
If I had not been wounded as I am.
Ah that the deadly pangs I suffer now   360
Would lend an hour's licence to my tongue,

331 *Prevented* deprived
333 *issue* conclusion
335 *their* the gods'
336 *With virtue* as a consequence
337 *league* treaty
    to in accordance with
353 *conceit* imagination

To make discourse of some sweet accidents
Have chanced thy merits in this worthless bondage,
And that I might be privy to the state
Of thy deserved contentment and thy love.   365
But making now a virtue of thy sight
To drive all sorrow from my fainting soul,
Since death denies me further cause of joy,
Deprived of care, my heart with comfort dies
Since thy desirèd hand shall close mine eyes.   [*Dies*] 370

Enter TAMBURLAINE *leading in the* SOLDAN, TECHELLES,
THERIDAMAS, USUMCASANE *with others*

TAMBURLAINE
Come, happy father of Zenocrate,
A title higher than thy Soldan's name;
Though my right hand have thus enthrallèd thee,
Thy princely daughter here shall set thee free –
She that hath calmed the fury of my sword,   375
Which had ere this been bathed in streams of blood
As vast and deep as Euphrates or Nile.
ZENOCRATE
O sight thrice welcome to my joyful soul,
To see the king my father issue safe
From dangerous battle of my conquering love!   380
SOLDAN
Well met, my only dear Zenocrate,
Though with the loss of Egypt and my crown.
TAMBURLAINE
'Twas I, my lord, that gat the victory,
And therefore grieve not at your overthrow,
Since I shall render all into your hands   385
And add more strength to your dominions
Than ever yet confirmed th'Egyptian crown.
The god of war resigns his room to me,
Meaning to make me general of the world;
Jove viewing me in arms looks pale and wan,   390
Fearing my power should pull him from his throne;
Where'er I come the Fatal Sisters sweat,
And grisly Death, by running to and fro

362 *sweet accidents* favourable occurrences
363 *Have ... merits* that have taken place as a result of your merits
366 *thy sight* i.e. my sight of you
380 *of* with
387 *confirmed* established
392 *Fatal Sisters* the three Fates

To do their ceaseless homage to my sword;
And here in Afric, where it seldom rains,   395
Since I arrived with my triumphant host,
Have swelling clouds drawn from wide gasping wounds
Been oft resolved in bloody purple showers,
A meteor that might terrify the earth
And make it quake at every drop it drinks.   400
Millions of souls sit on the banks of Styx,
Waiting the back return of Charon's boat;
Hell and Elysium swarm with ghosts of men
That I have sent from sundry foughten fields
To spread my fame through hell and up to heaven.   405
And see, my lord, a sight of strange import,
Emperors and kings lie breathless at my feet:
The Turk and his great empress, as it seems,
Left to themselves while we were at the fight,
Have desperately dispatched their slavish lives;   410
With them Arabia too hath left his life –
All sights of power to grace my victory.
And such are objects fit for Tamburlaine,
Wherein as in a mirror may be seen
His honour that consists in shedding blood   415
When men presume to manage arms with him.

SOLDAN
Mighty hath God and Mahomet made thy hand,
Renownèd Tamburlaine, to whom all kings
Of force must yield their crowns and emperies;
And I am pleased with this my overthrow   420
If, as beseems a person of thy state,
Thou hast with honour used Zenocrate.

TAMBURLAINE
Her state and person wants no pomp you see,
And for all blot of foul inchastity,
I record heaven, her heavenly self is clear.   425
Then let me find no further time to grace
Her princely temples with the Persian crown.
But here these kings that on my fortunes wait,
And have been crowned for provèd worthiness
Even by this hand that shall establish them,   430

397–400 According to Renaissance meteorology, the sun could draw up blood from
    where great quantities had been spilt and transform it to a bloody rain.
399 *meteor* meteorological phenomenon
419 *Of force* perforce, by necessity
423 *wants* lack
425 *record* call to witness

Shall now, adjoining all their hands with mine,
Invest her here my Queen of Persia.
What saith the noble Soldan and Zenocrate?

SOLDAN
I yield with thanks and protestations
Of endless honour to thee for her love.   435

TAMBURLAINE
Then doubt I not but fair Zenocrate
Will soon consent to satisfy us both.

ZENOCRATE
Else should I much forget myself, my lord.

THERIDAMAS
Then let us set the crown upon her head
That hath long lingered for so high a seat.   440

TECHELLES
My hand is ready to perform the deed,
For now her marriage time shall work us rest.

USUMCASANE
And here's the crown, my lord; help set it on.

TAMBURLAINE
Then sit thou down, divine Zenocrate,
And here we crown thee Queen of Persia   445
And all the kingdoms and dominions
That late the power of Tamburlaine subdued.
As Juno, when the giants were suppressed
That darted mountains at her brother Jove,
So looks my love, shadowing in her brows   450
Triumphs and trophies for my victories;
Or as Latona's daughter bent to arms,
Adding more courage to my conquering mind.
To gratify thee, sweet Zenocrate,
Egyptians, Moors, and men of Asia,   455
From Barbary unto the Western Indie,
Shall pay a yearly tribute to thy sire;
And from the bounds of Afric to the banks
Of Ganges shall his mighty arm extend.
And now, my lords and loving followers,   460
That purchased kingdoms by your martial deeds,

435 *for her love* for your love of her
442 *work us* bring about for us
448 *giants* Titans
450 *shadowing* portraying
452 *Latona's daughter* Artemis the huntress
454 *thee* ed. (the O1)
456 *From . . . Indie* from north Africa to the Ganges

Cast off your armour, put on scarlet robes,
Mount up your royal places of estate,
Environèd with troops of noblemen,
And there make laws to rule your provinces;   465
Hang up your weapons on Alcides' post,
For Tamburlaine takes truce with all the world.
Thy first betrothèd love, Arabia,
Shall we with honour, as beseems, entomb
With this great Turk and his fair emperess.   470
Then after all these solemn exequies
We will our celebrated rites of marriage solemnize.

                                                         [*Exeunt*]

466 *Alcides' post* the doorpost of the temple of Hercules (Alcides)
469 *as beseems* as is fitting
472 *celebrated* performed with customary observances (*O.E.D.*). Most editors cut this
    extra-metrical word, despite its presence in all the early texts, but the sonorous
    ring it gives to the final line is eminently suitable to the occasion.

Tamburlaine the Greate.

VVith his impaſsionate furie , for the
death of his Lady and Loue faire Zenocrate : his forme of exhortation and diſcipline
to his three Sonnes ,and the manner of
his owne death.

The ſecond part.

LONDON
Printed *by* E. A, *for* Ed. White, *and are* *to be ſolde*
at his Shop neere the little North doore of Saint Paules
Church at the Signe of the Gun.
1 6 0 6.

[DRAMATIS PERSONAE

PROLOGUE
TAMBURLAINE, King of Persia
CALYPHAS ⎫
AMYRAS ⎬ his sons
CELEBINUS ⎭
THERIDAMAS, King of Argier
TECHELLES, King of Fez
USUMCASANE, King of Morocco
ORCANES, King of Natolia
KING OF JERUSALEM
KING OF SORIA
KING OF TREBIZON
GAZELLUS, Viceroy of Byron
URIBASSA
SIGISMUND, King of Hungary
FREDERICK ⎫
BALDWIN ⎬ peers of Hungary
CALLAPINE, son of Bajazeth and prisoner of Tamburlaine
ALMEDA, his keeper
KING OF AMASIA
GOVERNOR OF BABYLON
CAPTAIN OF BALSERA
His SON
Another CAPTAIN
MAXIMUS
PERDICAS
LORDS, CITIZENS, SOLDIERS, PIONERS, PHYSICIANS, MESSENGERS,
and ATTENDANTS

ZENOCRATE, wife of Tamburlaine
OLYMPIA, wife of the Captain of Balsera
Turkish CONCUBINES]

THE PROLOGUE

The general welcomes Tamburlaine received
When he arrivèd last upon our stage,
Hath made our poet pen his second part,
Where death cuts off the progress of his pomp
And murd'rous Fates throws all his triumphs down.　　　　5
But what became of fair Zenocrate,
And with how many cities' sacrifice
He celebrated her sad funeral,
Himself in presence shall unfold at large.

8 *sad* ed. (said O1)

TAMBURLAINE THE GREAT

Act I, Scene i

[Enter] ORCANES, *King of Natolia*; GAZELLUS, *Viceroy of Byron*; URIBASSA, *and their train, with drums and trumpets*

ORCANES

Egregious viceroys of these eastern parts,
Placed by the issue of great Bajazeth
And sacred lord, the mighty Callapine,
Who lives in Egypt prisoner to that slave
Which kept his father in an iron cage: 5
Now have we marched from fair Natolia
Two hundred leagues, and on Danubius' banks
Our warlike host in complete armour rest,
Where Sigismund the King of Hungary
Should meet our person to conclude a truce.   10
What, shall we parley with the Christian,
Or cross the stream and meet him in the field?

GAZELLUS

King of Natolia, let us treat of peace,
We all are glutted with the Christians' blood
And have a greater foe to fight against –   15
Proud Tamburlaine, that now in Asia

I, i, s.d.2 URIBASSA ed. (Upibassa O1)
I, i, s.d.2 *train* The train, or group of followers, consisted of whatever extras could be recruited for various large and impressive scenes (see, for example, the opening stage directions for Part Two, I,v; II,i; II,ii; III,iii; etc.). A quick change of costume could transform a journeyman actor from Turk to Christian, or from Egyptian soldier to Tamburlaine loyalist. The numbers were small, but strategic placement onstage could give the impression of a large army just off. In the opening chorus of *Henry V*, Shakespeare appeals to his audience to compensate for the inadequacies of state representation: 'Piece out our imperfections with your thoughts – / Into a thousand parts divide one man.' Since the Rose stage, where *Tamburlaine* was performed during the 1590s, was considerably smaller than that at the Globe, the discrepancy might have seemed less glaring there, since the crowded Rose stage could more easily have given the impression of large numbers pressing at the sides. See Introduction pp. xxix–xxx.
1 *Egregious* Distinguished
2 *issue* offspring
6 *Natolia* a more extensive area of Asia Minor than the present-day Anatolia
11 *parley* ed. (parle O1)

Near Guyron's head doth set his conquering feet,
And means to fire Turkey as he goes.
'Gainst him my lord must you address your power.

URIBASSA

Besides, King Sigismund hath brought from Christen-
    dom   20
More than his camp of stout Hungarians,
Slavonians, Almains, Rutters, Muffs, and Danes,
That with the halberd, lance, and murdering axe,
Will hazard that we might with surety hold.

[ORCANES]

Though from the shortest northern parallel,   25
Vast Gruntland, compassed with the frozen sea,
Inhabited with tall and sturdy men,
Giants as big as hugy Polypheme,
Millions of soldiers cut the arctic line,
Bringing the strength of Europe to these arms,   30
Our Turkey blades shall glide through all their throats,
And make this champion mead a bloody fen.
Danubius' stream that runs to Trebizon,
Shall carry wrapped within his scarlet waves,
As martial presents to our friends at home,   35
The slaughtered bodies of these Christians.
The Terrene main wherein Danubius falls
Shall by this battle be the bloody sea.

---

17 *Guyron* Guiron, a town on the upper Euphrates, north-east of Aleppo
22 *Almains* Germans
   Rutters horsemen
   Muffs a derogatory term for Swiss or Germans
23 *halberd* a long-handled spear with an axe-edge
25 *shortest . . . parallel* the smallest circle of latitude described on the globe toward
   the north
26 *Gruntland* Greenland
   frozen sea Arctic Ocean
27–8 *Inhabited . . . Giants* a popular belief in Marlowe's day
28 *Polypheme* the Cyclops in Homer's *Odyssey*
29 *cut . . . line* cross the Arctic Circle from the north
32 *champion mead* level grassland
33–41 'Marlowe sees the waters of the Danube sweeping from the river-mouths in
   two strong currents, the one racing across the Black Sea to Trebizond, the other
   swirling southward to the Bosphorus, and so onward to the Hellespont and the
   Aegean; both currents bear the slaughtered bodies of Christian soldiers, the one
   to bring proof of victory to the great Turkish town, the other to strike terror to
   the Italian merchants cruising round the Isles of Greece.' (E. Seaton, 'Marlowe's
   Map', p. 33.)
37 *Terrene main* the Mediterranean

The wand'ring sailors of proud Italy
Shall meet those Christians fleeting with the tide,   40
Beating in heaps against their argosies,
And make fair Europe mounted on her bull,
Trapped with the wealth and riches of the world,
Alight and wear a woeful mourning weed.

GAZELLUS
Yet, stout Orcanes, prorex of the world,   45
Since Tamburlaine hath mustered all his men,
Marching from Cairo northward with his camp
To Alexandria and the frontier towns,
Meaning to make a conquest of our land,
'Tis requisite to parley for a peace   50
With Sigismund the King of Hungary,
And save our forces for the hot assaults
Proud Tamburlaine intends Natolia.

ORCANES
Viceroy of Byron, wisely hast thou said:
My realm, the centre of our empery,   55
Once lost, all Turkey would be overthrown,
And for that cause the Christians shall have peace.
Slavonians, Almains, Rutters, Muffs, and Danes,
Fear not Orcanes, but great Tamburlaine –
Nor he, but Fortune that hath made him great.   60
We have revolted Grecians, Albanese,
Sicilians, Jews, Arabians, Turks, and Moors,
Natolians, Sorians, black Egyptians,
Illyrians, Thracians, and Bithynians,
Enough to swallow forceless Sigismund,   65
Yet scarce enough t'encounter Tamburlaine.
He brings a world of people to the field:

40 *fleeting* floating
41 *argosies* merchant ships
42 Zeus, in the form of a bull, carried Europa, the daughter of Agenor, King of Phoenicia, across the sea to Crete.
43 *Trapped* adorned
44 *weed* garment
45 *prorex* viceroy
47 *Cairo* ed. (Cairon O1)
50 *parley* ed. (parle O1)
54 *Byron* a town near Babylon
55 *empery* empire
59 *Fear* frighten
61 *Albanese* Albanians
63 *Sorians* Syrians
64 *Illyrians* O3, Q (Illicians O1)

From Scythia to the oriental plage
Of India, where raging Lantchidol
Beats on the regions with his boisterous blows   70
That never seaman yet discoverèd,
All Asia is in arms with Tamburlaine;
Even from the midst of fiery Cancer's tropic
To Amazonia under Capricorn
And thence as far as Archipelago,   75
All Afric is in arms with Tamburlaine.
Therefore, viceroys, the Christians must have peace.

Act I, Scene ii

[*Enter*] SIGISMUND, FREDERICK, BALDWIN, *and their train,*
with drums and trumpets

SIGISMUND

Orcanes, as our legates promised thee,
We with our peers have crossed Danubius' stream
To treat of friendly peace or deadly war:
Take which thou wilt, for as the Romans used,
I here present thee with a naked sword.   5
Wilt thou have war, then shake this blade at me,
If peace, restore it to my hands again
And I will sheathe it to confirm the same.

ORCANES

Stay, Sigismund, forgett'st thou I am he
That with the cannon shook Vienna walls,   10
And made it dance upon the continent,
As when the massy substance of the earth
Quiver about the axle-tree of heaven?
Forgett'st thou that I sent a shower of darts,
Mingled with powdered shot and feathered steel,   15
So thick upon the blink-eyed burghers' heads,
That thou thyself, then County Palatine,

68 *oriental plage* eastern shore
69 *Lantchidol* an arm of the Indian Ocean
73–4 *from . . . Capricorn* from the Canaries, the centre of the Tropic of Cancer, to
   the region known as Amazonia, near the supposed sources of the Nile
75 *thence . . . Archipelago* northward to the Aegean islands
I, ii Though this is not really a different scene, most editors follow O1 in beginning
   a new scene here.
13 *axle-tree of heaven* See note to Part One, IV, ii, 50 above.
16 *blink-eyed* unable to look steadily upon the missiles
17 *County* Count

The King of Boheme, and the Austric Duke,
Sent heralds out, which basely on their knees
In all your names desired a truce of me?   20
Forgett'st thou that to have me raise my siege
Wagons of gold were set before my tent,
Stamped with the princely fowl that in her wings
Carries the fearful thunderbolts of Jove?
How canst thou think of this and offer war?   25

SIGISMUND
Vienna was besieged, and I was there,
Then County Palatine, but now a king;
And what we did was in extremity.
But now, Orcanes, view my royal host,
That hides these plains and seems as vast and wide   30
As doth the desert of Arabia
To those that stand on Badgeth's lofty tower,
Or as the ocean to the traveller
That rests upon the snowy Appenines:
And tell me whether I should stoop so low,   35
Or treat of peace with the Natolian king?

GAZELLUS
Kings of Natolia and of Hungary,
We came from Turkey to confirm a league,
And not to dare each other to the field;
A friendly parley might become ye both.   40

FREDERICK
And we from Europe to the same intent,
Which if your general refuse or scorn,
Our tents are pitched, our men stand in array,
Ready to charge you ere you stir your feet.

ORCANES
So prest are we, but yet if Sigismund   45
Speak as a friend and stand not upon terms,
Here is his sword, let peace be ratified
On these conditions specified before,
Drawn with advice of our ambassadors.

SIGISMUND
Then here I sheathe it, and give thee my hand,   50
Never to draw it out or manage arms
Against thyself or thy confederates,

18 *Austric* Austrian
23 *princely fowl* the eagle
32 *Badgeth* Baghdad
40 *parley* ed. (parle O1)
45 *prest* ready

But whilst I live will be at truce with thee.

ORCANES

But, Sigismund, confirm it with an oath,
And swear in sight of heaven and by thy Christ.   55

SIGISMUND

By him that made the world and saved my soul,
The son of God and issue of a maid,
Sweet Jesus Christ, I solemnly protest
And vow to keep this peace inviolable.

ORCANES

By sacred Mahomet, the friend of God,   60
Whose holy Alcoran remains with us,
Whose glorious body when he left the world
Closed in a coffin mounted up the air
And hung on stately Mecca's temple roof,
I swear to keep this truce inviolable,   65
Of whose conditions and our solemn oaths
Signed with our hands, each shall retain a scroll
As memorable witness of our league.
Now, Sigismund, if any Christian king
Encroach upon the confines of thy realm,   70
Send word Orcanes of Natolia
Confirmed this league beyond Danubius' stream,
And they will, trembling, sound a quick retreat,
So am I feared among all nations.

SIGISMUND

If any heathen potentate or king   75
Invade Natolia, Sigismund will send
A hundred thousand horse trained to the war
And backed by stout lancers of Germany
The strength and sinews of th'imperial seat.

ORCANES

I thank thee, Sigismund, but when I war   80
All Asia Minor, Africa, and Greece
Follow my standard and my thund'ring drums.
Come let us go and banquet in our tents –
I will dispatch chief of my army hence
To fair Natolia and to Trebizon,   85
To stay my coming 'gainst proud Tamburlaine.
Friend Sigismund, and peers of Hungary,
Come banquet and carouse with us a while,

58 *protest* swear
70 *confines* borders
84 *chief* most
86 *stay* await

And then depart we to our territories.   *Exeunt*

Act I, Scene iii

[Enter] CALLAPINE *with* ALMEDA, *his keeper*

CALLAPINE
Sweet Almeda, pity the ruthful plight
Of Callapine, the son of Bajazeth,
Born to be monarch of the western world,
Yet here detained by cruel Tamburlaine.

ALMEDA
My lord I pity it, and with my heart   5
Wish your release, but he whose wrath is death,
My sovereign lord, renownèd Tamburlaine,
Forbids you further liberty than this.

CALLAPINE
Ah, were I now but half so eloquent
To paint in words what I'll perform in deeds,   10
I know thou wouldst depart from hence with me.

ALMEDA
Not for all Afric, therefore move me not.

CALLAPINE
Yet hear me speak, my gentle Almeda.

ALMEDA
No speech to that end, by your favour sir.

CALLAPINE
By Cairo runs –   15

ALMEDA
No talk of running, I tell you sir.

CALLAPINE
A little further, gentle Almeda.

ALMEDA
Well sir, what of this?

CALLAPINE
By Cairo runs to Alexandria bay
Darote's streams, wherein at anchor lies   20
A Turkish galley of my royal fleet,
Waiting my coming to the river side,
Hoping by some means I shall be released:

3 *western world* Turkish empire
12 *move* urge
15 *Cairo* ed. and so throughout (Cario O1)
20 *Darote's streams* the Nile from Cairo to Alexandria, which runs by the town of
Darote

Which when I come aboard will hoist up sail,
And soon put forth into the Terrene sea,   25
Where 'twixt the isles of Cyprus and of Crete,
We quickly may in Turkish seas arrive.
Then shalt thou see a hundred kings and more
Upon their knees all bid me welcome home.
Amongst so many crowns of burnished gold,   30
Choose which thou wilt, all are at thy command;
A thousand galleys manned with Christian slaves
I freely give thee, which shall cut the straits
And bring armadoes from the coast of Spain,
Fraughted with gold of rich America;   35
The Grecian virgins shall attend on thee,
Skilful in music and in amorous lays,
As fair as was Pygmalion's ivory girl,
Or lovely Iö metamorphosèd.
With naked negroes shall thy coach be drawn,   40
And as thou rid'st in triumph through the streets,
The pavement underneath thy chariot wheels
With Turkey carpets shall be coverèd,
And cloth of Arras hung about the walls,
Fit objects for thy princely eye to pierce.   45
A hundred bassoes clothed in crimson silk
Shall ride before thee on Barbarian steeds,
And when thou goest, a golden canopy
Enchased with precious stones, which shine as bright
As that fair veil that covers all the world   50
When Phoebus leaping from his hemisphere
Descendeth downward to th'antipodes.
And more than this, for all I cannot tell.

ALMEDA
How far hence lies the galley, say you?

34 *armadoes* warships
35 *Fraughted* laden
37 *lays* songs
38 *Pygmalion's ivory girl* Galatea, the statue created by the sculptor Pygmalion and
   brought to life by Aphrodite
39 *Iö* daughter of Inachus, King of Argos. She was loved by Zeus and transformed
   into a milk white heifer.
44 *cloth of Arras* rich tapestry
46 *bassoes* pashas
48 *goest* walk
49 *Enchased* adorned
50 *fair veil* i.e. the stars
51 *Phoebus* the sun
52 *antipodes* the opposite side of the earth

CALLAPINE
    Sweet Almeda, scarce half a league from hence.   55
ALMEDA
    But need we not be spied going aboard?
CALLAPINE
    Betwixt the hollow hanging of a hill
    And crooked bending of a craggy rock,
    The sails wrapped up, the mast and tacklings down,
    She lies so close that none can find her out.   60
ALMEDA
    I like that well; but tell me, my lord, if I should let you
    go, would you be as good as your word? Shall I be made
    a king for my labour?
CALLAPINE
    As I am Callapine the emperor,
    And by the hand of Mahomet I swear,   65
    Thou shalt be crowned a king and be my mate.
ALMEDA
    Then here I swear, as I am Almeda,
    Your keeper under Tamburlaine the Great
    (For that's the style and title I have yet),
    Although he sent a thousand armèd men   70
    To intercept this haughty enterprise,
    Yet would I venture to conduct your grace
    And die before I brought you back again.
CALLAPINE
    Thanks, gentle Almeda, then let us haste,
    Lest time be past and ling'ring let us both.   75
ALMEDA
    When you will my lord, I am ready.
CALLAPINE
    Even straight; and farewell cursèd Tamburlaine.
    Now go I to revenge my father's death.   *Exeunt*

56 *need we not* shall we not inevitably
60 *close* concealed
66 *mate* equal
69 *style* designation
71 *haughty* grand
75 *let* hinder
77 *straight* immediately

Act I, Scene iv

[*Enter*] TAMBURLAINE *with* ZENOCRATE, *and his three*
sons, CALYPHAS, AMYRAS, *and* CELEBINUS,
with drums and trumpets

TAMBURLAINE
Now, bright Zenocrate, the world's fair eye,
Whose beams illuminate the lamps of heaven,
Whose cheerful looks do clear the cloudy air
And clothe it in a crystal livery,
Now rest thee here on fair Larissa plains,   5
Where Egypt and the Turkish empire parts,
Between thy sons that shall be emperors,
And every one commander of a world.
ZENOCRATE
Sweet Tamburlaine, when wilt thou leave these arms
And save thy sacred person free from scathe   10
And dangerous chances of the wrathful war?
TAMBURLAINE
When heaven shall cease to move on both the poles
And when the ground whereon my soldiers march
Shall rise aloft and touch the hornèd moon,
And not before, my sweet Zenocrate;   15
Sit up and rest thee like a lovely queen.
So, now she sits in pomp and majesty,
When these my sons, more precious in mine eyes
Than all the wealthy kingdoms I subdued,
Placed by her side, look on their mother's face.   20
But yet methinks their looks are amorous,
Not martial as the sons of Tamburlaine.
Water and air being symbolized in one
Argue their want of courage and of wit;
Their hair as white as milk and soft as down,   25
Which should be like the quills of porcupines,
As black as jet, and hard as iron or steel,
Bewrays they are too dainty for the wars.
Their fingers made to quaver on a lute,
Their arms to hang about a lady's neck,   30

5 *Larissa* a sea-coast town south of Gaza
10 *scathe* harm
21 *amorous* loving, gentle
23–4 Being overbalanced in the phlegmatic and sanguine humours (water and
    blood), the boys lack the bile and choler which might give them courage and
    wit.
28 *Bewrays* betrays, reveals

Their legs to dance and caper in the air,
Would make me think them bastards, not my sons,
But that I know they issued from thy womb,
That never looked on man but Tamburlaine.

ZENOCRATE
My gracious lord, they have their mother's looks,   35
But when they list, their conquering father's heart:
This lovely boy, the youngest of the three,
Not long ago bestrid a Scythian steed,
Trotting the ring and tilting at a glove,
Which when he tainted with his slender rod,   40
He reined him straight and made him so curvet,
As I cried out for fear he should have fall'n.

TAMBURLAINE
Well done, my boy, thou shalt have shield and lance,
Armour of proof, horse, helm, and curtle-axe,
And I will teach thee how to charge thy foe   45
And harmless run among the deadly pikes.
If thou wilt love the wars and follow me,
Thou shalt be made a king and reign with me,
Keeping in iron cages emperors.
If thou exceed thy elder brothers' worth   50
And shine in complete virtue more than they,
Thou shalt be king before them, and thy seed
Shall issue crownèd from their mother's womb.

CELEBINUS
Yes father, you shall see me if I live
Have under me as many kings as you,   55
And march with such a multitude of men
As all the world shall tremble at their view.

TAMBURLAINE
These words assure me, boy, thou art my son.
When I am old and cannot manage arms,
Be thou the scourge and terror of the world.   60

AMYRAS
Why may not I, my lord, as well as he,
Be termed the scourge and terror of the world?

36 *list* wish, choose
39 *Trotting ... glove* jousting exercises
40 *tainted* struck (a technical term in tilting)
41 *curvet* leap, spring
44 *proof* tested strength
   curtle-axe heavy slashing sword
51 *virtue* manly qualities

TAMBURLAINE
Be all a scourge and terror to the world,
Or else you are not sons of Tamburlaine.
CALYPHAS
But while my brothers follow arms, my lord,   65
Let me accompany my gracious mother,
They are enough to conquer all the world
And you have won enough for me to keep.
TAMBURLAINE
Bastardly boy, sprung from some coward's loins,
And not the issue of great Tamburlaine,   70
Of all the provinces I have subdued
Thou shalt not have a foot, unless thou bear
A mind courageous and invincible:
For he shall wear the crown of Persia
Whose head hath deepest scars, whose breast most   75
    wounds,
Which being wroth, sends lightning from his eyes,
And in the furrows of his frowning brows
Harbours revenge, war, death and cruelty.
For in a field whose superficies
Is covered with a liquid purple veil   80
And sprinkled with the brains of slaughtered men,
My royal chair of state shall be advanced,
And he that means to place himself therein
Must armèd wade up to the chin in blood.
ZENOCRATE
My lord, such speeches to our princely sons   85
Dismays their minds before they come to prove
The wounding troubles angry war affords.
CELEBINUS
No madam, these are speeches fit for us,
For if his chair were in a sea of blood
I would prepare a ship and sail to it,   90
Ere I would lose the title of a king.
AMYRAS
And I would strive to swim through pools of blood
Or make a bridge of murdered carcasses
Whose arches should be framed with bones of Turks,
Ere I would lose the title of a king.   95
TAMBURLAINE
Well, lovely boys, you shall be emperors both,

76 *wroth* enraged
79 *superficies* ed. (superfluities O1) surface
86 *prove* find out by experience

Stretching your conquering arms from east to west;
And, sirrah, if you mean to wear a crown,
When we shall meet the Turkish deputy
And all his viceroys, snatch it from his head,   100
And cleave his pericranion with thy sword.

CALYPHAS
If any man will hold him, I will strike,
And cleave him to the channel with my sword.

TAMBURLAINE
Hold him and cleave him too, or I'll cleave thee,
For we will march against them presently.   105
Theridamas, Techelles, and Casane
Promised to meet me on Larissa plains
With hosts apiece against this Turkish crew,
For I have sworn by sacred Mahomet
To make it parcel of my empery.   110
The trumpets sound, Zenocrate, they come.

Act I, Scene v

Enter THERIDAMAS *and his train with drums and trumpets*

TAMBURLAINE
Welcome Theridamas, King of Argier.

THERIDAMAS
My lord the great and mighty Tamburlaine,
Arch-monarch of the world, I offer here
My crown, myself, and all the power I have,
In all affection at thy kingly feet.   5

TAMBURLAINE
Thanks, good Theridamas.

THERIDAMAS
Under my colours march ten thousand Greeks,
And of Argier and Afric's frontier towns
Twice twenty thousand valiant men-at-arms,
All which have sworn to sack Natolia;   10
Five hundred brigandines are under sail,
Meet for your service on the sea, my lord,
That launching from Argier to Tripoli

101 *pericranion* skull
103 *channel* throat
110 *parcel ... empery* part of my empire
  I, v As at I, ii, this is not really a new scene.
  8 *Argier* Algiers
 11 *brigandines* brigantines, small vessels which could be either sailed or rowed

Will quickly ride before Natolia
And batter down the castles on the shore.   15
TAMBURLAINE
Well said, Argier, receive thy crown again.

Act I, Scene vi

Enter TECHELLES *and* USUMCASANE *together*

TAMBURLAINE
Kings of Morocco and of Fez, welcome.
USUMCASANE
Magnificent and peerless Tamburlaine,
I and my neighbour King of Fez have brought
To aid thee in this Turkish expedition
A hundred thousand expert soldiers: 5
From Azamor to Tunis near the sea
Is Barbary unpeopled for thy sake,
And all the men in armour under me,
Which with my crown I gladly offer thee.
TAMBURLAINE
Thanks, King of Morocco, take your crown again.   10
TECHELLES
And mighty Tamburlaine, our earthly god,
Whose looks make this inferior world to quake,
I here present thee with the crown of Fez,
And with an host of Moors trained to the war,
Whose coal-black faces make their foes retire   15
And quake for fear, as if infernal Jove,
Meaning to aid thee in these Turkish arms,
Should pierce the black circumference of hell
With ugly Furies bearing fiery flags,
And millions of his strong tormenting spirits.   20
From strong Tesella unto Biledull,
All Barbary is unpeopled for thy sake.
TAMBURLAINE
Thanks, King of Fez, take here thy crown again.

I, vi Again, not really a new scene.
 1 *Morocco* ed., and so throughout (Moroccus O1)
   Fez ed., and so throughout (Fesse O1)
 6 *Azamor* a town in North Africa
16 *infernal Jove* Pluto. The Furies were in his service.
17 *thee* ed. (them O1)
   these O3, Q (this O1)
21 *Tesella, Biledull* a town and a province in North Africa

Your presence, loving friends and fellow kings,
Makes me to surfeit in conceiving joy; 25
If all the crystal gates of Jove's high court
Were opened wide, and I might enter in
To see the state and majesty of heaven,
It could not more delight me than your sight.
Now will we banquet on these plains a while, 30
And after march to Turkey with our camp,
In numbers more than are the drops that fall
When Boreas rents a thousand swelling clouds.
And proud Orcanes of Natolia
With all his viceroys shall be so afraid, 35
That though the stones as at Deucalion's flood
Were turned to men, he should be overcome.
Such lavish will I make of Turkish blood
That Jove shall send his wingèd messenger
To bid me sheathe my sword and leave the field; 40
The sun, unable to sustain the sight,
Shall hide his head in Thetis' watery lap
And leave his steeds to fair Boötes' charge –
For half the world shall perish in this fight.
But now, my friends, let me examine ye, 45
How have ye spent your absent time from me?

USUMCASANE

My lord, our men of Barbary have marched
Four hundred miles with armour on their backs
And lain in leaguer fifteen months and more,
For since we left you at the Soldan's court, 50
We have subdued the southern Guallatia,
And all the land unto the coast of Spain.
We kept the narrow Strait of Gibraltar,
And made Canaria call us kings and lords,
Yet never did they recreate themselves 55
Or cease one day from war and hot alarms,

---

31 *camp* army
33 *Boreas* the north wind
36–7 Deucalion and his wife Pyrrha were the sole survivors of a flood sent by Zeus
　　to exterminate the human race. They repopulated the earth by casting stones to
　　the ground, from which sprang men and women.
38 *lavish* spilling, squandering
39 *wingèd messenger* Mercury
42 *Thetis* a sea goddess
43 *Boötes* a northern constellation
49 *lain in leaguer* been on campaign
51 *Guallatia* Gualata, a province in North Africa, south-west of the Sahara
54 *Canaria* the Canary Islands

And therefore let them rest a while my lord.

TAMBURLAINE

They shall, Casane, and 'tis time i'faith.

TECHELLES

And I have marched along the river Nile
To Machda, where the mighty Christian priest   60
Called John the Great sits in a milk-white robe,
Whose triple mitre I did take by force
And made him swear obedience to my crown.
From thence unto Cazates did I march,
Where Amazonians met me in the field,   65
With whom (being women) I vouchsafed a league,
And with my power did march to Zanzibar,
The western part of Afric, where I viewed
The Ethiopian sea, rivers and lakes,
But neither man nor child in all the land.   70
Therefore I took my course to Manico,
Where unresisted I removed my camp,
And by the coast of Byather at last
I came to Cubar, where the negroes dwell,
And conquering that, made haste to Nubia;   75
There, having sacked Borno the kingly seat,
I took the king, and led him bound in chains
Unto Damascus, where I stayed before.

TAMBURLAINE

Well done Techelles. What saith Theridamas?

THERIDAMAS

I left the confines and the bounds of Afric   80
And made a voyage into Europe,
Where by the river Tyros I subdued
Stoka, Padalia, and Codemia.
Then crossed the sea and came to Oblia,

59–75 Marlowe constructs Techelles's route on the map of Ortelius from northern
    Africa southward to Zanzibar and northward again to Nubia. Techelles's journey
    takes him down the Nile to Machda, an Abyssinian town, where he defeats
    Prester John ('John the Great'), a legendary priest-king supposed to rule a vast
    empire; he then continues down to Cazates, a town near where the Nile rises out
    of Lake Victoria; he then invades the province of Zanzibar (not the island but an
    area on the west coast of Africa), and makes his way northward from there
    through central and west Africa ('Manico', 'Byather', and 'Cubar') across to
    Nubia.
65 *Amazonians* Amazons
66 *league* alliance
69 *Ethiopian sea* the South Atlantic
76 *Borno* the chief town of Nubia
78 *Damascus* ed., and so throughout (Damasco O1)

   And Nigra Silva, where the devils dance,   85
   Which in despite of them I set on fire.
   From thence I crossed the gulf called by the name
   Mare Majore of th'inhabitants:
   Yet shall my soldiers make no period
   Until Natolia kneel before your feet.   90

TAMBURLAINE
   Then will we triumph, banquet and carouse,
   Cooks shall have pensions to provide us cates
   And glut us with the dainties of the world,
   Lachryma Christi and Calabrian wines
   Shall common soldiers drink in quaffing bowls,   95
   Ay, liquid gold when we have conquered him,
   Mingled with coral and with orient pearl.
   Come let us banquet and carouse the whiles.   *Exeunt*

Act II, Scene i

[Enter] SIGISMUND, FREDERICK, BALDWIN,
with their train

SIGISMUND
   Now say, my lords of Buda and Bohemia,
   What motion is it that inflames your thoughts
   And stirs your valours to such sudden arms?

FREDERICK
   Your majesty remembers, I am sure,
   What cruel slaughter of our Christian bloods   5
   These heathenish Turks and pagans lately made
   Betwixt the city Zula and Danubius,
   How through the midst of Varna and Bulgaria

82–6 Theridamas's journey takes him across the Dneister river (the 'Tyros'), the
   southern boundary of the province of Podalia, north-west of the Black Sea. There
   he subdues the towns of Stoka and Codemia, and passing through the Black
   Forest, or *Nigra Silva*, he destroys the town of Oblia. On Ortelius's map the
   Nigra Silva resembles a body of water (hence the confusion of l. 84).
88 *Mare Majore* the Black Sea
89 *period* pause
92 *cates* delicacies
94 *Lachryma Christi* a sweet wine of southern Italy
97 *orient* ed. (orientall O1) lustrous
 1 *Buda* a city on the Danube, now part of Budapest
 2 *motion* emotion
 7 *Zula* a town which Ortelius locates north of the Danube
 8 *Varna* a city in north-east Bulgaria

And almost to the very walls of Rome,
They have not long since massacred our camp.   10
It resteth now then that your majesty
Take all advantages of time and power
And work revenge upon these infidels.
Your highness knows, for Tamburlaine's repair,
That strikes a terror to all Turkish hearts,   15
Natolia hath dismissed the greatest part
Of all his army pitched against our power
Betwixt Cutheia and Orminius' mount,
And sent them marching up to Belgasar,
Acantha, Antioch, and Caesarea,   20
To aid the kings of Soria and Jerusalem.
Now then, my lord, advantage take hereof
And issue suddenly upon the rest,
That in the fortune of their overthrow
We may discourage all the pagan troop   25
That dare attempt to war with Christians.

SIGISMUND

But calls not then your grace to memory
The league we lately made with King Orcanes,
Confirmed by oaths and articles of peace,
And calling Christ for record of our truths?   30
This should be treachery and violence
Against the grace of our profession.

BALDWIN

No whit my lord: for with such infidels,
In whom no faith nor true religion rests,
We are not bound to those accomplishments   35
The holy laws of Christendom enjoin;
But as the faith which they profanely plight
Is not by necessary policy
To be esteemed assurance for ourselves,
So what we vow to them should not infringe   40
Our liberty of arms and victory.

9 *Rome* possibly Constantinople
11 *resteth* remains
14 *repair* arrival
18 *Orminius' mount* Mt. Horminius in Bithynia
18–20 *Cutheia, Belgasar, Acantha* towns in Anatolia
32 *profession* oath
33 *No whit* Not in the least
35 *accomplishments* performances of obligation
37 *plight* pledge themselves to
38 *policy* statecraft

SIGISMUND
    Though I confess the oaths they undertake
    Breed little strength to our security,
    Yet those infirmities that thus defame
    Their faiths, their honours, and their religion,   45
    Should not give us presumption to the like.
    Our faiths are sound and must be consummate,
    Religious, righteous, and inviolate.

FREDERICK
    Assure your grace 'tis superstition
    To stand so strictly on dispensive faith,   50
    And should we lose the opportunity
    That God hath given to venge our Christians' death
    And scourge their foul blasphemous paganism,
    As fell to Saul, to Balaam, and the rest,
    That would not kill and curse at God's command,   55
    So surely will the vengeance of the Highest
    And jealous anger of his fearful arm
    Be poured with rigour on our sinful heads,
    If we neglect this offered victory.

SIGISMUND
    Then arm, my lords, and issue suddenly,   60
    Giving commandment to our general host
    With expedition to assail the pagan,
    And take the victory our God hath given.   *Exeunt*

Act II, Scene ii

[*Enter*] ORCANES, GAZELLUS, URIBASSA, *with their train*

ORCANES
    Gazellus, Uribassa, and the rest,
    Now will we march from proud Orminius' mount
    To fair Natolia, where our neighbour kings
    Expect our power and our royal presence
    T'encounter with the cruel Tamburlaine,   5
    That nigh Larissa sways a mighty host
    And with the thunder of his martial tools

47 *consummate* ed. (consinuate O1) perfect
50 *dispensive faith* oath which may be set aside by special dispensation on the part
    of the church
54 Saul failed to kill King Agag and his flocks (I *Samuel* 15), but Balaam obeyed
    God in refusing to curse the children of Israel (*Numbers* 22–4); so Frederick's
    appeal to scriptural authority is confused.
62 *expedition* speed

Makes earthquakes in the hearts of men and heaven.

GAZELLUS
And now come we to make his sinews shake
With greater power than erst his pride hath felt –   10
An hundred kings by scores will bid him arms,
And hundred thousands subjects to each score:
Which if a shower of wounding thunderbolts
Should break out of the bowels of the clouds
And fall as thick as hail upon our heads   15
In partial aid of that proud Scythian,
Yet should our courages and steelèd crests
And numbers more than infinite of men
Be able to withstand and conquer him.

URIBASSA
Methinks I see how glad the Christian king   20
Is made for joy of your admitted truce,
That could not but before be terrified
With unacquainted power of our host.

Enter a MESSENGER

MESSENGER
Arm, dread sovereign and my noble lords!
The treacherous army of the Christians,   25
Taking advantage of your slender power,
Comes marching on us and determines straight
To bid us battle for our dearest lives.

ORCANES
Traitors, villains, damnèd Christians!
Have I not here the articles of peace   30
And solemn covenants we have both confirmed,
He by his Christ, and I by Mahomet?

GAZELLUS
Hell and confusion light upon their heads
That with such treason seek our overthrow,
And cares so little for their prophet Christ!   35

ORCANES
Can there be such deceit in Christians,
Or treason in the fleshly heart of man,
Whose shape is figure of the highest God?
Then if there be a Christ, as Christians say,
But in their deeds deny him for their Christ,   40

---

10 *erst* hitherto
11 *bid him arms* challenge him to fight
16 *partial* biased
38 *figure* image

If he be son to everliving Jove
And hath the power of his outstretched arm,
If he be jealous of his name and honour
As is our holy prophet Mahomet,
Take here these papers as our sacrifice   45
And witness of thy servant's perjury.
                    [*He tears up the articles of peace*]
Open, thou shining veil of Cynthia,
And make a passage from th'empyreal heaven,
That he that sits on high and never sleeps,
Nor in one place is circumscriptible,   50
But everywhere fills every continent
With strange infusion of his sacred vigour,
May in his endless power and purity
Behold and venge this traitor's perjury.
Thou Christ that art esteemed omnipotent,   55
If thou wilt prove thyself a perfect God
Worthy the worship of all faithful hearts,
Be now revenged upon this traitor's soul
And make the power I have left behind
(Too little to defend our guiltless lives)   60
Sufficient to discomfort and confound
The trustless force of those false Christians.
To arms, my lords, on Christ still let us cry –
If there be Christ, we shall have victory.   [*Exeunt*]

Act II, Scene iii

Sound to the battle, and SIGISMUND *comes out wounded*

SIGISMUND
Discomfited is all the Christian host
And God hath thundered vengeance from on high
For my accursed and hateful perjury.
O just and dreadful punisher of sin,
Let the dishonour of the pains I feel   5
In this my mortal well-deservèd wound
End all my penance in my sudden death,
And let this death wherein to sin I die

47 *Cynthia* the moon
Scene iii ed. (O1 omits)
 1 *Discomfited* Routed
 8 *wherein . . . die* which absolves me from my sin

Conceive a second life in endless mercy!

[*Dies*]

Enter ORCANES, GAZELLUS, URIBASSA, *with others*

ORCANES
Now lie the Christians bathing in their bloods,   10
And Christ or Mahomet hath been my friend.
GAZELLUS
See here the perjured traitor Hungary,
Bloody and breathless for his villainy.
ORCANES
Now shall his barbarous body be a prey
To beasts and fowls, and all the winds shall breathe   15
Through shady leaves of every senseless tree
Murmurs and hisses for his heinous sin.
Now scalds his soul in the Tartarian streams
And feeds upon the baneful tree of hell,
That Zoacum, that fruit of bitterness   20
That in the midst of fire is ingraft,
Yet flourisheth as Flora in her pride,
With apples like the heads of damnèd fiends.
The devils there in chains of quenchless flame
Shall lead his soul through Orcus' burning gulf   25
From pain to pain, whose change shall never end.
What sayest thou yet, Gazellus, to his foil,
Which we referred to justice of his Christ
And to his power, which here appears as full
As rays of Cynthia to the clearest sight?   30
GAZELLUS
'Tis but the fortune of the wars, my lord,
Whose power is often proved a miracle.
ORCANES
Yet in my thoughts shall Christ be honourèd,
Not doing Mahomet an injury
Whose power had share in this our victory.   35
And since this miscreant hath disgraced his faith
And died a traitor both to heaven and earth,

18 *Tartarian* of Tartarus, the region of hell where the worst sinners were punished
20 *Zoacum* (or Ezecum) a tree of hell described in the Koran, XXXVII, 60–4
22 *Flora* the Roman goddess of springtime and flowers
25 *Orcus* Hades. Marlowe here fuses Muslim, Christian, and Greek notions of hell.
27 *foil* defeat
29 *his* Christ's
30 *rays of Cynthia* moonlight
32 *proved* asserted to be
36 *miscreant* vile wretch

We will both watch and ward shall keep his trunk
Amidst these plains for fowls to prey upon.
Go Uribassa, give it straight in charge.   40

URIBASSA
I will my lord.
             Exit URIBASSA [*and others, with* SIGISMUND's *body*]

ORCANES
And now, Gazellus, let us haste and meet
Our army and our brother of Jerusalem,
Of Soria, Trebizon, and Amasia,
And happily with full Natolian bowls   45
Of Greekish wine now let us celebrate
Our happy conquest and his angry fate.   *Exeunt*

Act II, Scene iv

The arras is drawn, and ZENOCRATE *lies in her bed of state,*
TAMBURLAINE *sitting by her; three* PHYSICIANS *about*
her bed, tempering potions. THERIDAMAS,
TECHELLES, USUMCASANE, *and the three sons* [CALYPHAS,
AMYRAS, CELEBINUS]

TAMBURLAINE
Black is the beauty of the brightest day –
The golden ball of heaven's eternal fire
That danced with glory on the silver waves
Now wants the fuel that inflamed his beams,
And all with faintness and for foul disgrace   5
He binds his temples with a frowning cloud,
Ready to darken earth with endless night.
Zenocrate that gave him light and life,
Whose eyes shot fire from their ivory bowers
And tempered every soul with lively heat,   10
Now by the malice of the angry skies,
Whose jealousy admits no second mate,
Draws in the comfort of her latest breath

38 *will . . . ward* decree that continuous guard
40 *give . . . charge* command it immediately
43 *Our army* i.e. the main body of our army
44 *Amasia* a district of Anatolia in northern Asia Minor
47 *angry* grievous
  II, iv, s.d.1 *arras* A curtain across the 'discovery space' or inner stage (see Introduction p. xxx) is here opened, revealing Zenocrate in her bed. It is then closed at
  the end of the scene.
  9 *bowers* i.e. the places where they were set

All dazzled with the hellish mists of death.
Now walk the angels on the walls of heaven   15
As sentinels to warn th'immortal souls
To entertain divine Zenocrate.
Apollo, Cynthia, and the ceaseless lamps
That gently looked upon this loathsome earth
Shine downwards now no more, but deck the heavens   20
To entertain divine Zenocrate.
The crystal springs whose taste illuminates
Refinèd eyes with an eternal sight,
Like trièd silver runs through Paradise
To entertain divine Zenocrate.   25
The cherubins and holy seraphins
That sing and play before the King of Kings
Use all their voices and their instruments
To entertain divine Zenocrate.
And in this sweet and curious harmony,   30
The god that tunes this music to our souls
Holds out his hand in highest majesty
To entertain divine Zenocrate.
Then let some holy trance convey my thoughts
Up to the palace of th'empyreal heaven   35
That this my life may be as short to me
As are the days of sweet Zenocrate.
Physicians, will no physic do her good?

PHYSICIAN
My lord, your majesty shall soon perceive –
And if she pass this fit, the worst is past.   40

TAMBURLAINE
Tell me, how fares my fair Zenocrate?

ZENOCRATE
I fare, my lord, as other empresses,
That when this frail and transitory flesh
Hath sucked the measure of that vital air
That feeds the body with his dated health,   45
Wanes with enforced and necessary change.

TAMBURLAINE
May never such a change transform my love,

---

17 *entertain* welcome
18 *Apollo, Cynthia* the sun, the moon
23 *Refinèd* given clearer sight
24 *trièd* purified
30 *curious* exquisite
35 *th'empyreal heaven* See note to Part One, II, vii, 15.
45 *dated* having its preordained end

In whose sweet being I repose my life,
Whose heavenly presence beautified with health
Gives light to Phoebus and the fixèd stars,   50
Whose absence makes the sun and moon as dark
As when opposed in one diameter
Their spheres are mounted on the serpent's head,
Or else descended to his winding train.
Live still my love and so conserve my life,   55
Or dying be the author of my death.

ZENOCRATE
Live still my lord, O let my sovereign live,
And sooner let the fiery element
Dissolve, and make your kingdom in the sky,
Than this base earth should shroud your majesty: 60
For should I but suspect your death by mine,
The comfort of my future happiness
And hope to meet your highness in the heavens,
Turned to despair, would break my wretched breast
And fury would confound my present rest.   65
But let me die, my love, yet let me die,
With love and patience let your true love die:
Your grief and fury hurts my second life.
Yet let me kiss my lord before I die
And let me die with kissing of my lord.   70
But since my life is lengthened yet a while,
Let me take leave of these my loving sons,
And of my lords whose true nobility
Have merited my latest memory.
Sweet sons farewell, in death resemble me,   75
And in your lives your father's excellency.
Some music, and my fit will cease, my lord.
                                        They call music

TAMBURLAINE
Proud fury and intolerable fit,
That dares torment the body of my love
And scourge the Scourge of the immortal God!   80

50 *Phoebus* the sun
51 *makes* O3, Q (make O1)
52 *opposed . . . diameter* i.e. when the earth is directly between the sun and the moon,
   or when the moon is directly between the sun and the earth
53–4 The 'serpent' is the constellation Draco (the Dragon). The moon's path
   intersects the ecliptic (thus causing an eclipse) at two points, the Dragon's head
   and tail ('train').
56 *author* Q (anchor O1)
58 *the fiery element* the sphere of fire, separating the earth from the planetary bodies
68 *my second life* my life after death

Now are those spheres where Cupid used to sit,
Wounding the world with wonder and with love,
Sadly supplied with pale and ghastly death,
Whose darts do pierce the centre of my soul.
Her sacred beauty hath enchanted heaven   85
And, had she lived before the siege of Troy,
Helen, whose beauty summoned Greece to arms
And drew a thousand ships to Tenedos,
Had not been named in Homer's Iliads –
Her name had been in every line he wrote.   90
Or had those wanton poets for whose birth
Old Rome was proud but gazed a while on her,
Nor Lesbia, nor Corinna had been named –
Zenocrate had been the argument
Of every epigram or elegy.   95

The music sounds, and she dies

What, is she dead? Techelles, draw thy sword
And wound the earth that it may cleave in twain,
And we descend into th'infernal vaults
To hale the Fatal Sisters by the hair
And throw them in the triple moat of hell   100
For taking hence my fair Zenocrate.
Casane and Theridamas, to arms!
Raise cavalieros higher than the clouds
And with the cannon break the frame of heaven,
Batter the shining palace of the sun   105
And shiver all the starry firmament,
For amorous Jove hath snatched my love from hence,
Meaning to make her stately queen of heaven.
What god soever holds thee in his arms,
Giving thee nectar and ambrosia,   110
Behold me here, divine Zenocrate,
Raving, impatient, desperate and mad,
Breaking my steelèd lance with which I burst
The rusty beams of Janus' temple doors,
Letting out death and tyrannizing war   115

81 *those spheres* her eyes
88 *Tenedos* a small island near Troy
90 *Her* Zenocrate's
93 *Lesbia ... Corinna* women celebrated in the love poetry of Catullus and Ovid
94 *argument* subject, theme
99 *hale* drag
    Fatal Sisters the three goddesses who govern human destiny
103 *cavalieros* mounds on which cannon were placed
114 *Janus' temple doors* The doors of the temple of Janus in Rome were open in time
    of war, closed in time of peace.

To march with me under this bloody flag,
And if thou pitiest Tamburlaine the Great,
Come down from heaven and live with me again!

THERIDAMAS
Ah, good my lord, be patient, she is dead,
And all this raging cannot make her live.   120
If words might serve, our voice hath rent the air,
If tears, our eyes have watered all the earth,
If grief, our murdered hearts have strained forth blood.
Nothing prevails, for she is dead, my lord.

TAMBURLAINE
For she is dead? Thy words do pierce my soul.   125
Ah sweet Theridamas, say so no more –
Though she be dead, yet let me think she lives,
And feed my mind that dies for want of her.
Where'er her soul be, thou shalt stay with me
Embalmed with cassia, ambergris, and myrrh,   130
Not lapped in lead but in a sheet of gold,
And till I die thou shalt not be interred.
Then in as rich a tomb as Mausolus'
We both will rest and have one epitaph,
Writ in as many several languages   135
As I have conquered kingdoms with my sword.
This cursèd town will I consume with fire
Because this place bereft me of my love:
The houses burnt will look as if they mourned,
And here will I set up her statue   140
And march about it with my mourning camp,
Drooping and pining for Zenocrate.

                              The arras is drawn [*Exeunt*]

129 *thou* i.e. Zenocrate's body
130 *cassia* a fragrant shrub
      ambergris an odiferous substance used in perfumery
131 *lapped in lead* placed in a leaden coffin
133 *Mausolus* King of Caria, whose widow (also his sister) built for him a costly
      monument, called Mausoleum, at Halicarnassus
140 *statue* O3, Q (stature O1). Some editors emend to 'statua' for metrical reasons
      (see note in *O.E.D.*)

Act III, Scene i

Enter the KINGS OF TREBIZON *and* SORIA, *one bringing*
a sword, and another a sceptre. Next [ORCANES, *King*
of] *Natolia and* [KING OF] JERUSALEM *with the imperial*
crown. After, CALLAPINE, *and after him* [ALMEDA *and*]
other Lords. ORCANES *and* JERUSALEM *crown*
[CALLAPINE] *and the other*[s] *give him the sceptre*

ORCANES
 Callapinus Cyricelibes, otherwise Cybelius, son and suc-
 cessive heir to the late mighty emperor Bajazeth, by the
 aid of God and his friend Mahomet, Emperor of Natolia,
 Jerusalem, Trebizon, Soria, Amasia, Thracia, Illyria,
 Carmonia, and all the hundred and thirty kingdoms late   5
 contributory to his mighty father. Long live Callapinus,
 Emperor of Turkey!
CALLAPINE
 Thrice worthy kings of Natolia, and the rest,
 I will requite your royal gratitudes
 With all the benefits my empire yields;   10
 And were the sinews of th'imperial seat
 So knit and strengthened as when Bajazeth,
 My royal lord and father, filled the throne,
 Whose cursèd fate hath so dismembered it,
 Then should you see this thief of Scythia,   15
 This proud usurping King of Persia,
 Do us such honour and supremacy,
 Bearing the vengeance of our father's wrongs,
 As all the world should blot our dignities
 Out of the book of base-born infamies.   20
 And now I doubt not but your royal cares
 Hath so provided for this cursèd foe
 That, since the heir of mighty Bajazeth
 (An emperor so honoured for his virtues)
 Revives the spirits of true Turkish hearts   25
 In grievous memory of his father's shame,
 We shall not need to nourish any doubt
 But that proud Fortune, who hath followed long
 The martial sword of mighty Tamburlaine,
 Will now retain her old inconstancy,   30
 And raise our honours to as high a pitch
 In this our strong and fortunate encounter.

5 *Carmonia* Carmania, south-east of Natolia and north of Syria
19 *blot our dignities* delete our noble names

For so hath heaven provided my escape
From all the cruelty my soul sustained,
By this my friendly keeper's happy means,   35
That Jove, surcharged with pity of our wrongs,
Will pour it down in showers on our heads,
Scourging the pride of cursèd Tamburlaine.

ORCANES
I have a hundred thousand men in arms;
Some, that in conquest of the perjured Christian,   40
Being a handful to a mighty host,
Think them in number yet sufficient
To drink the river Nile or Euphrates,
And, for their power, enow to win the world.

KING OF JERUSALEM
And I as many from Jerusalem,   45
Judea, Gaza, and Scalonia's bounds,
That on Mount Sinai with their ensigns spread
Look like the parti-coloured clouds of heaven
That show fair weather to the neighbour morn.

KING OF TREBIZON
And I as many bring from Trebizon,   50
Chio, Famastro, and Amasia,
All bord'ring on the Mare Major sea,
Riso, Sancina, and the bord'ring towns
That touch the end of famous Euphrates,
Whose courages are kindled with the flames   55
The cursèd Scythian sets on all their towns,
And vow to burn the villain's cruel heart.

KING OF SORIA
From Soria with seventy thousand strong,
Ta'en from Aleppo, Soldino, Tripoli,
And so unto my city of Damascus,   60
I march to meet and aid my neighbour kings,
All which will join against this Tamburlaine,
And bring him captive to your highness' feet.

ORCANES
Our battle then in martial manner pitched
According to our ancient use shall bear   65
The figure of the semi-circled moon,
Whose horns shall sprinkle through the tainted air

44 *enow* enough
46 *Scalonia's* ed. (Scalonians O1–3). Ascalon, a town near Jerusalem
47 *ensigns* banners
52 *Mare Major sea* the Black Sea
65 *use* custom

The poisoned brains of this proud Scythian.

CALLAPINE

Well then, my noble lords, for this my friend
That freed me from the bondage of my foe,   70
I think it requisite and honourable
To keep my promise and to make him king,
That is a gentleman, I know, at least.

ALMEDA

That's no matter, sir, for being a king, for Tamburlaine
came up of nothing.   75

KING OF JERUSALEM

Your majesty may choose some 'pointed time,
Performing all your promise to the full:
'Tis naught for your majesty to give a kingdom.

CALLAPINE

Then will I shortly keep my promise, Almeda.

ALMEDA

Why, I thank your majesty.   *Exeunt*   80

Act III, Scene ii

[*Enter*] TAMBURLAINE *with* USUMCASANE, *and his three sons*
[CALYPHAS, AMYRAS, *and* CELEBINUS]; *four* [*Attendants*]
bearing the hearse of ZENOCRATE, *and the drums*
sounding a doleful march; [*the town burning*]

TAMBURLAINE

So, burn the turrets of this cursèd town,
Flame to the highest region of the air
And kindle heaps of exhalations
That, being fiery meteors, may presage
Death and destruction to th'inhabitants.   5

III, ii, s.d.4 Exactly how the burning of the town might have been handled on the
open Elizabethan stage is uncertain. Perhaps fireworks were used to simulate
flames or to produce realistic smoke (as they had been in medieval drama),
perhaps a symbolic backdrop was hoisted up or fiery streamers hung from the
tiring house wall, or perhaps, if it could be managed, an emblematic structure of
some kind, representing a city with 'turrets' (line 1), was actually burned. Such
spectacular effects were not unknown in civic and courtly pageants during the
16th and 17th centuries.

2 *highest ... air* the uppermost limit of the atmosphere, next to the sphere of the
moon

3–4 *kindle ... meteors* may the rising flames create meteors, traditionally portents
of disaster

Over my zenith hang a blazing star,
That may endure till heaven be dissolved,
Fed with the fresh supply of earthly dregs,
Threat'ning a death and famine to this land.
Flying dragons, lightning, fearful thunderclaps,   10
Singe these fair plains and make them seem as black
As is the island where the Furies mask,
Compassed with Lethe, Styx, and Phlegethon,
Because my dear Zenocrate is dead.

CALYPHAS
This pillar placed in memory of her,   15
Where in Arabian, Hebrew, Greek, is writ,
'This town being burnt by Tamburlaine the Great,
Forbids the world to build it up again.'

AMYRAS
And here this mournful streamer shall be placed,
Wrought with the Persian and Egyptian arms   20
To signify she was a princess born
And wife unto the monarch of the East.

CELEBINUS
And here this table as a register
Of all her virtues and perfections.

TAMBURLAINE
And here the picture of Zenocrate   25
To show her beauty which the world admired,
Sweet picture of divine Zenocrate,
That hanging here will draw the gods from heaven
And cause the stars fixed in the southern arc,
Whose lovely faces never any viewed   30
That have not passed the centre's latitude,
As pilgrims travel to our hemisphere,
Only to gaze upon Zenocrate.
Thou shalt not beautify Larissa plains
But keep within the circle of mine arms.   35
At every town and castle I besiege,

6 *zenith* the highest point of the sun's course, which Tamburlaine compares to the
   high point of his own fortunes
12 *island ... mask* The underworld is thought of as an island, presumably because
   it is ringed with rivers. The Furies hide ('mask') there until called into the upper
   world.
13 *Lethe ... Phlegethon* rivers of the underworld
20 *Wrought* embroidered
23 *table* tablet
29 *arc* hemisphere
31 *centre's latitude* equator
34 *Thou* i.e. Zenocrate's picture

Thou shalt be set upon my royal tent,
And when I meet an army in the field
Those looks will shed such influence in my camp
As if Bellona, goddess of the war,   40
Threw naked swords and sulphur balls of fire
Upon the heads of all our enemies.
And now, my lords, advance your spears again,
Sorrow no more, my sweet Casane, now;
Boys, leave to mourn – this town shall ever mourn,   45
Being burnt to cinders for your mother's death.

CALYPHAS
If I had wept a sea of tears for her,
It would not ease the sorrow I sustain.

AMYRAS
As is that town, so is my heart consumed
With grief and sorrow for my mother's death.   50

CELEBINUS
My mother's death hath mortified my mind
And sorrow stops the passage of my speech.

TAMBURLAINE
But now my boys, leave off, and list to me,
That mean to teach you rudiments of war:
I'll have you learn to sleep upon the ground,   55
March in your armour thorough watery fens,
Sustain the scorching heat and freezing cold,
Hunger and thirst, right adjuncts of the war.
And after this, to scale a castle wall,
Besiege a fort, to undermine a town,   60
And make whole cities caper in the air.
Then next, the way to fortify your men:
In champion grounds what figure serves you best,
For which the quinque-angle form is meet,
Because the corners there may fall more flat   65

---

39 *Those* ed. (Whose O1)
40 *Bellona* the Roman goddess of war
41 *sulphur . . . fire* primitive incendiary bombs
56 *thorough* O2–3, Q (throwe O1)
58 *thirst* Q (cold O1)
62–90 A close paraphrase of Paul Ive's *Practice of Fortification* (1589). See Paul Kocher, 'Marlowe's Art of War', *Studies in Philology*, xxxix (1942), 207–25.
63 *champion* level and open
64–7 *For . . . desperate* and for which types of ground (i.e. rough and uneven, as distinct from 'champion') the pentagonal formation ('quinque-angle') will be most suitable, since its 'flat' and 'sharp' angles can be placed where most appropriate for either attack or defence
64 *which* ed. (with O1)

Whereas the fort may fittest be assailed,
And sharpest where th'assault is desperate.
The ditches must be deep, the counterscarps
Narrow and steep, the walls made high and broad,
The bulwarks and the rampires large and strong,   70
With cavalieros and thick counterforts,
And room within to lodge six thousand men.
It must have privy ditches, countermines,
And secret issuings to defend the ditch.
It must have high argins and covered ways   75
To keep the bulwark fronts from battery,
And parapets to hide the musketeers,
Casemates to place the great artillery,
And store of ordnance that from every flank
May scour the outward curtains of the fort,   80
Dismount the cannon of the adverse part,
Murder the foe and save the walls from breach.
When this is learned for service on the land,
By plain and easy demonstration
I'll teach you how to make the water mount   85
That you may dry-foot march through lakes and pools,
Deep rivers, havens, creeks and little seas,
And make a fortress in the raging waves,
Fenced with the concave of a monstrous rock,
Invincible by nature of the place.   90
When this is done, then are ye soldiers,
And worthy sons of Tamburlaine the Great.

CALYPHAS
My lord, but this is dangerous to be done –
We may be slain or wounded ere we learn.

66 *Whereas* where
68 *counterscarps* the outer walls of the ditch surrounding a fort
70 *bulwarks* projecting earthworks built round the angles of a fort
   rampires ramparts supporting the walls from within
71 *cavalieros* mounds for heavy guns
73 *countermines* underground tunnels
75 *argins* earthworks
   covered ways protected passages
78 *Casemates* chambers within the ramparts of a fort
79 *ordnance* ammunition
80 *scour* rake with gun-shot
   curtains walls connecting the towers
81 *Dismount* knock out
   adverse part adversary
82 *the walls* ed. (their walles O1)
85 *mount* rise

TAMBURLAINE

Villain, art thou the son of Tamburlaine   95
And fear'st to die, or with a curtle-axe
To hew thy flesh and make a gaping wound?
Hast thou beheld a peal of ordnance strike
A ring of pikes, mingled with shot and horse,
Whose shattered limbs, being tossed as high as heaven, 100
Hang in the air as thick as sunny motes,
And canst thou, coward, stand in fear of death?
Hast thou not seen my horsemen charge the foe,
Shot through the arms, cut overthwart the hands,
Dyeing their lances with their streaming blood,   105
And yet at night carouse within my tent
Filling their empty veins with airy wine
That, being concocted, turns to crimson blood,
And wilt thou shun the field for fear of wounds?
View me thy father that hath conquered kings   110
And with his host marched round about the earth
Quite void of scars and clear from any wound,
That by the wars lost not a dram of blood,
And see him lance his flesh to teach you all.
                                          He cuts his arm
A wound is nothing be it ne'er so deep,   115
Blood is the god of war's rich livery.
Now look I like a soldier, and this wound
As great a grace and majesty to me,
As if a chair of gold enamellèd,
Enchased with diamonds, sapphires, rubies,   120
And fairest pearl of wealthy India,
Were mounted here under a canopy,
And I sat down clothed with the massy robe
That late adorned the Afric potentate
Whom I brought bound unto Damascus' walls.   125
Come, boys, and with your fingers search my wound
And in my blood wash all your hands at once,
While I sit smiling to behold the sight.
Now, my boys, what think you of a wound?

98 *peal of ordnance* discharge of cannon
99 *A ring ... horse* a ring of pike-men closely flanked by infantry and cavalry
101 *sunny motes* particles of dust in the sunlight
107–8 Wine, when digested ('concocted'), was thought to replenish a dwindling blood
    supply.
111 *marched* O3, Q (martch O1)
120 *Enchased* adorned
123 *massy* weighty
124 *Afric potentate* i.e. Bajazeth, so called from his African conquests

CALYPHAS

　I know not what I should think of it. Methinks 'tis a　130
　pitiful sight.

CELEBINUS

　'Tis nothing: give me a wound, father.

AMYRAS

　And me another, my lord.

TAMBURLAINE

　Come, sirrah, give me your arm.

CELEBINUS

　Here, father, cut it bravely as you did your own.　　135

TAMBURLAINE

　It shall suffice thou dar'st abide a wound.
　My boy, thou shalt not lose a drop of blood
　Before we meet the army of the Turk.
　But then run desperate through the thickest throngs,
　Dreadless of blows, of bloody wounds and death,　　140
　And let the burning of Larissa walls,
　My speech of war, and this my wound you see
　Teach you, my boys, to bear courageous minds,
　Fit for the followers of great Tamburlaine.
　Usumcasane, now come let us march　　　　　　145
　Towards Techelles and Theridamas,
　That we have sent before to fire the towns,
　The towers and cities of these hateful Turks,
　And hunt that coward, faint-heart runaway,
　With that accursèd traitor Almeda,　　　　　　150
　Till fire and sword have found them at a bay.

USUMCASANE

　I long to pierce his bowels with my sword
　That hath betrayed my gracious sovereign,
　That cursed and damnèd traitor Almeda.

TAMBURLAINE

　Then let us see if coward Callapine　　　　　155
　Dare levy arms against our puissance,
　That we may tread upon his captive neck
　And treble all his father's slaveries.　　　　　*Exeunt*

---

135 *bravely* well
151 *at a bay* at bay

Act III, Scene iii

[*Enter*] TECHELLES, THERIDAMAS, *and their train*
[SOLDIERS *and* PIONERS]

THERIDAMAS
  Thus have we marched northward from Tamburlaine
  Unto the frontier point of Soria:
  And this is Balsera, their chiefest hold,
  Wherein is all the treasure of the land.
TECHELLES
  Then let us bring our light artillery,   5
  Minions, falc'nets, and sakers, to the trench,
  Filling the ditches with the walls' wide breach,
  And enter in, to seize upon the gold –
  How say ye soldiers, shall we not?
SOLDIERS
  Yes, my lord, yes, come let's about it.   10
THERIDAMAS
  But stay a while; summon a parley, drum,
  It may be they will yield it quietly,
  Knowing two kings, the friends to Tamburlaine,
  Stand at the walls with such a mighty power.

        Summon the battle. [*Enter above*] CAPTAIN
          with his wife [OLYMPIA] *and* SON

CAPTAIN
  What require you my masters?   15
THERIDAMAS
  Captain, that thou yield up thy hold to us.
CAPTAIN
  To you? Why, do you think me weary of it?
TECHELLES
  Nay Captain, thou art weary of thy life
  If thou withstand the friends of Tamburlaine.
THERIDAMAS
  These pioners of Argier in Africa,   20
  Even in the cannon's face shall raise a hill
  Of earth and faggots higher than thy fort
  And over thy argins and covered ways

III, iii, s.d. *Pioners* advance guard of trench-diggers
  3 *Balsera* probably Passera, a town near the Natolian frontier
    hold stronghold
  6 *Minions . . . sakers* small cannons
 11 *parley* ed. (parle O1)
 13 *friends* O3, Q (friend O1)
 14 s.d.1 *Summon the battle* Drums call the troops (*battle*) to a parley

Shall play upon the bulwarks of thy hold
Volleys of ordnance till the breach be made,   25
That with his ruin fills up all the trench.
And when we enter in, not heaven itself
Shall ransom thee, thy wife, and family.

TECHELLES
Captain, these Moors shall cut the leaden pipes
That bring fresh water to thy men and thee,   30
And lie in trench before thy castle walls
That no supply of victual shall come in,
Nor any issue forth but they shall die:
And therefore Captain, yield it quietly.

CAPTAIN
Were you that are the friends of Tamburlaine   35
Brothers to holy Mahomet himself,
I would not yield it: therefore do your worst.
Raise mounts, batter, intrench, and undermine,
Cut off the water, all convoys that can,
Yet I am resolute, and so farewell.   [*Exeunt above*]   40

THERIDAMAS
Pioners away, and where I stuck the stake
Intrench with those dimensions I prescribed;
Cast up the earth towards the castle wall,
Which till it may defend you, labour low,
And few or none shall perish by their shot.   45

PIONERS
We will my lord.   *Exeunt* [PIONERS]

TECHELLES
A hundred horse shall scout about the plains
To spy what force comes to relieve the hold.
Both we, Theridamas, will intrench our men,
And with the Jacob's staff measure the height   50
And distance of the castle from the trench,
That we may know if our artillery
Will carry full point blank unto their walls.

THERIDAMAS
Then see the bringing of our ordinance
Along the trench into the battery,   55

---

26 *trench* defensive ditch around the outer walls
38 *intrench* surround with trenches
39 *that can* that you can
50 *Jacob's staff* a gunner's quadrant
54 *ordinance* Marlowe's usual spelling of 'ordnance' here retained for the sake of the
metre

Where we will have gabions of six foot broad
To save our cannoneers from musket shot,
Betwixt which shall our ordnance thunder forth
And with the breach's fall, smoke, fire, and dust,
The crack, the echo, and the soldier's cry   60
Make deaf the air and dim the crystal sky.

TECHELLES
Trumpets and drums, alarum presently!
And, soldiers, play the men, the hold is yours.

                                            [*Exeunt*]

Act III, Scene iv

Enter the CAPTAIN *with his wife* [OLYMPIA] *and* SON

OLYMPIA
Come, good my lord, and let us haste from hence
Along the cave that leads beyond the foe –
No hope is left to save this conquered hold.

CAPTAIN
A deadly bullet gliding through my side
Lies heavy on my heart, I cannot live.   5
I feel my liver pierced and all my veins,
That there begin and nourish every part,
Mangled and torn, and all my entrails bathed
In blood that straineth from their orifex.
Farewell sweet wife! Sweet son farewell! I die.   10

                                            [*Dies*]

OLYMPIA
Death, whither art thou gone that both we live?
Come back again, sweet Death, and strike us both!
One minute end our days and one sepulchre
Contain our bodies! Death, why com'st thou not?
Well, this must be the messenger for thee.   15

                                  [*Drawing a knife*]

Now, ugly Death, stretch out thy sable wings
And carry both our souls where his remains.

---

56 *gabions* ed. (Galions O1) great baskets filled with earth, used in defence and to
   steady cannons
62 *alarum* call to arms
   presently at once
63 *hold* O3 (holds O1)
   Scene iv ed. (O1 omits)
 2 *cave* underground passage
 9 *orifex* orifice, breach

Tell me, sweet boy, art thou content to die?
These barbarous Scythians full of cruelty,
And Moors in whom was never pity found,   20
Will hew us piecemeal, put us to the wheel,
Or else invent some torture worse than that.
Therefore die by thy loving mother's hand,
Who gently now will lance thy ivory throat
And quickly rid thee both of pain and life.   25

SON

Mother dispatch me or I'll kill myself,
For think ye I can live and see him dead?
Give me your knife, good mother, or strike home –
The Scythians shall not tyrannize on me.
Sweet mother, strike, that I may meet my father.   30

                                   She stabs him

OLYMPIA

Ah sacred Mahomet, if this be sin,
Entreat a pardon of the God of heaven
And purge my soul before it come to thee.

        [*She burns the bodies of her husband and son*]

        Enter THERIDAMAS, TECHELLES *and all their train*

THERIDAMAS

How now madam, what are you doing?

OLYMPIA

Killing myself, as I have done my son,   35
Whose body with his father's I have burnt,
Lest cruel Scythians should dismember him.

TECHELLES

'Twas bravely done, and like a soldier's wife.
Thou shalt with us to Tamburlaine the Great,
Who when he hears how resolute thou wert   40
Will match thee with a viceroy or a king.

OLYMPIA

My lord deceased was dearer unto me
Than any viceroy, king, or emperor,
And for his sake here will I end my days.

---

21 *the wheel* an instrument of torture
33 s.d. Although it has been argued that the Rose and other early theatres did not
    have a stage trap, the staging here seems to require one to simulate a pit in which
    Olympia can place the bodies of her dead husband and son. Fireworks and smoke
    under the stage could then furnish the desired effect (see Introduction, p. xxx).
    Actually burning the bodies onstage would seem to surpass the ingenuity and
    technical resources even of modern producers.

THERIDAMAS
    But lady go with us to Tamburlaine   45
    And thou shalt see a man greater than Mahomet,
    In whose high looks is much more majesty
    Than from the concave superficies
    Of Jove's vast palace the empyreal orb,
    Unto the shining bower where Cynthia sits   50
    Like lovely Thetis in a crystal robe;
    That treadeth fortune underneath his feet
    And makes the mighty god of arms his slave;
    On whom Death and the Fatal Sisters wait
    With naked swords and scarlet liveries;   55
    Before whom, mounted on a lion's back,
    Rhamnusia bears a helmet full of blood
    And strews the way with brains of slaughtered men;
    By whose proud side the ugly Furies run,
    Harkening when he shall bid them plague the world; 60
    Over whose zenith clothed in windy air,
    And eagle's wings joined to her feathered breast,
    Fame hovereth, sounding of her golden trump,
    That to the adverse poles of that straight line
    Which measureth the glorious frame of heaven,   65
    The name of mighty Tamburlaine is spread.
    And him, fair lady, shall thy eyes behold.
    Come.
OLYMPIA
    Take pity of a lady's ruthful tears,
    That humbly craves upon her knees to stay   70
    And cast her body in the burning flame
    That feeds upon her son's and husband's flesh.
TECHELLES
    Madam, sooner shall fire consume us both
    Than scorch a face so beautiful as this,
    In frame of which nature hath showed more skill   75
    Than when she gave eternal chaos form,
    Drawing from it the shining lamps of heaven.

47–51 'In Tamburlaine's looks there dwells more majesty than is to be found through-
    out the heavens, from the hollow roof ['concave superficies'] of Jove's palace to
    the shining bower where the moon sits veiled in a crystal robe like Thetis the
    ocean goddess' (Ellis-Fermor).
49 *empyreal orb* heavenly sphere
57 *Rhamnusia* Nemesis
61 *zenith* crest; the highest point in his career
64–5 *adverse . . . heaven* the diameter of the sphere of heaven
67–8 lineation ed.
75 *frame* forming, fashioning

THERIDAMAS
    Madam, I am so far in love with you
    That you must go with us, no remedy.
OLYMPIA
    Then carry me I care not where you will,   80
    And let the end of this my fatal journey
    Be likewise end to my accursèd life.
TECHELLES
    No madam, but the beginning of your joy –
    Come willingly therefore.
THERIDAMAS
    Soldiers, now let us meet the general   85
    Who by this time is at Natolia,
    Ready to charge the army of the Turk.
    The gold, the silver, and the pearl ye got
    Rifling this fort, divide in equal shares.
    This lady shall have twice so much again   90
    Out of the coffers of our treasury.   *Exeunt*

Act III, Scene v

[*Enter*] CALLAPINE, ORCANES, JERUSALEM, TREBIZON,
SORIA, ALMEDA, *with their train*
[*and* MESSENGER *to them*]

MESSENGER
    Renownèd emperor, mighty Callapine,
    God's great lieutenant over all the world:
    Here at Aleppo with an host of men
    Lies Tamburlaine, this King of Persia,
    In number more than are the quivering leaves   5
    Of Ida's forest, where your highness' hounds
    With open cry pursues the wounded stag,
    Who means to girt Natolia's walls with siege,
    Fire the town and overrun the land.
CALLAPINE
    My royal army is as great as his,   10
    That from the bounds of Phrygia to the sea
    Which washeth Cyprus with his brinish waves,
    Covers the hills, the valleys, and the plains.
    Viceroys and peers of Turkey, play the men,

    6 *Ida's forest* probably Mt. Ida near Troy
    8 *Natolia* Asia Minor, but here apparently a city
    11 *Phrygia* an inland district of Natolia

Whet all your swords to mangle Tamburlaine, 15
His sons, his captains, and his followers –
By Mahomet, not one of them shall live.
The field wherein this battle shall be fought
Forever term the Persians' sepulchre,
In memory of this our victory. 20

ORCANES
Now he that calls himself the Scourge of Jove,
The emperor of the world and earthly god,
Shall end the warlike progress he intends
And travel headlong to the lake of hell,
Where legions of devils (knowing he must die 25
Here in Natolia by your highness' hands)
All brandishing their brands of quenchless fire,
Stretching their monstrous paws, grin with their teeth,
And guard the gates to entertain his soul.

CALLAPINE
Tell me, viceroys, the number of your men 30
And what our army royal is esteemed.

KING OF JERUSALEM
From Palestina and Jerusalem,
Of Hebrews three score thousand fighting men
Are come since last we showed your majesty.

ORCANES
So from Arabia Desert and the bounds 35
Of that sweet land whose brave metropolis
Re-edified the fair Semiramis,
Came forty thousand warlike foot and horse,
Since last we numbered to your majesty.

KING OF TREBIZON
From Trebizon in Asia the Less, 40
Naturalized Turks and stout Bithynians
Came to my bands full fifty thousand more
That, fighting, knows not what retreat doth mean,
Nor e'er return but with the victory,
Since last we numbered to your majesty. 45

KING OF SORIA
Of Sorians from Halla is repaired,
And neighbour cities of your highness' land,

---

36 *metropolis* Babylon, whose walls were supposedly built by Semiramis
40 *Asia the Less* Asia Minor
41 *stout* bold
   Bithynians Bithynia was the north-western region of Asia Minor.
46 *Halla* a town to the south-east of Aleppo
   is repaired have travelled

Ten thousand horse and thirty thousand foot,
Since last we numbered to your majesty.
So that the army royal is esteemed   50
Six hundred thousand valiant fighting men.

CALLAPINE
Then welcome, Tamburlaine, unto thy death.
Come puissant viceroys, let us to the field,
The Persians' sepulchre, and sacrifice
Mountains of breathless men to Mahomet,   55
Who now with Jove opens the firmament
To see the slaughter of our enemies.

[*Enter*] TAMBURLAINE *with his three sons* [CALYPHAS,
AMYRAS, *and* CELEBINUS], USUMCASANE, *with other*[s]

TAMBURLAINE
How now Casane! See a knot of kings,
Sitting as if they were a-telling riddles.

USUMCASANE
My lord, your presence makes them pale and wan –   60
Poor souls they look as if their deaths were near.

TAMBURLAINE
Why so he is, Casane, I am here,
But yet I'll save their lives and make them slaves.
Ye petty kings of Turkey, I am come,
As Hector did into the Grecian camp   65
To overdare the pride of Graecia
And set his warlike person to the view
Of fierce Achilles, rival of his fame.
I do you honour in the simile,
For if I should as Hector did Achilles   70
(The worthiest knight that ever brandished sword)
Challenge in combat any of you all,
I see how fearfully ye would refuse,
And fly my glove as from a scorpion.

ORCANES
Now thou art fearful of thy army's strength   75
Thou wouldst with overmatch of person fight;
But, shepherd's issue, base-born Tamburlaine,
Think of thy end, this sword shall lance thy throat.

TAMBURLAINE
Villain, the shepherd's issue, at whose birth

65–8 There is no such episode in the *Iliad*, but Marlowe could have found it in the
    post-Homeric Troy tales, such as Lydgate's *Troy Book*.
74 *glove* challenge. To throw down a glove was to issue a chivalric challenge.
76 *with ... fight* fight personally, out of confidence in your superior strength

Heaven did afford a gracious aspect   80
And joined those stars that shall be opposite
Even till the dissolution of the world,
And never meant to make a conqueror
So famous as is mighty Tamburlaine,
Shall so torment thee and that Callapine   85
That like a roguish runaway suborned
That villain there, that slave, that Turkish dog,
To false his service to his sovereign,
As ye shall curse the birth of Tamburlaine.

CALLAPINE
Rail not, proud Scythian, I shall now revenge   90
My father's vile abuses and mine own.

KING OF JERUSALEM
By Mahomet, he shall be tied in chains,
Rowing with Christians in a brigandine
About the Grecian isles to rob and spoil,
And turn him to his ancient trade again.   95
Methinks the slave should make a lusty thief.

CALLAPINE
Nay, when the battle ends, all we will meet
And sit in council to invent some pain
That most may vex his body and his soul.

TAMBURLAINE
Sirrah, Callapine, I'll hang a clog about your neck for   100
running away again, you shall not trouble me thus to
come and fetch you.
But as for you, viceroy, you shall have bits
And harnessed like my horses draw my coach,
And when ye stay be lashed with whips of wire;   105
I'll have you learn to feed on provender
And in a stable lie upon the planks.

ORCANES
But Tamburlaine, first thou shalt kneel to us
And humbly crave a pardon for thy life.

KING OF TREBIZON
The common soldiers of our mighty host   110

---

80 *gracious aspect* favourable conjunction of the heavenly bodies
81–2 *And joined ... world* which conjunction will never again be seen
86 *suborned* bribed
88 *false* betray
93 *brigandine* small ship
96 *lusty* vigorous
100 *for* to prevent
106 *provender* fodder

Shall bring thee bound unto the general's tent.

KING OF SORIA

And all have jointly sworn thy cruel death,
Or bind thee in eternal torments' wrath.

TAMBURLAINE

Well sirs, diet yourselves, you know I shall have occasion
shortly to journey you.   115

CELEBINUS

See father, how Almeda the jailor looks upon us.

TAMBURLAINE

Villain, traitor, damnèd fugitive,
I'll make thee wish the earth had swallowed thee:
Seest thou not death within my wrathful looks?
Go villain, cast thee headlong from a rock,   120
Or rip thy bowels and rend out thy heart
T'appease my wrath, or else I'll torture thee,
Searing thy hateful flesh with burning irons
And drops of scalding lead, while all thy joints
Be racked and beat asunder with the wheel.   125
For if thou livest, not any element
Shall shroud thee from the wrath of Tamburlaine.

CALLAPINE

Well, in despite of thee he shall be king:
Come, Almeda, receive this crown of me.
I here invest thee King of Ariadan,   130
Bordering on Mare Roso near to Mecca.

ORCANES

What, take it man!

ALMEDA

[*To* TAMBURLAINE] Good my lord, let me take it.

CALLAPINE

Dost thou ask him leave? Here, take it.

TAMBURLAINE

Go to, sirrah, take your crown, and make up the half 135
dozen. So sirrah, now you are a king you must give arms.

ORCANES

So he shall, and wear thy head in his scutcheon.

---

113 Perhaps 'thee' should read 'them', and the line would then refer to the terms of
the soldiers' oath (see Cunningham).
114 *diet yourselves* feed yourselves well
115 *journey* drive (as horses)
130 *Ariadan* a town on the Red Sea coast of Arabia, south of Mecca
131 *Mare Roso* the Red Sea
137 *scutcheon* heraldic shield

TAMBURLAINE

No, let him hang a bunch of keys on his standard to put
him in remembrance he was a jailor, that when I take
him, I may knock out his brains with them, and lock you   140
in the stable when you shall come sweating from my
chariot.

KING OF TREBIZON

Away, let us to the field, that the villain may be slain.

TAMBURLAINE

[*To an attendant*] Sirrah, prepare whips, and bring my
chariot to my tent: for as soon as the battle is done, I'll   145
ride in triumph through the camp.

Enter THERIDAMAS, TECHELLES, *and their train*

How now, ye petty kings, lo, here are bugs
Will make the hair stand upright on your heads
And cast your crowns in slavery at their feet.
Welcome, Theridamas and Techelles both,   150
See ye this rout and know ye this same king?

THERIDAMAS

Ay, my lord, he was Callapine's keeper.

TAMBURLAINE

Well, now you see he is a king; look to him Theridamas,
when we are fighting, lest he hide his crown as the foolish
King of Persia did.   155

KING OF SORIA

No, Tamburlaine, he shall not be put to that exigent, I
warrant thee.

TAMBURLAINE

You know not, sir.
But now, my followers and my loving friends,
Fight as you ever did, like conquerors,   160
The glory of this happy day is yours:
My stern aspect shall make fair Victory,
Hovering betwixt our armies, light on me,
Loaden with laurel wreaths to crown us all.

TECHELLES

I smile to think how, when this field is fought   165
And rich Natolia ours, our men shall sweat
With carrying pearl and treasure on their backs.

138 *standard* the distinctive flag of a nobleman
147 *bugs* bugbears, objects of terror to children
151 *rout* rabble
154 See Part One, II, iv, 10–15.
164 *Loaden* laden

TAMBURLAINE
      You shall be princes all immediately:
      Come fight, ye Turks, or yield us victory.
ORCANES
      No, we will meet thee, slavish Tamburlaine.   *Exeunt* 170

Act IV, Scene i

Alarm. AMYRAS *and* CELEBINUS *issue from the tent
where* CALYPHAS *sits asleep*

[AMYRAS]
      Now in their glories shine the golden crowns
      Of these proud Turks, much like so many suns
      That half dismay the majesty of heaven;
      Now brother, follow we our father's sword
      That flies with fury swifter than our thoughts   5
      And cuts down armies with his conquering wings.
CELEBINUS
      Call forth our lazy brother from the tent,
      For if my father miss him in the field,
      Wrath kindled in the furnace of his breast
      Will send a deadly lightning to his heart.   10
AMYRAS
      Brother ho! What, given so much to sleep
      You cannot leave it when our enemies' drums
      And rattling cannons thunder in our ears
      Our proper ruin and our father's foil?
CALYPHAS
      Away, ye fools, my father needs not me,   15
      Nor you, in faith, but that you will be thought
      More childish valorous than manly wise.
      If half our camp should sit and sleep with me,
      My father were enough to scar the foe:
      You do dishonour to his majesty   20
      To think our helps will do him any good.
AMYRAS
      What, dar'st thou then be absent from the fight,
      Knowing my father hates thy cowardice

      IV, i, s.d. *issue* ed. (issues O1)
       6 *conquering* ed. (conquerings O1)
      14 *proper* own
         foil defeat
      19 *were* ed. (ware O1)

And oft hath warned thee to be still in field,
When he himself amidst the thickest troops   25
Beats down our foes, to flesh our taintless swords?

CALYPHAS
I know, sir, what it is to kill a man –
It works remorse of conscience in me;
I take no pleasure to be murderous
Nor care for blood when wine will quench my thirst.   30

CELEBINUS
O cowardly boy! Fie, for shame, come forth!
Thou dost dishonour manhood and thy house.

CALYPHAS
Go, go tall stripling, fight you for us both,
And take my other toward brother here,
For person like to prove a second Mars.   35
'Twill please my mind as well to hear both you
Have won a heap of honour in the field,
And left your slender carcasses behind,
As if I lay with you for company.

AMYRAS
You will not go then?   40

CALYPHAS
You say true.

AMYRAS
Were all the lofty mounts of Zona Mundi
That fill the midst of farthest Tartary
Turned into pearl and proffered for my stay,
I would not bide the fury of my father   45
When made a victor in these haughty arms
He comes and finds his sons have had no shares
In all the honours he proposed for us.

CALYPHAS
Take you the honour, I will take my ease,
My wisdom shall excuse my cowardice: 50
I go into the field before I need?
                    Alarm, and AMYRAS *and* CELEBINUS *run in*
The bullets fly at random where they list.
And should I go and kill a thousand men,

24 *still* constantly
26 *to flesh ... swords* to fight our first battle
33 *tall* brave
34 *toward* forward, promising
42 *Zona Mundi* a mountain range in Tartary, an area of central Asia east of the
   Caspian
52 *list* like

I were as soon rewarded with a shot
And sooner far than he that never fights.   55
And should I go and do nor harm nor good,
I might have harm, which all the good I have
Joined with my father's crown would never cure.
I'll to cards. Perdicas!

[*Enter* PERDICAS]

PERDICAS

                    Here my lord.

CALYPHAS

Come, thou and I will go to cards to drive away the   60
time.

PERDICAS

Content, my lord, but what shall we play for?

CALYPHAS

Who shall kiss the fairest of the Turks' concubines first,
when my father hath conquered them.

PERDICAS

Agreed i'faith.   65

                                   They play [*in the tent*]

CALYPHAS

They say I am a coward, Perdicas, and I fear as little
their taratantaras, their swords or their cannons, as I do
a naked lady in a net of gold, and for fear I should be
afraid, would put it off and come to bed with me.

PERDICAS

Such a fear, my lord, would never make ye retire.   70

CALYPHAS

I would my father would let me be put in the front of
such a battle once, to try my valour.

                                                  Alarm

What a coil they keep, I believe there will be some hurt
done anon amongst them.

                Enter TAMBURLAINE, THERIDAMAS, TECHELLES,
                USUMCASANE, AMYRAS, CELEBINUS, *leading the*
                Turkish KINGS [OF NATOLIA, JERUSALEM,
                TREBIZON, *and* SORIA; *and* SOLDIERS]

---

65 s.d. The staging here, as at the beginning of the scene, requires an inner area to
    serve as the tent, visible to the audience but removed from the main playing area
67 *taratantaras* bugle calls
68 *and* i.e. who
73 *coil* commotion

TAMBURLAINE

See now, ye slaves, my children stoops your pride   75
And leads your glories sheep-like to the sword.
Bring them, my boys, and tell me if the wars
Be not a life that may illustrate gods,
And tickle not your spirits with desire
Still to be trained in arms and chivalry?   80

AMYRAS

Shall we let go these kings again, my lord,
To gather greater numbers 'gainst our power,
That they may say it is not chance doth this,
But matchless strength and magnanimity?

TAMBURLAINE

No, no Amyras, tempt not fortune so,   85
Cherish thy valour still with fresh supplies
And glut it not with stale and daunted foes.
But where's this coward, villain, not my son,
But traitor to my name and majesty?
          He goes in [*the tent*] *and brings* [CALYPHAS] *out*
Image of sloth and picture of a slave,   90
The obloquy and scorn of my renown,
How may my heart, thus fired with mine eyes,
Wounded with shame and killed with discontent,
Shroud any thought may hold my striving hands
From martial justice on thy wretched soul?   95

THERIDAMAS

Yet pardon him I pray your majesty.

TECHELLES, USUMCASANE

Let all of us entreat your highness' pardon.
          [*They kneel*]

TAMBURLAINE

Stand up, ye base unworthy soldiers,
Know ye not yet the argument of arms?

AMYRAS

Good my lord, let him be forgiven for once   100
And we will force him to the field hereafter.

TAMBURLAINE

Stand up, my boys, and I will teach ye arms,
And what the jealousy of wars must do.

---

75 *stoops* humble
78 *illustrate* adorn, shed lustre upon
94 *Shroud* shelter, harbour
   may which may
99 *argument of arms* necessity of military life
103 *jealousy* zeal

O Samarcanda, where I breathèd first
And joyed the fire of this martial flesh, 105
Blush, blush fair city at thine honour's foil
And shame of nature which Jaertis' stream,
Embracing thee with deepest of his love,
Can never wash from thy distainèd brows.
Here Jove, receive his fainting soul again, 110
A form not meet to give that subject essence
Whose matter is the flesh of Tamburlaine,
Wherein an incorporeal spirit moves
Made of the mould whereof thyself consists
Which makes me valiant, proud, ambitious, 115
Ready to levy power against thy throne,
That I might move the turning spheres of heaven –
For earth and all this airy region
Cannot contain the state of Tamburlaine.
　　　　　　　　　　　　[*Stabs* CALYPHAS]
By Mahomet, thy mighty friend, I swear, 120
In sending to my issue such a soul,
Created of the massy dregs of earth,
The scum and tartar of the elements,
Wherein was neither courage, strength, or wit,
But folly, sloth, and damnèd idleness: 125
Thou hast procured a greater enemy
Than he that darted mountains at thy head,
Shaking the burden mighty Atlas bears,
Whereat thou trembling hidd'st thee in the air,

---

104 *Samarcanda* Samarkand, Tamburlaine's birthplace
105 *joyed* took delight in
106 *foil* disgrace
107 *which* ed. (with O1)
　　　Jaertis' stream the river Jaxartes, which flows west from Tartary to the Caspian
　　　Sea
109 *distainèd* stained, dishonoured
110–14 *Here Jove ... consists* Ellis-Fermor paraphrases: 'Here Jove receive again the
　　　soul of Calyphas, a spirit (i.e. "form" almost in the sense of "idea") not worthy
　　　to be the immortal part (essence) of that subject whose mortal part (matter) is
　　　derived from the flesh of Tamburlaine – in whom moves an immortal spirit of
　　　the same mould as thine own.' She observes that 'form', 'subject', 'essence', and
　　　'matter' are used in strict accordance with the tradition of sixteenth-century
　　　Aristotelian logic.
120 *thy* i.e. Jove's
121 *In ... soul* by sending such a soul as Calyphas to be my child
123 *tartar* dregs (as of a wine cask)
127 *he ... head* the Titans who warred against Jove
128 *Atlas* the Titan who was condemned to bear the heavens on his shoulders

Clothed with a pitchy cloud for being seen.   130
And now ye cankered curs of Asia,
That will not see the strength of Tamburlaine
Although it shine as brightly as the sun,
Now you shall feel the strength of Tamburlaine
And by the state of his supremacy   135
Approve the difference 'twixt himself and you.

ORCANES
Thou showest the difference 'twixt ourselves and thee
In this thy barbarous damnèd tyranny.

KING OF JERUSALEM
Thy victories are grown so violent
That shortly heaven, filled with the meteors   140
Of blood and fire thy tyrannies have made,
Will pour down blood and fire on thy head,
Whose scalding drops will pierce thy seething brains,
And with our bloods revenge our bloods on thee.

TAMBURLAINE
Villains, these terrors and these tyrannies   145
(If tyrannies war's justice ye repute)
I execute, enjoined me from above,
To scourge the pride of such as heaven abhors;
Nor am I made arch-monarch of the world,
Crowned and invested by the hand of Jove,   150
For deeds of bounty or nobility.
But since I exercise a greater name,
The scourge of God and terror of the world,
I must apply myself to fit those terms
In war, in blood, in death, in cruelty,   155
And plague such peasants as resist in me
The power of heaven's eternal majesty.
Theridamas, Techelles, and Casane,
Ransack the tents and the pavilions
Of these proud Turks and take their concubines,   160
Making them bury this effeminate brat,
For not a common soldier shall defile
His manly fingers with so faint a boy.
Then bring those Turkish harlots to my tent

130 *for being seen* to avoid being seen
136 *Approve* find out by experience
140–44 See Part One, V, ii, 397–400 and note.
146 *repute* regard as
156 *resist in* ed. (resisting O1)
163 *faint* faint-hearted

And I'll dispose them as it likes me best.   165
Meanwhile take him in.
SOLDIERS   We will my lord.

[*Exeunt* SOLDIERS *with the body of* CALYPHAS]
KING OF JERUSALEM
O damnèd monster, nay a fiend of hell,
Whose cruelties are not so harsh as thine,
Nor yet imposed with such a bitter hate!
ORCANES
Revenge it, Rhadamanth and Aeacus,   170
And let your hates extended in his pains
Expel the hate wherewith he pains our souls!
KING OF TREBIZON
May never day give virtue to his eyes,
Whose sight composed of fury and of fire
Doth send such stern affections to his heart!   175
KING OF SORIA
May never spirit, vein, or artier feed
The cursèd substance of that cruel heart,
But, wanting moisture and remorseful blood,
Dry up with anger and consume with heat!
TAMBURLAINE
Well, bark ye dogs. I'll bridle all your tongues   180
And bind them close with bits of burnished steel
Down to the channels of your hateful throats,
And with the pains my rigour shall inflict
I'll make ye roar, that earth may echo forth
The far resounding torments ye sustain,   185
As when an herd of lusty Cimbrian bulls
Run mourning round about the females' miss,
And stung with fury of their following,
Fill all the air with troublous bellowing.
I will with engines never exercised   190
Conquer, sack, and utterly consume

165 *likes* pleases
170 *Rhadamanth and Aeacus* with Minos, the judges of the Greek underworld
173 *virtue* power
175 *affections* emotions
176 *artier* artery
178 *remorseful* compassionate
186 *Cimbrian* The Cimbri were a Celtic people who defeated several Roman armies in
    the second century B.C. Marlowe's association of the Cimbri with bulls apparently
    derives from Spenser's *Faerie Queene*, I, viii, 11.
187 *females' miss* i.e. the loss of their mates
188 *their following* following them

Your cities and your golden palaces,
And with the flames that beat against the clouds
Incense the heavens and make the stars to melt,
As if they were the tears of Mahomet   195
For hot consumption of his country's pride.
And till by vision or by speech I hear
Immortal Jove say 'Cease, my Tamburlaine,'
I will persist a terror to the world,
Making the meteors, that like armèd men   200
Are seen to march upon the towers of heaven,
Run tilting round about the firmament
And break their burning lances in the air
For honour of my wondrous victories.
Come, bring them in to our pavilion.   *Exeunt* 205

Act IV, Scene ii

[Enter] OLYMPIA *alone*

[OLYMPIA]
Distressed Olympia, whose weeping eyes
Since thy arrival here beheld no sun,
But closed within the compass of a tent
Hath stained thy cheeks and made thee look like death,
Devise some means to rid thee of thy life,   5
Rather than yield to his detested suit
Whose drift is only to dishonour thee.
And since this earth, dewed with thy brinish tears,
Affords no herbs whose taste may poison thee,
Nor yet this air, beat often with thy sighs,   10
Contagious smells and vapours to infect thee,
Nor thy close cave a sword to murder thee,
Let this invention be the instrument.
                              [Taking out a vial]

Enter THERIDAMAS

THERIDAMAS
Well met, Olympia, I sought thee in thy tent
But when I saw the place obscure and dark,   15
Which with thy beauty thou wast wont to light,

194 *Incense* set on fire
202 *tilting* jousting
  7 *drift* intention
 12 *close cave* place of confinement

Enraged I ran about the fields for thee,
Supposing amorous Jove had sent his son,
The wingèd Hermes, to convey thee hence.
But now I find thee and that fear is past.   20
Tell me Olympia, wilt thou grant my suit?

OLYMPIA
My lord and husband's death, with my sweet son's,
With whom I buried all affections
Save grief and sorrow which torment my heart,
Forbids my mind to entertain a thought   25
That tends to love, but meditate on death,
A fitter subject for a pensive soul.

THERIDAMAS
Olympia, pity him in whom thy looks
Have greater operation and more force
Than Cynthia's in the watery wilderness,   30
For with thy view my joys are at the full,
And ebb again as thou depart'st from me.

OLYMPIA
Ah pity me, my lord, and draw your sword,
Making a passage for my troubled soul,
Which beats against this prison to get out   35
And meet my husband and my loving son.

THERIDAMAS
Nothing but still thy husband and thy son?
Leave this, my love, and listen more to me,
Thou shalt be stately queen of fair Argier
And, clothed in costly cloth of massy gold,   40
Upon the marble turrets of my court
Sit like to Venus in her chair of state,
Commanding all thy princely eye desires;
And I will cast off arms and sit with thee
Spending my life in sweet discourse of love.   45

OLYMPIA
No such discourse is pleasant in mine ears
But that where every period ends with death
And every line begins with death again –
I cannot love, to be an emperess.

THERIDAMAS
Nay lady, then if nothing will prevail   50
I'll use some other means to make you yield –

19 *Hermes* Zeus's herald and messenger
30 *Cynthia's ... wilderness* i.e. the power of the moon to govern the tides
47 *period* sentence
49 *emperess* Original spelling here and elsewhere retained for the sake of the metre.

Such is the sudden fury of my love,
I must and will be pleased and you shall yield.
Come to the tent again.

OLYMPIA
Stay, good my lord, and will you save my honour,   55
I'll give your grace a present of such price
As all the world cannot afford the like.

THERIDAMAS
What is it?

OLYMPIA
An ointment which a cunning alchemist
Distillèd from the purest balsamum   60
And simplest extracts of all minerals,
In which th'essential form of marble stone,
Tempered by science metaphysical
And spells of magic from the mouths of spirits,
With which if you but 'noint your tender skin,   65
Nor pistol, sword, nor lance can pierce your flesh.

THERIDAMAS
Why madam, think ye to mock me thus palpably?

OLYMPIA
To prove it, I will 'noint my naked throat
Which, when you stab, look on your weapon's point
And you shall see't rebated with the blow.   70

THERIDAMAS
Why gave you not your husband some of it,
If you loved him, and it so precious?

OLYMPIA
My purpose was, my lord, to spend it so,
But was prevented by his sudden end,
And for a present easy proof hereof   75
That I dissemble not, try it on me.

THERIDAMAS
I will, Olympia, and will keep it for
The richest present of this eastern world.
                              She [a]noints her throat

OLYMPIA
Now stab, my lord, and mark your weapon's point
That will be blunted if the blow be great.   80

---

55 *and will you* and if you will
61 *simplest extracts* in alchemy, the pure elements
63 *metaphysical* supernatural, the science that went beyond physical knowledge
70 *rebated* blunted
71–2 lineation ed. (O1 prints as prose)

THERIDAMAS
  Here then, Olympia.
                              [*He stabs her and she dies*]
    What, have I slain her? Villain, stab thyself,
    Cut off this arm that murderèd my love,
    In whom the learnèd rabbis of this age
    Might find as many wondrous miracles   85
    As in the theoria of the world.
    Now hell is fairer than Elysium,
    A greater lamp than that bright eye of heaven,
    From whence the stars do borrow all their light,
    Wanders about the black circumference,   90
    And now the damnèd souls are free from pain
    For every Fury gazeth on her looks:
    Infernal Dis is courting of my love,
    Inventing masks and stately shows for her,
    Opening the doors of his rich treasury   95
    To entertain this queen of chastity,
    Whose body shall be tombed with all the pomp
    The treasure of my kingdom may afford.
                              Exit, taking her away

Act IV, Scene iii

[*Enter*] TAMBURLAINE *drawn in his chariot by* TREBIZON
and SORIA *with bits in their mouths, reins in his left hand,*
in his right hand a whip, with which he scourgeth them.
  TECHELLES, THERIDAMAS, USUMCASANE, AMYRAS,
CELEBINUS; [ORCANES, *King of*] *Natolia, and* JERUSALEM,
      led by five or six common SOLDIERS

TAMBURLAINE
  Holla, ye pampered jades of Asia!
    What, can ye draw but twenty miles a day,
    And have so proud a chariot at your heels
    And such a coachman as great Tamburlaine?
    But from Asphaltis, where I conquered you,   5

84 *rabbis* scholarly authorities
86 *theoria* observation, survey
87 *Elysium* ed. (Elisian O1) paradise or heaven in Greek mythology
93 *Dis* Hades, Pluto, god of the underworld
94 *masks* lavish entertainment
IV, iii, s.d. 6 *led by* ed. (led by with O1)
 1 *jades* horses (a contemptuous term)
 5 *Asphaltis* a bituminous lake near Babylon

To Byron here where thus I honour you?
The horse that guide the golden eye of heaven
And blow the morning from their nosterils,
Making their fiery gait above the clouds,
Are not so honoured in their governor   10
As you, ye slaves, in mighty Tamburlaine.
The headstrong jades of Thrace Alcides tamed,
That King Aegeus fed with human flesh
And made so wanton that they knew their strengths,
Were not subdued with valour more divine   15
Than you by this unconquered arm of mine.
To make you fierce and fit my appetite,
You shall be fed with flesh as raw as blood
And drink in pails the strongest muscadel –
If you can live with it, then live, and draw   20
My chariot swifter than the racking clouds;
If not, then die like beasts, and fit for naught
But perches for the black and fatal ravens.
Thus am I right the scourge of highest Jove,
And see the figure of my dignity   25
By which I hold my name and majesty.

AMYRAS

Let me have coach, my lord, that I may ride
And thus be drawn with these two idle kings.

TAMBURLAINE

Thy youth forbids such ease my kingly boy,
They shall tomorrow draw my chariot,   30
While these their fellow kings may be refreshed.

ORCANES

O thou that sway'st the region under earth
And art a king as absolute as Jove,
Come as thou didst in fruitful Sicily,
Surveying all the glories of the land,   35
And as thou took'st the fair Proserpina,
Joying the fruit of Ceres' garden plot,
For love, for honour, and to make her queen,

---

6 *Byron* a city near Babylon
7 *horse* a plural form
8 *nosterils* O1's spelling retained for the sake of the metre
12 *Alcides* Hercules. The passage refers to one of his twelve labours.
19 *muscadel* strong sweet wine
21 *racking* scudding before the wind
24 *right* indeed
25 *figure* image
32 *thou* Pluto, god of the underworld, who carried off Proserpina, the daughter of
   Ceres, goddess of the harvest

So for just hate, for shame, and to subdue
This proud contemner of thy dreadful power,   40
Come once in fury and survey his pride,
Haling him headlong to the lowest hell.

THERIDAMAS
Your majesty must get some bits for these
To bridle their contemptuous cursing tongues,
That like unruly never-broken jades   45
Break through the hedges of their hateful mouths
And pass their fixèd bounds exceedingly.

TECHELLES
Nay, we will break the hedges of their mouths
And pull their kicking colts out of their pastures.

USUMCASANE
Your majesty already hath devised   50
A mean as fit as may be to restrain
These coltish coach-horse tongues from blasphemy.

CELEBINUS
How like you that, sir king? Why speak you not?

KING OF JERUSALEM
Ah cruel brat, sprung from a tyrant's loins,
How like his cursèd father he begins   55
To practise taunts and bitter tyrannies!

TAMBURLAINE
Ay Turk, I tell thee, this same boy is he
That must, advanced in higher pomp than this,
Rifle the kingdoms I shall leave unsacked
If Jove esteeming me too good for earth   60
Raise me to match the fair Aldebaran,
Above the threefold astracism of heaven,
Before I conquer all the triple world.
Now fetch me out the Turkish concubines,
I will prefer them for the funeral   65
They have bestowed on my abortive son.
                    The CONCUBINES *are brought in*
Where are my common soldiers now that fought
So lion-like upon Asphaltis' plains?

45–52 The simile compares the tongues of the captive kings to unruly horses leaping
        over hedges.
49 *pull ... pastures* i.e. their over-active tongues will be cut out
61 *Aldebaran* a bright star in the constellation of Taurus, one of the fixed stars of
        heaven and associated with Mars by Ptolemy
62 *threefold astracism* an asterism, or cluster, of three stars in the constellation Taurus
63 *triple world* composed of Asia, Africa, and Europe
65 *prefer* promote, reward

SOLDIERS
    Here my lord.
TAMBURLAINE
    Hold ye, tall soldiers, take ye queens apiece –   70
    I mean such queens as were kings' concubines.
    Take them, divide them and their jewels too,
    And let them equally serve all your turns.
SOLDIERS
    We thank your majesty.
TAMBURLAINE
    Brawl not, I warn you, for your lechery,   75
    For every man that so offends shall die.
ORCANES
    Injurious tyrant, wilt thou so defame
    The hateful fortunes of thy victory
    To exercise upon such guiltless dames
    The violence of thy common soldiers' lust?   80
TAMBURLAINE
    Live continent then, ye slaves, and meet not me
    With troops of harlots at your slothful heels.
CONCUBINES
    O pity us my lord, and save our honours.
TAMBURLAINE
    Are ye not gone, ye villains, with your spoils?
                    They [SOLDIERS] *run away with the* LADIES
KING OF JERUSALEM
    O merciless infernal cruelty!   85
TAMBURLAINE
    Save your honours? 'Twere but time indeed
    Lost long before you knew what honour meant.
THERIDAMAS
    It seems they meant to conquer us, my lord,
    And make us jesting pageants for their trulls.
TAMBURLAINE
    And now themselves shall make our pageant,   90
    And common soldiers jest with all their trulls.
    Let them take pleasure soundly in their spoils
    Till we prepare our march to Babylon,
    Whither we next make expedition.

70 *tall* brave
70–1 *queens . . . queens* Tamburlaine puns on 'queens' and 'queans' (whores).
81 *continent* ed. (content O1) chaste
89 *pageants* spectacles
      trulls whores
94 *expedition* haste

TECHELLES

Let us not be idle then, my lord,   95
But presently be prest to conquer it.

TAMBURLAINE

We will Techelles. Forward then ye jades!
Now crouch, ye kings of greatest Asia,
And tremble when ye hear this scourge will come
That whips down cities and controlleth crowns,   100
Adding their wealth and treasure to my store.
The Euxine Sea, north to Natolia,
The Terrene, west, the Caspian, north-northeast,
And on the south, Sinus Arabicus,
Shall all be loaden with the martial spoils   105
We will convey with us to Persia.
Then shall my native city Samarcanda
And crystal waves of fresh Jaertis' stream,
The pride and beauty of her princely seat,
Be famous through the furthest continents –   110
For there my palace royal shall be placed,
Whose shining turrets shall dismay the heavens
And cast the fame of Ilion's tower to hell.
Thorough the streets with troops of conquered kings
I'll ride in golden armour like the sun,   115
And in my helm a triple plume shall spring,
Spangled with diamonds dancing in the air,
To note me emperor of the three-fold world –
Like to an almond tree ymounted high
Upon the lofty and celestial mount   120
Of ever-green Selinus, quaintly decked
With blooms more white than Erycina's brows,
Whose tender blossoms tremble every one
At every little breath that thorough heaven is blown.
Then, in my coach, like Saturn's royal son   125

---

 96 *presently* quickly
    prest ready
102 *Euxine Sea* the Black Sea
104 *Sinus Arabicus* the Red Sea
108 *Jaertis' stream* See note to Part Two, IV, i, 107 above.
113 *Ilion* Troy
119–24 *Like . . . blown* This passage has been adapted from Spenser's *Faerie Queene*,
    I, vii, 32, which Marlowe might have seen in manuscript.
121 *ever-green* ed. (every greene O1)
    Selinus a town in Sicily
122 *Erycina* a name for Venus derived from her temple on Mt. Eryx in Sicily
125 *Saturn's royal son* Jove

Mounted his shining chariot, gilt with fire,
And drawn with princely eagles through the path
Paved with bright crystal and enchased with stars,
When all the gods stand gazing at his pomp,
So will I ride through Samarcanda streets,   130
Until my soul dissevered from this flesh
Shall mount the milk-white way and meet him there.
To Babylon my lords, to Babylon!   *Exeunt*

Act V, Scene i

Enter the GOVERNOR OF BABYLON *upon the walls with*
[MAXIMUS *and*] *others*

GOVERNOR
    What saith Maximus?
MAXIMUS
    My lord, the breach the enemy hath made
    Gives such assurance of our overthrow
    That little hope is left to save our lives
    Or hold our city from the conqueror's hands.   5
    Then hang out flags, my lord, of humble truce,
    And satisfy the people's general prayers
    That Tamburlaine's intolerable wrath
    May be suppressed by our submission.
GOVERNOR
    Villain, respects thou more thy slavish life   10
    Than honour of thy country or thy name?
    Is not my life and state as dear to me,
    The city and my native country's weal,
    As anything of price with thy conceit?
    Have we not hope, for all our battered walls,   15
    To live secure and keep his forces out,
    When this our famous lake of Limnasphaltis
    Makes walls afresh with every thing that falls
    Into the liquid substance of his stream,
    More strong than are the gates of death or hell?   20
    What faintness should dismay our courages,
    When we are thus defenced against our foe

126 *chariot* ed. (chariots O1)
127 *path* the Milky Way, mentioned again in l. 132
128 *enchased* set with
132 *him* i.e. Jove
14 *As . . . conceit* as anything which you may regard as valuable
17 *Limnasphaltis* the bituminous lake of Babylon

And have no terror but his threat'ning looks?

Enter another [CITIZEN *above*], *kneeling to the* GOVERNOR

[FIRST CITIZEN]
My lord, if ever you did deed of ruth
And now will work a refuge to our lives,   25
Offer submission, hang up flags of truce,
That Tamburlaine may pity our distress
And use us like a loving conqueror.
Though this be held his last day's dreadful siege,
Wherein he spareth neither man nor child,   30
Yet are there Christians of Georgia here
Whose state he ever pitied and relieved,
Will get his pardon if your grace would send.

GOVERNOR
How is my soul environèd,
And this eternized city Babylon   35
Filled with a pack of faint-heart fugitives
That thus entreat their shame and servitude!

[*Enter a second* CITIZEN]

[SECOND CITIZEN]
My lord, if ever you will win our hearts,
Yield up the town, save our wives and children,
For I will cast myself from off these walls   40
Or die some death of quickest violence,
Before I bide the wrath of Tamburlaine.

GOVERNOR
Villains, cowards, traitors to our state,
Fall to the earth and pierce the pit of hell
That legions of tormenting spirits may vex   45
Your slavish bosoms with continual pains.
I care not, nor the town will never yield
As long as any life is in my breast.

Enter [*below*] THERIDAMAS *and* TECHELLES,
with other SOLDIERS

[THERIDAMAS]
Thou desperate governor of Babylon,
To save thy life, and us a little labour,   50
Yield speedily the city to our hands,
Or else be sure thou shalt be forced with pains
More exquisite than ever traitor felt.

35 *eternized* immortalized

GOVERNOR
 Tyrant, I turn the traitor in thy throat,
 And will defend it in despite of thee.   55
 Call up the soldiers to defend these walls.
TECHELLES
 Yield, foolish governor, we offer more
 Than ever yet we did to such proud slaves
 As durst resist us till our third day's siege:
 Thou seest us prest to give the last assault,   60
 And that shall bide no more regard of parley.
GOVERNOR
 Assault and spare not, we will never yield.
 Alarm, and they scale the walls. [GOVERNOR *and* CITIZENS
       exeunt, pursued by THERIDAMUS'S *army*]

  Enter TAMBURLAINE [*all in black drawn in his chariot*
 by the KINGS OF TREBIZON *and* SORIA], *with* USUMCASANE,
 AMYRAS, *and* CELEBINUS, *with others; the two spare Kings*
     [ORCANES *and* JERUSALEM]

TAMBURLAINE
 The stately buildings of fair Babylon
 Whose lofty pillars, higher than the clouds,
 Were wont to guide the seaman in the deep,   65
 Being carried thither by the cannon's force,
 Now fill the mouth of Limnasphaltis lake
 And make a bridge unto the battered walls.
 Where Belus, Ninus, and great Alexander
 Have rode in triumph, triumphs Tamburlaine, 70
 Whose chariot wheels have burst th'Assyrians' bones,
 Drawn with these kings on heaps of carcasses.
 Now in the place where fair Semiramis,
 Courted by kings and peers of Asia,
 Hath trod the measures, do my soldiers march, 75
 And in the streets where brave Assyrian dames
 Have rid in pomp like rich Saturnia,
 With furious words and frowning visages
 My horsemen brandish their unruly blades.

 69 Belus was the son of Neptune and legendary founder of Babylon. Ninus, the
   founder of Nineveh, married Semiramis, who rebuilt Babylon. Alexander the
   Great conquered Babylon in 331 B.C.
 71 *burst* broken
 75 *measures* stately dances
 76 *brave* finely arrayed, splendid
 77 *Saturnia* Juno

Enter THERIDAMAS *and* TECHELLES [*below*], *bringing the*
GOVERNOR OF BABYLON

Who have ye there, my lords?   80
THERIDAMAS
  The sturdy governor of Babylon,
  That made us all the labour for the town,
  And used such slender reckoning of your majesty.
TAMBURLAINE
  Go bind the villain, he shall hang in chains
  Upon the ruins of this conquered town.   85
  Sirrah, the view of our vermilion tents,
  Which threatened more than if the region
  Next underneath the element of fire
  Were full of comets and of blazing stars
  Whose flaming trains should reach down to the earth,   90
  Could not affright you; no, nor I myself,
  The wrathful messenger of mighty Jove,
  That with his sword hath quailed all earthly kings,
  Could not persuade you to submission,
  But still the ports were shut: villain I say,   95
  Should I but touch the rusty gates of hell,
  The triple-headed Cerberus would howl
  And wake black Jove to crouch and kneel to me;
  But I have sent volleys of shot to you,
  Yet could not enter till the breach was made.   100
GOVERNOR
  Nor if my body could have stopped the breach
  Shouldst thou have entered, cruel Tamburlaine.
  'Tis not thy bloody tents can make me yield,
  Nor yet thyself, the anger of the Highest,
  For though thy cannon shook the city walls,   105
  My heart did never quake, or courage faint.
TAMBURLAINE
  Well now I'll make it quake: go draw him up,
  Hang him in chains upon the city walls
  And let my soldiers shoot the slave to death.
GOVERNOR
  Vile monster, born of some infernal hag,   110
  And sent from hell to tyrannize on earth,
  Do all thy worst: nor death nor Tamburlaine,

87–8 *region . . . fire* the air
93 *quailed* overpowered
95 *ports* gates
97 *Cerberus* the three-headed dog of hell
98 *black Jove* Pluto, ruler of the underworld

Torture or pain, can daunt my dreadless mind.
TAMBURLAINE
Up with him then, his body shall be scarred.
GOVERNOR
But Tamburlaine, in Limnasphaltis lake   115
There lies more gold than Babylon is worth,
Which when the city was besieged I hid –
Save but my life and I will give it thee.
TAMBURLAINE
Then, for all your valour, you would save your life.
Whereabout lies it?   120
GOVERNOR
Under a hollow bank, right opposite
Against the western gate of Babylon.
TAMBURLAINE
Go thither some of you and take his gold.
                        [*Exeunt some* ATTENDANTS]
The rest forward with execution.
Away with him hence, let him speak no more: 125
I think I make your courage something quail.
            [*Exeunt* ATTENDANTS *with* GOVERNOR OF BABYLON]
When this is done we'll march from Babylon
And make our greatest haste to Persia.
These jades are broken-winded and half tired,
Unharness them, and let me have fresh horse.   130
    [ATTENDANTS *unharness Kings of* TREBIZON *and* SORIA]
So, now their best is done to honour me,
Take them, and hang them both up presently.
KING OF TREBIZON
Vile tyrant, barbarous bloody Tamburlaine!
TAMBURLAINE
Take them away, Theridamas, see them dispatched.
THERIDAMAS
I will my lord.   135
    [*Exit* THERIDAMAS *with the* KINGS OF TREBIZON *and* SORIA]
TAMBURLAINE
Come, Asian viceroys, to your tasks a while
And take such fortune as your fellows felt.
ORCANES
First let thy Scythian horse tear both our limbs
Rather than we should draw thy chariot
And like base slaves abject our princely minds   140

132 *presently* immediately
137 *take ... felt* share the fate of your fellow kings
140 *abject* abase

To vile and ignominious servitude.

KING OF JERUSALEM
Rather lend me thy weapon, Tamburlaine,
That I may sheathe it in this breast of mine.
A thousand deaths could not torment our hearts
More than the thought of this doth vex our souls.   145

AMYRAS
They will talk still, my lord, if you do not bridle them.

TAMBURLAINE
Bridle them and let me to my coach.

They bridle them. [The GOVERNOR OF BABYLON *appears
hanging in chains on the walls. Enter* THERIDAMAS]

AMYRAS
See now, my lord, how brave the captain hangs.

TAMBURLAINE
'Tis brave indeed my boy, well done!
Shoot first, my lord, and then the rest shall follow.   150

THERIDAMAS
Then have at him to begin withal.

THERIDAMAS *shoots*

GOVERNOR
Yet save my life and let this wound appease
The mortal fury of great Tamburlaine.

TAMBURLAINE
No, though Asphaltis lake were liquid gold
And offered me as ransom for thy life,   155
Yet shouldst thou die; shoot at him all at once.

They shoot

So, now he hangs like Bagdet's governor,
Having as many bullets in his flesh
As there be breaches in her battered wall.
Go now and bind the burghers hand and foot   160
And cast them headlong in the city's lake:
Tartars and Persians shall inhabit there,

147 s.d. The soldiers who exited with the Governor at l. 126 re-appear above (having
   mounted an inner staircase to the second level), thrust their victim out of the
   window or over the edge of the balcony and fasten him with chains to the tiring
   house wall. The shooting was presumably done with muskets (l. 158) and
   appropriate jets of pig's blood would no doubt have punctuated the grisly scene.
   On the modern stage, spectacular effects with arrows have also been managed
   (see Introduction, p. xxxi). At the end of the scene, directed by the now sick
   Tamburlaine (l. 215), the soldiers return to remove the body. The staging invites
   us to link Tamburlaine's treachery to the Governor with his sudden distemper.
151 *have . . . withal* I'll have a go at him for a start.
157 *Bagdet's* Baghdad's

And to command the city, I will build
A citadel that all Africa,
Which hath been subject to the Persian king,   165
Shall pay me tribute for in Babylon.

TECHELLES

What shall be done with their wives and children, my
lord?

TAMBURLAINE

Techelles, drown them all, man, woman, and child,
Leave not a Babylonian in the town.

TECHELLES

I will about it straight; come soldiers.   170

Exit [with SOLDIERS]

TAMBURLAINE

Now Casane, where's the Turkish Alcoran
And all the heaps of superstitious books
Found in the temples of that Mahomet,
Whom I have thought a god? They shall be burnt.

USUMCASANE

Here they are, my lord.   175

TAMBURLAINE

Well said, let there be a fire presently.

[They light a fire]

In vain, I see, men worship Mahomet:
My sword hath sent millions of Turks to hell,
Slew all his priests, his kinsmen, and his friends,
And yet I live untouched by Mahomet.   180
There is a God full of revenging wrath,
From whom the thunder and the lightning breaks,
Whose scourge I am, and him will I obey.
So, Casane, fling them in the fire.

[They burn the books]

Now Mahomet, if thou have any power,   185
Come down thyself and work a miracle,
Thou art not worthy to be worshippèd
That suffers flames of fire to burn the writ
Wherein the sum of thy religion rests.
Why send'st thou not a furious whirlwind down   190

---

171 *Alcoran* Koran
176 s.d. Again here, as with the burning of the bodies in III, iv, a trap might have
     been used. But a simpler expedient would have been a brazier of some sort in
     which a fire could be quickly kindled. The books, flung into the fire on Tam-
     burlaine's orders (l. 184), would then continue to burn onstage during his chal-
     lenge to Mahomet and the subsequent onset of his distemper – producing a
     telling ironic effect.

To blow thy Alcoran up to thy throne,
Where men report thou sitt'st by God himself,
Or vengeance on the head of Tamburlaine
That shakes his sword against thy majesty
And spurns the abstracts of thy foolish laws?   195
Well, soldiers, Mahomet remains in hell –
He cannot hear the voice of Tamburlaine.
Seek out another godhead to adore,
The God that sits in heaven, if any god,
For he is God alone, and none but he.   200

[*Enter* TECHELLES]

TECHELLES
I have fulfilled your highness' will, my lord:
Thousands of men drowned in Asphaltis lake
Have made the water swell above the banks,
And fishes fed by human carcasses,
Amazed, swim up and down upon the waves,   205
As when they swallow asafoetida,
Which makes them fleet aloft and gasp for air.
TAMBURLAINE
Well then, my friendly lords, what now remains
But that we leave sufficient garrison
And presently depart to Persia,   210
To triumph after all our victories.
THERIDAMAS
Ay, good my lord, let us in haste to Persia,
And let this captain be removed the walls
To some high hill about the city here.
TAMBURLAINE
Let it be so, about it soldiers.   215
But stay, I feel myself distempered suddenly.
TECHELLES
What is it dares distemper Tamburlaine?
TAMBURLAINE
Something, Techelles, but I know not what;
But forth ye vassals! Whatsoe'er it be,
Sickness or death can never conquer me.   *Exeunt* 220

---

195 *abstracts* written summaries
204 *fed* ed. (feed O1)
206 *asafoetida* a resinous gum with a strong odour, used in cooking and medicine
207 *fleet* float
216 *distempered* sick, disordered

Act V, Scene ii

Enter CALLAPINE, [KING OF] AMASIA,
[CAPTAIN, SOLDIERS,] *with drums and trumpets*

CALLAPINE
King of Amasia, now our mighty host
Marcheth in Asia Major, where the streams
Of Euphrates and Tigris swiftly runs,
And here may we behold great Babylon,
Circled about with Limnasphaltis lake,   5
Where Tamburlaine with all his army lies,
Which being faint and weary with the siege,
We may lie ready to encounter him
Before his host be full from Babylon,
And so revenge our latest grievous loss,   10
If God or Mahomet send any aid.

KING OF AMASIA
Doubt not, my lord, but we shall conquer him.
The monster that hath drunk a sea of blood
And yet gapes still for more to quench his thirst,
Our Turkish swords shall headlong send to hell,   15
And that vile carcass drawn by warlike kings
The fowls shall eat, for never sepulchre
Shall grace that base-born tyrant Tamburlaine.

CALLAPINE
When I record my parents' slavish life,
Their cruel death, mine own captivity,   20
My viceroys' bondage under Tamburlaine,
Methinks I could sustain a thousand deaths
To be revenged of all his villainy.
Ah sacred Mahomet, thou that hast seen
Millions of Turks perish by Tamburlaine,   25
Kingdoms made waste, brave cities sacked and burnt,
And but one host is left to honour thee:
Aid thy obedient servant Callapine
And make him after all these overthrows
To triumph over cursèd Tamburlaine.   30

KING OF AMASIA
Fear not, my lord, I see great Mahomet
Clothèd in purple clouds, and on his head
A chaplet brighter than Apollo's crown,

9 *full from Babylon* i.e. fully recuperated from the siege
19 *record* recall
33 *chaplet* wreath or garland

Marching about the air with armèd men
To join with you against this Tamburlaine.   35
[CAPTAIN]
Renownèd general, mighty Callapine,
Though God himself and holy Mahomet
Should come in person to resist your power,
Yet might your mighty host encounter all
And pull proud Tamburlaine upon his knees   40
To sue for mercy at your highness' feet.
CALLAPINE
Captain, the force of Tamburlaine is great,
His fortune greater, and the victories
Wherewith he hath so sore dismayed the world
Are greatest to discourage all our drifts;   45
Yet when the pride of Cynthia is at full,
She wanes again, and so shall his, I hope,
For we have here the chief selected men
Of twenty several kingdoms at the least.
Nor plowman, priest, nor merchant stays at home: 50
All Turkey is in arms with Callapine
And never will we sunder camps and arms
Before himself or his be conquerèd.
This is the time that must eternize me
For conquering the tyrant of the world.   55
Come, soldiers, let us lie in wait for him,
And if we find him absent from his camp
Or that it be rejoined again at full,
Assail it and be sure of victory.   *Exeunt*

Act V, Scene iii

[*Enter*] THERIDAMAS, TECHELLES, USUMCASANE

[THERIDAMAS]
Weep heavens, and vanish into liquid tears!
Fall stars that govern his nativity
And summon all the shining lamps of heaven
To cast their bootless fires to the earth
And shed their feeble influence in the air;   5
Muffle your beauties with eternal clouds,
For hell and darkness pitch their pitchy tents,

45 *drifts* purposes
49 *several* different
52 *sunder ... arms* give up our campaign
58 *Or that* before
 4 *bootless* unavailing

And death with armies of Cimmerian spirits
Gives battle 'gainst the heart of Tamburlaine.
Now, in defiance of that wonted love   10
Your sacred virtues poured upon his throne,
And made his state an honour to the heavens,
These cowards invisibly assail his soul
And threaten conquest on our sovereign.
But if he die your glories are disgraced,   15
Earth droops and says that hell in heaven is placed.

TECHELLES
O then, ye powers that sway eternal seats
And guide this massy substance of the earth,
If you retain desert of holiness,
As your supreme estates instruct our thoughts,   20
Be not inconstant, careless of your fame,
Bear not the burden of your enemies' joys,
Triumphing in his fall whom you advanced,
But as his birth, life, health and majesty
Were strangely blest and governèd by heaven,   25
So honour heaven, till heaven dissolvèd be,
His birth, his life, his health and majesty.

USUMCASANE
Blush, heaven, to lose the honour of thy name,
To see thy footstool set upon thy head,
And let no baseness in thy haughty breast   30
Sustain a shame of such inexcellence
To see the devils mount in angels' thrones,
And angels dive into the pools of hell.
And though they think their painful date is out,
And that their power is puissant as Jove's,   35
Which makes them manage arms against thy state,
Yet make them feel the strength of Tamburlaine,
Thy instrument and note of majesty,
Is greater far than they can thus subdue –
For if he die thy glory is disgraced,   40
Earth droops and says that hell in heaven is placed.

---

8 *Cimmerian* dark, infernal. See note to Part One, III, ii, 77 above.
19 *desert of holiness* that which deserves religious worship
20 *estates* ranks, authorities
22 *Bear . . . burden* do not join in the chorus
31 *Sustain . . . inexcellence* bear so vile a shame
34 i.e though the powers of darkness think their time of submission is over
38 *note* distinguishing mark

[*Enter* TAMBURLAINE, *drawn in his chariot by the captive Kings*,
ORCANES *and* JERUSALEM; AMYRAS, CELEBINUS, *and* PHYSICIANS]

TAMBURLAINE
    What daring god torments my body thus
    And seeks to conquer mighty Tamburlaine?
    Shall sickness prove me now to be a man
    That have been termed the terror of the world?   45
    Techelles and the rest, come take your swords
    And threaten him whose hand afflicts my soul;
    Come let us march against the powers of heaven
    And set black streamers in the firmament
    To signify the slaughter of the gods.   50
    Ah friends, what shall I do? I cannot stand –
    Come, carry me to war against the gods
    That thus envy the health of Tamburlaine.
THERIDAMAS
    Ah good my lord, leave these impatient words,
    Which add much danger to your malady.   55
TAMBURLAINE
    Why shall I sit and languish in this pain?
    No, strike the drums, and in revenge of this,
    Come let us charge our spears and pierce his breast
    Whose shoulders bear the axis of the world,
    That if I perish, heaven and earth may fade.   60
    Theridamas, haste to the court of Jove,
    Will him to send Apollo hither straight
    To cure me, or I'll fetch him down myself.
TECHELLES
    Sit still, my gracious lord, this grief will cease,
    And cannot last, it is so violent.   65
TAMBURLAINE
    Not last Techelles? No, for I shall die.
    See where my slave, the ugly monster Death,
    Shaking and quivering, pale and wan for fear,
    Stands aiming at me with his murdering dart,
    Who flies away at every glance I give,   70
    And when I look away comes stealing on.
    Villain away, and hie thee to the field!
    I and mine army come to load thy bark
    With souls of thousand mangled carcasses.

58 *charge* level
    his Atlas's, with whom Tamburlaine is compared in Part One, II, i, 10–11
62 *Apollo* the god of medicine
73 *bark* ship

Look where he goes! But see, he comes again   75
Because I stay. Techelles, let us march
And weary Death with bearing souls to hell.
PHYSICIAN
Pleaseth your majesty to drink this potion,
Which will abate the fury of your fit
And cause some milder spirits govern you.   80
TAMBURLAINE
Tell me, what think you of my sickness now?
PHYSICIAN
I viewed your urine and the hypostasis,
Thick and obscure, doth make your danger great;
Your veins are full of accidental heat
Whereby the moisture of your blood is dried –   85
The humidum and calor, which some hold
Is not a parcel of the elements
But of a substance more divine and pure,
Is almost clean extinguishèd and spent, .
Which being the cause of life imports your death.   90
Besides, my lord, this day is critical,
Dangerous to those whose crisis is as yours.
Your artiers which alongst the veins convey
The lively spirits which the heart engenders
Are parched and void of spirit, that the soul,   95
Wanting those organons by which it moves,
Cannot endure by argument of art.
Yet if your majesty may escape this day,
No doubt but you shall soon recover all.
TAMBURLAINE
Then will I comfort all my vital parts   100

76 *stay* delay
82 *hypostasis* sediment
84–97 The 'accidental [abnormal] heat' has parched Tamburlaine's arteries and
'dried up in his blood the radical moisture (*humidum*) which is necessary for the
preservation of his natural heat (*calor*).' This depletion of moisture and heat
prevents his soul's functions and slows his bodily activities by impeding the
circulation of 'spirits', thus threatening his death. (See Johnstone Parr, *Tamburlaine's Malady*, University AL, 1953, p. 15)
87 *parcel* part
91 *day is critical* i.e. the stars are in an unfavourable conjunction for effecting a cure
93 *artiers* arteries
96 *organons* organs of the body which act as instruments of the soul (here, perhaps,
in the sense of the fluid or 'spirits' that animate such organs)
97 *argument of art* i.e. the science of medicine

And live in spite of death above a day.

Alarm within. [*Enter a* MESSENGER]

MESSENGER
My lord, young Callapine that lately fled from your
majesty, hath now gathered a fresh army, and hearing
your absence in the field, offers to set upon us presently.

TAMBURLAINE
See, my physicians, now, how Jove hath sent   105
A present medicine to recure my pain.
My looks shall make them fly and might I follow
There should not one of all the villain's power
Live to give offer of another fight.

USUMCASANE
I joy, my lord, your highness is so strong   110
That can endure so well your royal presence
Which only will dismay the enemy.

TAMBURLAINE
I know it will Casane: draw you slaves!
In spite of death I will go show my face.

Alarm. TAMBURLAINE *goes in
and comes out again with all the rest*

Thus are the villains, cowards fled for fear,   115
Like summer's vapours vanished by the sun,
And could I but a while pursue the field,
That Callapine should be my slave again.
But I perceive my martial strength is spent;
In vain I strive and rail against those powers   120
That mean t'invest me in a higher throne,
As much too high for this disdainful earth.
Give me a map, then let me see how much
Is left for me to conquer all the world,
That these my boys may finish all my wants.   125
                              One brings a map

Here I began to march towards Persia,
Along Armenia and the Caspian Sea,
And thence unto Bithynia, where I took
The Turk and his great empress prisoners;
Then marched I into Egypt and Arabia,   130

106 *recure* cure
111 *endure* make sturdy or robust
112 *only* alone

And here not far from Alexandria,
Whereas the Terrene and the Red Sea meet,
Being distant less than full a hundred leagues,
I meant to cut a channel to them both
That men might quickly sail to India.   135
From thence to Nubia near Borno lake
And so along the Ethiopian sea,
Cutting the tropic line of Capricorn,
I conquered all as far as Zanzibar.
Then by the northern part of Africa   140
I came at last to Graecia, and from thence
To Asia, where I stay against my will,
Which is from Scythia, where I first began,
Backward and forwards near five thousand leagues.
Look here, my boys, see what a world of ground   145
Lies westward from the midst of Cancer's line,
Unto the rising of this earthly globe,
Whereas the sun declining from our sight
Begins the day with our antipodes:
And shall I die and this unconquerèd?   150
Lo here, my sons, are all the golden mines,
Inestimable drugs and precious stones,
More worth than Asia and the world beside;
And from th'Antarctic Pole eastward behold
As much more land, which never was descried,   155
Wherein are rocks of pearl that shine as bright
As all the lamps that beautify the sky:
And shall I die and this unconquerèd?
Here, lovely boys, what death forbids my life,
That let your lives command in spite of death.   160

AMYRAS

Alas my lord, how should our bleeding hearts,
Wounded and broken with your highness' grief,
Retain a thought of joy or spark of life?
Your soul gives essence to our wretched subjects,

132 *Whereas* where
134 *cut a channel* make a canal. The Suez Canal had been suggested before Marlowe's
      day.
146 *the midst of Cancer's line* just off the coast of north-west Africa where, according
      to Ortelius, the meridian 0° intersects the Tropic of Cancer
149 *antipodes* here, the inhabitants of the western hemisphere
154–5 *And from . . . descried* Australia, which had not yet been 'descried' (discovered)
      but about which rumours were current
162 *grief* suffering

Whose matter is incorporate in your flesh.   165

CELEBINUS
Your pains do pierce our souls, no hope survives,
For by your life we entertain our lives.

TAMBURLAINE
But sons, this subject, not of force enough
To hold the fiery spirit it contains,
Must part, imparting his impressions   170
By equal portions into both your breasts;
My flesh divided in your precious shapes
Shall still retain my spirit, though I die,
And live in all your seeds immortally.
Then now remove me, that I may resign   175
My place and proper title to my son:
[*To* AMYRAS] First take my scourge and my imperial
     crown,
And mount my royal chariot of estate,
That I may see thee crowned before I die.
Help me, my lords, to make my last remove.   180
          [*They help* TAMBURLAINE *out of his chariot*]

THERIDAMAS
A woeful change, my lord, that daunts our thoughts
More than the ruin of our proper souls.

TAMBURLAINE
Sit up, my son, let me see how well
Thou wilt become thy father's majesty.
                              They crown [AMYRAS]

AMYRAS
With what a flinty bosom should I joy   185
The breath of life and burden of my soul,
If, not resolved into resolvèd pains,
My body's mortifièd lineaments
Should exercise the motions of my heart,

164–5 *Your soul . . . flesh* Your soul has bequeathed an animating spirit ('essence') to
     our unhappy selves ('wretched subjects'), since our bodies are part of your flesh.
     See Introduction, pp. xxvii–xxviii.
167 *entertain* maintain
168 *subject* material body
170 *his impressions* its spiritual power
176 *proper* own (also l. 182)
177 *scourge* whip
185–90 *With . . . dignity* How hard my heart would be if I could enjoy my life and the
     possession of my own soul [i.e. with Tamburlaine about to die], or if my body

Pierced with the joy of any dignity!   190
O father, if the unrelenting ears
Of death and hell be shut against my prayers
And that the spiteful influence of heaven
Deny my soul fruition of her joy,
How should I step or stir my hateful feet   195
Against the inward powers of my heart,
Leading a life that only strives to die,
And plead in vain unpleasing sovereignty?

TAMBURLAINE
Let not thy love exceed thine honour, son,
Nor bar thy mind that magnanimity   200
That nobly must admit necessity:
Sit up, my boy, and with those silken reins
Bridle the steelèd stomachs of those jades.

THERIDAMAS
My lord, you must obey his majesty
Since fate commands and proud necessity.   205

AMYRAS   [mounting the chariot]
Heavens witness me with what a broken heart
And damnèd spirit I ascend this seat,
And send my soul, before my father die,
His anguish and his burning agony!

TAMBURLAINE
Now fetch the hearse of fair Zenocrate –   210
Let it be placed by this my fatal chair
And serve as parcel of my funeral.

USUMCASANE
Then feels your majesty no sovereign ease
Nor may our hearts, all drowned in tears of blood,
Joy any hope of your recovery?   215

did not dissolve into extreme pain and its afflicted limbs ('mortified lineaments')
were still able to carry out the promptings of a heart that could be touched to joy
by earthly dignities (adapted from Ellis-Fermor).
195–8 *How ... sovereignty* How could I act against the inner promptings of my
       heart, exercising unwanted sovereignty while my deepest desires pull me towards
       death?
200 *magnanimity* fortitude
203 *steelèd stomachs* obdurately proud spirits
207 *damnèd* condemned to suffer
208 *send* may the heavens send. Amyras wants to share in his father's death-agony.
212 *parcel* part

TAMBURLAINE

Casane no, the monarch of the earth
And eyeless monster that torments my soul,
Cannot behold the tears ye shed for me,
And therefore still augments his cruelty.

TECHELLES

Then let some god oppose his holy power	220
Against the wrath and tyranny of Death,
That his tear-thirsty and unquenchèd hate
May be upon himself reverberate.

They bring in the hearse [of ZENOCRATE]

TAMBURLAINE

Now eyes, enjoy your latest benefit,
And when my soul hath virtue of your sight,	225
Pierce through the coffin and the sheet of gold
And glut your longings with a heaven of joy.
So, reign my son, scourge and control those slaves,
Guiding thy chariot with thy father's hand.
As precious is the charge thou undertak'st	230
As that which Clymen's brain-sick son did guide
When wand'ring Phoebe's ivory cheeks were scorched
And all the earth like Aetna breathing fire.
Be warned by him, then learn with awful eye
To sway a throne as dangerous as his.	235
For if thy body thrive not full of thoughts
As pure and fiery as Phyteus' beams,
The nature of these proud rebelling jades
Will take occasion by the slenderest hair,
And draw thee piecemeal like Hippolytus	240
Through rocks more steep and sharp than Caspian cliffs.
The nature of thy chariot will not bear

216 *monarch of the earth* Death
222 *his* Death's
223 *be . . . reverberate* rebound
225 *when . . . sight* When (after death) Tamburlaine's soul, having been freed from
the body, will have the power of vision which in life belongs only to the eyes, he
will be able to see the spirit of Zenocrate.
231 *Clymen's* O2 (Clymeus O1)
Clymen's . . . son Phaëton, son of Apollo and Clymene. See note to Part One, IV,
ii, 49 above.
232 *Phoebe* the moon
234 *awful* awe-inspiring
237 *Phyteus* Pythius, another name for Apollo, the sun god
238 *these . . . jades* the conquered kings
239 *take . . . hair* seize the slightest opportunity
240 *Hippolytus* killed when his horses bolted and dragged him to death

A guide of baser temper than myself,
More than heaven's coach the pride of Phaëton.
Farewell my boys, my dearest friends farewell,   245
My body feels, my soul doth weep to see
Your sweet desires deprived my company,
For Tamburlaine the scourge of God must die.

                                                        [*Dies*]

AMYRAS
Meet heaven and earth, and here let all things end,
For earth hath spent the pride of all her fruit   250
And heaven consumed his choicest living fire.
Let earth and heaven his timeless death deplore,
For both their worths will equal him no more.

                                                     [*Exeunt*]

252 *timeless* untimely